PUBLIC POLICY AND THE QUALITY OF LIFE

PUBLIC POLICY AND THE QUALITY OF LIFE

Market Incentives versus Government Planning

Randall G. Holcombe

Contributions in Economics and Economic History,
Number 161

GREENWOOD PRESS
Westport, Connecticut • London

Library of Congress Cataloging-in-Publication Data

Holcombe, Randall G.
   Public policy and the quality of life : market incentives versus
government planning / Randall G. Holcombe.
     p.   cm. — (Contributions in economics and economic history,
ISSN 0084–9235 ; no. 161)
   Includes bibliographical references and index.
    ISBN 0–313–29358–9 (alk. paper)
    1. Quality of life—United States. 2. United States—Social
policy. 3. Regional planning—United States. 4. Environmental
policy—Social aspects—United States. 5. Land use—Social aspects—
United States. I. Title. II. Series.
HT123.H645   1995
306'.0973—dc20   94–25060

British Library Cataloguing in Publication Data is available.

Library of Congress Catalog Card Number: 94–25060
ISBN: 0–313–29358–9
ISSN: 0084–9235

First published in 1995

Greenwood Press, 88 Post Road West, Westport, CT 06881
An imprint of Greenwood Publishing Group, Inc.

Printed in the United States of America

The paper used in this book complies with the
Permanent Paper Standard issued by the National
Information Standards Organization (Z39.48–1984).

10 9 8 7 6 5 4 3 2 1

To Ross, Mark, and Connor,

with the hope that the ideas in this book
can help them and their generation
to have a better future

Contents

Preface

The quality of life has been rising for centuries in the United States
and in other developed nations, primarily because of the growth in the
production of material goods. However, as people become wealthier,
their quality of life is increasingly determined, not by the things their
money can buy, but by amenities that are collectively shared with
others in the society and, more importantly, that are collectively
produced as a result of public policy. In the past, increases in the
quality of life have come when governments have stepped aside and
allowed market economies to produce more goods and services and a
higher standard of living for their citizens. Laissez-faire was the policy
that improved the quality of life. Increasingly, people are ready to
argue that, while market economies are good at producing goods and
services, government intervention is needed to enhance the quality of
life. This book challenges that view by showing that the same market
forces that have been so successful at producing goods and services also
provide the best way to enhance the quality of life. Indeed, well-
intentioned government intervention is often counterproductive.

In the abstract, most people are willing to accept that nations are
more prosperous, standards of living are higher, and the quality of life
is better in market-oriented economies. This abstract perception was
reinforced by the overthrow of socialist governments in Eastern Europe
in 1989 and by the collapse of the Soviet Union in 1991. However, while
there is general agreement that the quality of life is better when
market solutions, rather than government planning, are relied on
whenever a specific issue arises, the policy reaction is consistently to
increase the government's control over the allocation of resources.
Thus, paradoxically, even though in general we agree on the desir-
ability of the market mechanism to allocate resources, the government
gets more involved, policy by policy. As a result, we are moving more
toward the central planning that caused the collapse of the Soviet

Union and away from the market economy that has been responsible for our prosperity in the past.

It is not logically inconsistent to argue that the market has done all it can to enhance the quality of life and that now it is time to turn to government. Thus, the issue requires careful analysis — the purpose of this book. After looking at the issue, the book concludes that the same market forces that have been responsible for our high material standard of living are also the most effective way to increase the quality of life in all areas.

I find it easy to see why people might think otherwise and why the siren song of government intervention is so powerful. Market allocation requires that many people's actions be influenced by appropriate incentives, but without government coercion, people can do whatever they want, and there are no guarantees about the effectiveness of policy. Government intervention, on the other hand, mandates the appropriate solution so that people have no choice but to respond appropriately. The flaw in this very appealing line of reasoning becomes apparent after studying the alternatives in more detail. An analysis of government decision-making shows that government intervention typically does not work as well as planned. However, with the appropriate market incentives, people are led as if by an invisible hand to undertake actions that benefit everybody — not because they are forced to, but because they want to.

The line of reasoning developed here is built on a foundation of work done by many others. Previous writers have discussed the advantages of allocating resources through markets rather than by government planning. This book extends that reasoning to issues that deal with the quality of life and that often are seen as the proper role of government within a mostly market-oriented economy. The specific policy issues discussed here have been analyzed in detail by others, too. This book uses those specific policy issues as examples within the more general framework of market allocation to show that the quality of life issues that are often thought of as the province of government are actually better addressed through the same market mechanism that has served developed nations so well in the past.

I wrote this book because of my genuine concern that our turn toward government planning to increase the quality of life is having the opposite effect. I am even more concerned that people do not recognize the negative side effects of government policies, so that problems caused by government intervention lead citizens to demand that the government enact more policies to try to solve the problems that were caused by the government in the first place. Although issues can be looked at one at a time, I hope the framework presented here conveys the idea that, in general, market incentives are preferable to government planning in enhancing the quality of life. If readers can develop a greater appreciation for the way in which market mechanisms can be used to increase the quality of life, they might be less inclined to demand government allocation of resources in these areas and also might be more quick to recognize the detrimental effects of many government policies that have already been put in place.

Acknowledgments

Many individuals have given me helpful comments, advice, and criticism as I have progressed on this project. My ideas were sharpened by comments from Charles Barrilleaux, Leslie Beitsch, Bruce Benson, John Cooper, Jim Gwartney, Lora Holcombe, Stan Marshall, John Metcalf, David Rasmussen, Tim Sass, Russell Sobel, Mike Stroup, and surely by others whom I have forgotten to mention. Most did not see the entire manuscript, and I confess that I did not always take the advice of my critics, so I alone must bear the responsibility for the final product. My wife, Lora, has been especially supportive throughout this project, and deserves special recognition. The book is dedicated to our three sons — Ross, Mark, and Connor — who provide us with a very personal reason to be concerned about the long-run effects of public policies on the quality of life.

PUBLIC POLICY AND
THE QUALITY OF LIFE

1

Introduction

At the beginning of the nineteenth century, Thomas Malthus wrote his influential "Essay on Population," which painted a bleak, but widely accepted, view of the future of humankind.[1] As Malthus saw it, population tended to increase exponentially, while the resources to support that population increased more slowly. As a result, most people would always be destined to live at a subsistence level, having barely enough resources to keep them alive. In the nearly two centuries since Malthus wrote his essay, the actual experience of humankind has been substantially different from his predictions, at least for much of the world. In developed countries where most citizens have more than enough income to allow them to live comfortably, public policy issues have shifted from how to provide enough food, clothing, and shelter to survive to how to improve the quality of life for those who never worry about having plenty to eat.

Although much public policy still deals with how to provide people with the essentials of life, an increasing amount of public policy is intended to provide a higher quality of life to those who have the essentials. Protection of the natural environment, housing and land use policies to improve the quality of life in developed areas, health policies to improve our physical well-being, and regulation to protect consumers from potentially dangerous products are all part of the public policy initiatives that have the stated goal of improving the quality of life.

The stated goals of public policy are often different from their actual effects for two reasons. First, people are not always able to foresee all of the effects of the policies they propose. A proposal to have the government test and approve drugs before they are allowed to be sold sounds like a policy that will save lives by preventing the use of potentially dangerous and inadequately tested drugs. However, people who might be helped by beneficial drugs cannot get them until they are approved, and some people will die before the drugs that could help them are legally available. Furthermore, a long and costly screening process may discourage the development of new drugs and will likely make them more expensive once they are available. Considering both sides of the issue, are we sure that government approval of drugs is beneficial to public health? This specific issue is considered further in Chapter 8, but it serves as an example of a public policy that has both benefits and costs. In order to fairly assess whether this public policy actually enhances the quality of life, the benefits and the costs must be weighed against each other. In many cases, while the benefits seem desirable, the costs are greater than the benefits, and the public policy lowers the quality of life.

The second reason why the stated goals of public policy can be different from their actual effects is that the stated goals may be easier to push through the political process than the actual goals of those who favor the policy. For example, someone might live in a house beside a lake in the woods and enjoy the natural scenery, so the individual would prefer that the rest of the lake remain undeveloped in order to preserve the view. However, it would be selfish for the individual to try to prevent others who owned lakefront lots from building on their property just to preserve his view. Few people would be sympathetic to the argument that others who own land around the lake should not be able to enjoy the same benefits as this landowner, so the individual might try to stop further development around the lake in the name of environmental protection. If nobody else were allowed to build on the lake, the individual's natural surroundings could be protected, with the cost borne by other landowners who were prevented from developing their land.

Environmental protection is a more politically acceptable defense for preventing new development than is enhancing one landowner's view at the expense of other landowners. Thus, individuals might argue that they favor certain policies because they further the public interest, when, in fact, their motivation is to provide private benefits to themselves. This example is not intended to minimize the importance of protecting the environment; the point is that in the name of environmental protection, people often pursue goals that provide little, if any, environmental benefit but provide large private benefits to certain individuals. Chapter 4 discusses policies to protect the environment, and Chapter 5 considers growth management and land use policies in more detail.

All of the quality of life issues discussed here are important. The provision of medical care and drugs, the protection of the environment, the provision of adequate housing, and the protection of consumers from dangerous products are examples of the issues that will be discussed. If these issues are important and if, as just noted, actual public policies do not always further their stated goals, then it is important to analyze public policies intended to improve the quality of life to see if they really will do as they say and to see if alternative policies might provide options that would do better than the policies that are currently being pursued.

The book will often be critical of current policies intended to improve the quality of life, so it is crucial to emphasize that this criticism is not because the stated goals of these policies are not considered important. On the contrary, the goals of these policies are very worthwhile, which is why it is imperative to identify the short-comings in current policies dealing with the quality of life and to point out how better policies could be designed and implemented. Environmental protection, urban growth patterns, and the provision of health care are a few of the vitally important quality of life issues considered. However, laws passed with the stated goal of improving the quality of life do not necessarily do so. Analysis is required to see if laws intended to improve the quality of life actually will produce their intended results. Often, the best method of improving the quality of life is not more government control but greater reliance on the market system that has been responsible for the phenomenal improvements in the quality of life in the two centuries since Malthus painted his dismal picture.

GOVERNMENTS, MARKETS, AND THE QUALITY OF LIFE

Improvement in the material well-being of much of the population of the world has largely been due to the private enterprise system that has relied on private property and trade in markets to give people the incentive to produce goods and services that are valuable to everyone. Although there was serious debate on the merits of central planning versus market economies in the middle of the twentieth century, by the end of the twentiethth century, almost everyone has seen that social-ism and central planning lead to impoverishment and chaos. Yet, while markets have propelled much of the world's economy away from the Malthusian specter of perpetual poverty, there is an increasing call for the government to become more involved in improving the quality of life. Critics of the market system argue that even though governments around the world have failed to provide for the material well-being of their citizens, government intervention and control is the answer to improving the quality of life in economies that rely on markets to provide goods and services.

There is an immediate reason to be suspicious about the claim that government planning can improve the quality of life considering that it has had such a poor record in other economic endeavors. Many of the problems that quality-of-life policies try to address seem to be the result of the greed of people who are engaged in market activities for their own profit rather than for the common good. If government pro-grams are not always the right solution, then unbridled capitalism does not always improve the quality of life either. The challenge is to get public policy to work in coordination with markets to produce a better quality of life.

There is undeniable evidence that markets work to improve the material standard of living. Why can they not work to improve the quality of life in other dimensions as well? One answer is that there are often no markets for those things that enhance the quality of life. Where is the market for environmental protection, for example? Almost uniformly, the public policy answer in these cases has been to establish regulations that prevent markets and then try to control the quality of life through central planning. The alternative is to create markets for quality-of-life issues and allow them to work. Markets for environmental protection can work, and markets for product quality, endangered species, and health care can work if they are allowed to. Often, problems are caused in these areas by government regulation, and the response to problems is always the call for more regulation.

THE DEMAND FOR GOVERNMENT INTERVENTION

The call for government regulation to solve problems often stems from the idea that something should be done, coupled with the idea that, in theory, it would be possible for someone with a great deal of wisdom, the ability to put the public interest ahead of any personal interests, and the absolute power of a dictator to implement the appropriate solution. In practice, government-implemented solutions rarely work out as well as their supporters had hoped. Consider why.

First, it is easy to find things in the real world that are not perfect and to say that something should be done to correct the problems. However, for every ten people who see the same problem, there will be ten different ideal solutions. Thus, government action could not possibly solve most problems to the satisfaction of everybody because, while people tend to agree on the problems, they disagree on what would be the appropriate solutions. This is the nature of politics. With collective action, one solution is implemented for everybody, and, whatever that solution is, some people will not like it. Thus, the person who argues that the government should do something to solve a problem must, realistically, be prepared to face the fact that if the government does take action, its action is not likely to be the one that individual would have chosen.

Second, political solutions are necessarily the product of compromise, so in many cases, what course of action the government takes is not determined by choosing one person's solution over another's but, rather, is a compromise that takes bits and pieces of everyone's proposals and combines them. This may be desirable in some instances, but in other cases, compromise cripples policy proposals so that compromise policies work worse than if another option had been taken.

In a majority rule system, however, compromise is necessary in order to get the approval of a majority of the voters. The government is not a monolithic benevolent dictator but, rather, a collection of individuals linked together by political institutions where compromise is necessary to implement policies. Thus, in the end, nobody is likely to get the policy he or she really would have liked.

Third, the government does not always know what is the right solution to a problem. It is easier to identify problems than it is to identify ways to successfully deal with those problems, and, perhaps because of some of the reasons just noted, the government does not always find the right solution and often makes matters worse rather than better. That alone is a good reason for taking a close look at ways in which public policies can enhance the quality of life.

Fourth, because of the way that government is structured, those in the government do not always have the incentive to solve problems. Their personal concerns might override the public interest when they make decisions affecting public policy.

INCENTIVES IN GOVERNMENT

The quick reaction to seeing a problem and thinking that the government should do something implicitly assumes that the government will act in the public interest, but the government is not a single entity with public-spirited motivations. Rather, it is a group of individuals who undoubtedly want to further the public interest but also want to take care of their own interests. People who work in government are no better and no worse than people who work in the private sector. Everyone, whether in the public or private sector, wants to further the public interest, but everyone has to look out for themselves, too. Thus, any analysis of the policy-making process must take account of the incentives facing policy makers and not simply assume that they will further the public interest — especially when the public interest conflicts with their own personal interests.[2]

With this in mind, consider the interests of individuals in government. Elected officials face the reality of having to retain enough political support in order to be reelected. Thus, they must consider the political popularity of their decisions in addition to their judgment regarding the public interest. Selfish elected officials might think only in terms of how many additional votes or campaign contributions they can get from a particular policy, but even the most public-spirited elected official must consider how his decisions will affect his reelection prospects. Public-spirited elected officials can only act in the public interest if they get reelected, after all. Thus, political support for public policy decisions is always an important consideration. Chapter 2 investigates more thoroughly the relationship between politics and public policy.

Most government employees are not elected, but work in the bureaucracy, relatively insulated from electoral politics. Like elected officials, these bureaucrats undoubtedly want to further the public interest, but must consider their own interests, too. Chapter 2 also examines the role that bureaucratic incentives play in determining public policy outcomes. The bottom line is that one cannot assume that the government will automatically produce public policy that furthers the public interest. Rather, one must analyze the political process that produces public policy in order to determine what types of policies are likely to be produced. In many cases, the system is biased to create policies that favor the private interests of individuals who have political power rather than favor the public interest.

THE SIGNS OF PROGRESS

The standard of living in developed nations has improved tremendously since Malthus wrote about a future in which most of the population would be doomed to a life at the subsistence level — a world in which starvation would be a primary form of population control. In parts of the world, starvation is still a very real threat, but those nations tend to be dictatorships with centrally planned economies. Economic freedom and reliance on markets to allocate resources produce higher standards of living. That is what has made the difference between North and South Korea and between East and West Germany. That is what caused Eastern Europe to lag behind Western Europe before Eastern Europeans overthrew their dictatorial governments in 1989. Will the standard of living in Eastern Europe now approach that of Western Europe? It will for those countries that adopt private property, markets, and freedom of exchange.

In developed countries in the nineteenth century and in less developed countries today, hiking and canoeing were methods of transportation. Hunting and fishing were ways to produce food. Now, in developed countries, they are forms of recreation. This is some indication of the progress that has been made.[3] When Malthus wrote, and for all of history before Malthus's time, obesity was a sign of wealth. Only a wealthy person could obtain enough food to become overweight. Today, in countries like the United States, the most common nutritional problem of poor people is obesity. It is a sign of progress when even poor people can afford enough food to overeat.

In the United States, people can be categorized as below poverty level and yet have indoor plumbing, telephones, electricity, and cars. The twentieth century has seen significant increases in life spans and significant decreases in work hours. None of this is intended to minimize the plight of the poor. Certainly, we should want public policy in the United States and around the world to improve the well-being of those who are least well-off. The point is, those who are least well-off are much better-off now than they would have been a century ago, and this is especially true in market economies.

At the end of the twentieth century, it is apparent around the world that improvements in the standard of living can be produced by abandoning centrally planned economic systems and embracing market systems. The signs of progress in market economies are obvious. This is true not only in the production of goods and services but also in other quality-of-life areas that affect all citizens. Environmental degradation has been much more severe in socialist countries than in capitalist ones. Health care for all citizens has been much better in market economies. Housing has been much better in market economies. What does this say about the role of government in dealing with quality-of-life issues in market economies that already have a high standard of living for most citizens? The thesis developed throughout this volume is that increased reliance on market incentives rather than government planning is the way to enhance the quality of life. The same market mechanisms that can efficiently produce goods and services can also be employed to enhance the quality of life.

This conclusion is not inescapable. It is conceivable that markets are better at producing goods and services, while government planning is better at enhancing the quality of life. Thus, it is important to understand the underlying issues, to understand how markets work, and to understand how they can be applied to these quality-of-life issues in order to see that government planning will be as counterproductive in enhancing the quality of life as it has proven to be at producing goods and services.

REDISTRIBUTION TO THE RICH

Some issues that might normally be thought of as enhancing the quality of life are cultural amenities, such as art museums, symphony orchestras, and operas. These amenities are distinctly outside the bounds of this study because they are fundamentally redistribution to the rich. Overwhelmingly, these types of cultural activities tend to appeal to upper income people, although often they are subsidized heavily by general tax revenues. Why should general tax dollars be used to subsidize symphony orchestras but not rock concerts? Why should general tax dollars be used to subsidize golf courses but not bowling alleys? Essentially, these are special interest expenditures that benefit those consumers who enjoy those activities but are paid for by the general public.

Even though these activities are publicly funded, they are often further rationed with user fees. Thus, the poor person who wants to play on the golf course will have to pay a greens fee, and the poor person who wants to attend the symphony will have to buy a ticket. Thus, lower income people are often priced out of these markets that are subsidized by everybody's tax dollars.

Are these activities just publicly subsidized consumption for the rich, or do they really serve a larger public purpose and enhance the quality of life for everyone? Of course, those people who like the symphony will argue for the importance of subsidizing it, but what justification is there in having country music fans subsidize symphonies? If their fans, who tend to be higher income people, cannot afford to have them pay their own way, then one must question the wisdom of funding these consumption activities through a public subsidy. These are interesting questions, but these issues fall outside the scope of analysis of this book. The quality-of-life issues considered here do not include programs that essentially are redistribution to the rich.

WHAT IS THE QUALITY OF LIFE?

One of the essential indicators of an individual's quality of life is the goods and services that the individual is able to consume. Another is the enjoyment of family and friends. Yet, these issues fall outside the quality-of-life indicators considered here because they are elements of the quality of life that individuals can produce for themselves. Government has proven to be inept at producing goods and services for its citizens, and government programs have yet to create friendships and enhance family ties.[4] Some aspects of the quality of life must be created collectively, however. Individual effort can do little to protect the environment, for example, and one person can have little impact on producing safe products or on reducing communicable diseases. Likewise, an individual can build a house but can have little impact on the overall design of a city. This volume is concerned with the quality-of-life issues in which cooperation among many individuals is required to enhance the quality of life.

The real problem in many of these quality-of-life issues is that the activities of one individual affect the quality of life of other individuals, so some form of cooperation is necessary to enhance the quality of life. An individual who damages his television set harms himself primarily, but an individual who dumps toxic waste or who has a communicable disease can potentially harm many other individuals. Does this mean that government intervention is necessary in order to preserve the quality of life or can the market mechanisms that create goods and services also be used to enhance the quality of life? That is the issue considered here.

THE PLAN OF ATTACK

The issues to be dealt with are complex, and the arguments are at times subtle. How can they best be analyzed? The plan of attack in this volume is to consider first the general idea that market mechanisms can be employed to enhance the quality of life. Government planning can be compared to market allocation of resources to show how markets are able to take advantage of more information than bureaucratically run governments and are better able to utilize that information to enhance the quality of life.

Markets are fundamentally better able to enhance the quality of life by producing and conserving those things that are socially valuable. With private property and market allocation of resources, owners have an incentive to preserve the value of what they own, whereas, when the government allocates resources, all decisions come down to who has more political power. Chapter 2 directly compares government planning with market allocation of resources, and Chapter 3 examines how markets can work to protect future resources.

Chapters 4–10 examine particular quality-of-life issues to see how the ideas developed in the first three chapters can be applied. Protection of the environment is an important public policy issue. Some other issues considered are growth management and land use planning, homelessness, the regulation of product quality, the drug problem, and health care. These specific issues were chosen because they tend to be among the more important quality-of-life issues, and because they tend to be among the more controversial issues. Seeing how markets can work in some of these more controversial areas can help toward understanding how markets can work in areas not directly considered.

A number of other areas might have been discussed but were not. Education is an area that could benefit from more market incentives, but much has been written already on the voucher system and privatizing education. Libraries and universities could be analyzed in a manner similar to elementary and secondary schools, but these two areas fall more into the category of redistribution to the rich. Upper income people usually get college educations and frequent the public libraries even though all taxpayers help to finance these institutions. The alleviation of poverty might also have been examined, but, again, much has been written about government redistribution programs.[5]

The topics covered here are not intended to be comprehensive in any sense but are intended to illustrate how market incentives can work to enhance the quality of life and how government intervention is often counterproductive. The idea of the first several chapters is to show that the principles depicted by these individual issues are applicable to quality-of-life issues in general.

CONCLUSION

The market system has a good record for enhancing the quality of life. Throughout history, those societies that relied on markets have seen the quality of life of their citizens increase, while government planning has proven to be a failure. However, while the merits of allocating resources through markets are recognized in the abstract, in many specific cases, people whose standard of living has been greatly enhanced by market economies argue that government intervention is needed to further enhance the quality of life.

The quality of life is in danger when people who have benefited so much from the market allocation of resources turn away from the market and try to produce other amenities through government. For example, when one turns to government to produce housing, to protect the environment, or to produce health care one is likely to find the quality of life in those areas lowered as a result. However, the real danger comes when people do not realize why there are housing shortages, environmental problems, and health care crises and turn to government to solve problems that are largely the result of government policies to begin with. If people do not realize that problems in these areas are caused by government policies, then one failed government policy leads to another as people demand government action to deal with government-created problems.

If government policies are to be determined through democratic decision making, then voters must understand the policy alternatives in order to choose the best policies. At the end of the twentieth century, the idea that government planning can be used to produce goods and services effectively has been discredited, but the threat of government planning is still present in issues dealing with the quality of life. In a democracy, it is important that this threat be understood widely, or else the nation could unwittingly choose public policies that will erode our quality of life. How long could misguided policy options be continued? It took the centrally planned economy in the Soviet Union 70 years to collapse. Would we recognize government-induced problems when they started to appear? Until the end of the 1980s, many experts were proclaiming central planning to be the most efficient way to allocate resources.

The arguments are important precisely because the negative effects of government planning can take a long time to appear and are not obviously recognizable as the result of government planning even when they do appear. With this introduction, it is time to develop a theoretical foundation for understanding the relationship between public policy and the quality of life.

NOTES

1.   The first edition of the "Essay on Population" was published anonymously in 1798. A much larger second edition was published in 1803, and Malthus continued publishing numerous revised editions containing additional evidence that he believed supported his views.

2.   This idea is discussed by James M. Buchanan, "Public Finance and Public Choice," *National Tax Journal* 28 (December 1975): 383–94.

3.   This point was made in Terry L. Anderson and Donald R. Leal, *Free Market Environmentalism* (San Francisco: Pacific Research Institute for Public Policy, 1991).

4.   Some have argued that government programs break down family ties in a number of ways. Welfare programs give families an incentive to break up, and the advent of Social Security and Medicare have lessened the intergenerational responsibilities between children and their parents as well as family bonds. Charles Murray, *Losing Ground* (New York: Basic Books, 1984) argues that government redistribution programs have served to break up families and, hence, have lowered the quality of life in this dimension.

5.   See Murray, *Losing Ground* for a good discussion of problems that have been produced by government programs to aid lower income individuals.

2

Planning versus Markets

Throughout much of the twentieth century, a debate extended from the most abstract quarters of academia to the most pragmatic areas of public policy about the relative merits of government versus markets in the allocation of resources. Those who argued in favor of government planning did not deny that markets could be productive in the allocation of resources but, rather, argued that government planning was superior to markets. Some argued that government planning should be used to augment markets in places where markets are weakest while others argued that markets be replaced completely by centrally planned economies.

In the abstract world of academics, both sides declared a victory in the debate and the issue never has been resolved. In the real world, the collapse of much of the centrally planned Eastern European economy in 1989, followed shortly thereafter by the break-up of the Soviet Union, has pushed public opinion away from central planning. The experiments with socialism in country after country have shown that markets produce a higher standard of living and a better quality of life than central planning.

The issue is not resolved completely, however, because while most people acknowledge readily the general superiority of markets they also see a significant role for government to play in the economy. This is particularly true in issues that involve the quality of life rather than merely the quantity of goods and services that people consume. The market is great at producing goods and services for private consumption, the argument goes, but falls down when it comes to producing the things for the collective good, such as a clean environment, an efficient mix of land uses in developed areas, the protection of endangered species, and the provision of health care. The list could go on. Thus, it is worthwhile to review the general arguments on both sides of the planning versus markets debate to see what principles might apply to these quality-of-life issues.

THE SOCIALIST CALCULATION DEBATE

The socialist calculation debate centers on the question of whether central planning can be used to aid in the allocation of resources. While the details of the debate are interesting in their own right, they are also very relevant to the applicability of government action to improve the quality of life. With hindsight, it is clear that centrally planned economies are not very good at producing goods and services, but, as late as the 1960s, very respected economists argued that central planning was superior to markets in the production of goods and services. It is important to see not only that they were wrong but also why they were wrong, because some of the same problems that governments have had in producing goods and services might also impede a government's ability to enhance the quality of life, despite the best intentions of everyone involved.

The socialist calculation debate began early in the twentieth century, shortly after the Russian revolution that created the Soviet Union, whose new leaders wanted to establish a centrally planned socialist economy. One problem they faced is that nobody knew how a centrally planned economy should be established or how it would operate. The intellectual foundations leading to the establishment of a socialist country were found in Karl Marx's treatise, *Capital*,[1] but *Capital* was a book about the failings of capitalism and offered little guidance as to how a socialist economy would actually be run. When the socialists in the Soviet Union were searching for answers, economist Ludwig von Mises made the claim that central planning could not work to allocate resources. The problem, as Mises saw it, was that prices and markets are necessary to provide the information about how resources should be allocated. Without prices and markets, there would be no indication about how much of any good should be produced, what production process would be most efficient, how much investment should be undertaken, or where resources used for investment should be allocated.[2]

Markets helped the early planned economy in the Soviet Union in two ways, Mises noted. First, some markets did remain in the Soviet Union; second, because most of the world still used markets, central planners could look at world prices as a guide to resource allocation in developing their plans. Prices in world markets would provide central planners in the Soviet Union with good information about how valuable various resources were. For example, by looking at world prices of steel and aluminum, Soviet planners could obtain information about the value of those goods in their economy, despite the internal lack of prices. If the whole world turned to central planning, Mises argued that there would be no way in which central planners could develop a workable plan.

In response to Mises' critique of central planning, Oskar Lange and Fred Taylor wrote a volume in which they explained how central planners could take advantage of the same principles that underlie the market in order to develop a centrally planned economy.[3] In brief, Lange and Taylor argued that central planners could create administered prices and allow plant managers to decide how much of various resources they wanted at those centrally planned prices. The planners would allocate budgets to the managers based upon administered prices for their output. If shortages of some goods developed, that would indicate that the administered prices for those goods should be raised; conversely, surpluses for goods would indicate that those prices should be lowered. Essentially, the central planners in Lange and Taylor's system would duplicate the functions of the market. With this response to Mises' criticisms of socialism, the socialists declared themselves winners in the socialist calculation debate.

A superficial critique of this type of market socialism is that central planning duplicates the functions of the market, so one might as well use real markets rather than going through all of the costs of erecting a central planning mechanism that probably will not do a very good job of mimicking markets. This critique opens the door for additional debate about the merits of markets versus central planning. Friedrich Hayek made a more telling critique in an article that argued that the socialists had fundamentally misunderstood the function of prices and markets.

HAYEK ON PRICES AND MARKETS

Hayek noted that, while the Lange and Taylor solution had some superficial plausibility in an economy in which the same goods are always produced the same way, the most important function of markets is to allow individuals to share valuable information at low cost.[4] All individuals in an economy have certain information that is specific to their own work, such as alternative methods of production, the local availability of resources, and the value of potential innovations (new methods of production or new goods that might be produced). For example, soft drink manufacturers might alter the proportions of sugar and corn syrup as sweeteners depending upon the relative availability of the two sweeteners, and seafood restaurants might change their menus and prices in response to the local availability of various fish. An assembly line worker might find a more efficient way of assembling a product, and an automobile engineer might determine that steel engine blocks should be phased out in favor of aluminum. These are but a few examples of the specific decentralized information available to every person in an economy. One challenge any economy faces is to make the best use of all of this decentralized information in order to allocate resources as efficiently as possible.

In a market economy, the profit motive gives people an incentive to act on this information and change their prices accordingly without consulting anyone. Then, others in the economy can use this information to make their own decisions about resource allocation. The soft drink manufacturer does not have to know any of the details about the production of corn or sugar in order to decide on proportions of sugar and corn syrup to use as a sweetener. The prices of the two sweeteners convey all the information he needs to know. If something happens in the corn market to make corn syrup less readily available than before, its price will rise, and that price increase is all the information the soft drink manufacturer needs in order to know that there is reason to conserve corn syrup more now than previously. To take advantage of all of the information like this in a centrally planned economy, everyone would have to be constantly passing information up the chain of command to the central planners, who then would have to modify the central plan accordingly and pass the information back down to those who need it. The problem with central planning is there is too much information for the central planners to digest and comprehend, and even if they could receive all this information, they would be unable to use it as effectively as the people who originally had it to begin with.

When seasonal variations cause flounder to become relatively more abundant than shrimp, the restaurant owner (or grocer) will be in a better position to determine how relative prices should change than the central planner. How should the relative prices of seafood and steak be adjusted? Even more difficult problems arise when product innovations must be factored in. When an engineer develops a more efficient product, should it be produced and built? The manufacturing firm will be in a better position to assess the costs of development and the expected benefits from producing the more efficient product.

For example, gold is a better conductor of electricity than lead. If an electrical engineer suggests that gold solder be used in battery-powered radios instead of lead solder to conserve battery power, should the switch to gold be made? The high cost of gold in the market compared to lead makes it obvious that except in the most unusual circumstance, lead solder should be used. However, how would a central planner determine this without markets to show the relative value of gold compared to lead? This example understates the magnitude of the problem because it would be a relatively simple task to simply make two radios, one with gold solder and one with lead, and compare their performances. It would be more costly if the engineer said he could develop transistors to replace tubes in radios, or if an engineer said he could develop a jet engine to replace a piston engine for an airplane. How would a central planner decide which potential innovations are worth pursuing? In these areas, where market participants have specific information on the potential value of innovations, markets fare far better than central planning.

Hayek's insights on the workings of the market are critical to understanding why central planning failed in socialist countries and why there are perils in trying to use government planning to enhance the quality of life. Every individual has certain specific knowledge that is difficult to share with the central planner and that would be difficult to use even if the information were available. When a state agency oversees a land use plan for a local community, for example, the agency cannot take advantage of all of the local knowledge available to the local residents. Likewise, a bureaucrat in Washington will be in an unlikely position to take account of all relevant local information when protecting the environment or deciding how a particular parcel of land should be used. Similarly, an individual's doctor will have better information about appropriate medical treatment in a specific case than a government health agency that plans a health policy but does not see the individual patients.

GOVERNMENT PLANNING IN THE ABSTRACT AND IN THE REAL WORLD

In the abstract, people can create what seem like great plans to deal with problems ranging from crime to the environment to educational improvement to urban design. Really, there is no limit to great plans. However, plans can never take account of every contingency, and, in the real world, many of the problems were assumed away to make the plan end up being very relevant to the plan's actual operation.[5] Using Hayek's insights, one can see that, in the real world, government plans are likely to work less well than can be foreseen, while markets are likely to work better than anticipated. This is because with a government plan, problems that were not foreseen in the plan will arise to hurt the ability of the plan to achieve its goals, whereas with markets, individuals have an incentive to bargain among themselves to overcome resource allocation problems when unforeseen problems arise.[6] As Hayek noted, markets are organized to make the best use of everyone's knowledge throughout the economy in a way that no central planner could.

Often, when people suggest that the government should get involved to solve a problem, they view the government as a benevolent dictator who thinks the same as they do. There are lots of people who will recognize the same problem, and there will be lots of people who will advocate getting the government involved to solve it. However, agreeing on the problem is not the same as agreeing on the solution, and the problems with government involvement begin here. While everyone agrees on the problem to be solved, there will be many different and conflicting opinions on what is the best solution. Those problems will be resolved through the political process, but as a result, some individuals who initially advocated government involvement will be dissatisfied with the government's actions and will work through the political process to modify the government's behavior. Trying to solve problems through the political process invites conflict.[7]

The problems only begin here, because, while people have an ideal view of what those in government ought to be doing, the people working in the government may not be doing what those outside the government think they ought to. With markets, businesses have an incentive to satisfy the desires of their customers because only by doing so will they earn the profits that will keep the businesses afloat. The more successful a business is at satisfying its customers, the more profitable it will be. Incentives are different in the government because the government is going to collect taxes to pay for its programs regardless of how well its customers are served.

Often, the incentives are perverse, so that the less well an agency does its job, the more money will flow into it. If environmental problems grow, for example, more money is likely to be appropriated to the Environmental Protection Agency (EPA). If the EPA solves several environmental problems, their services will be needed less, and their budget is likely to decrease. While one should not doubt the good intentions of EPA employees, one should also note that those who work for the EPA have less personal incentive to solve environmental problems than those who work for McDonalds have to serve a good hamburger. Rather than just viewing government bureaucracies as agencies that unwaveringly do the best thing, it is worthwhile to examine the incentives more closely to see if they really can be counted on to serve the public interest.

INCENTIVES IN BUREAUCRACY

To understand bureaucracy, one must first understand that the people who work in bureaucracies are the same type of people who work in other jobs. They are motivated by rewards that may include higher pay, more praise, or nicer working conditions, and they will be reluctant to act in ways that have a negative impact on their own personal well-being. Bureaucrats are just like the rest of us, so to understand how bureaucracies work, we must understand the incentives that face those who work in them.

An important difference between government bureaucracies and private sector firms is that private firms have an incentive to serve their customers in order to enhance their profits. Bureaucracies do not receive profits; rather, they are given a budget to undertake certain activities. Usually, there is no way in which a profit or loss could be calculated for a bureaucracy because customers do not pay for the bureau's service, and there is usually not a private sector firm with which the bureau's performance could be compared. In cases where direct comparisons can be made, bureaucracies do not fare well.[8] For many of government's activities, a comparison between private sector and public sector production may be irrelevant. Government often produces things for which the market is ill-suited, such as national defense. However, when market alternatives do exist, such as for those quality-of-life issues that are the subject of this volume, it is relevant to consider the relative efficiencies of the private and public sectors.

In an insightful study about bureaucracy, William Niskanen observed that while bureaucrats do not get rewarded for profits like private sector workers, they do tend to get greater rewards the larger their budgets are.[9] For one thing, bureaucratic salaries are typically a function of how many employees a bureaucrat supervises, as well as the bureau's total budget. Thus, a larger bureau will mean a larger salary, giving the bureaucrat an incentive to increase the bureau's budget and increase the number of people on the organization's payroll. There are direct financial rewards for increasing the bureau's budget.

Bureaucrats may not be motivated by money alone, however. Another factor might be the prestige of one's job, but, once again, the larger the organization that is being supervised, the more prestige will be attached to the job. Another motivating factor could be power, but, again, a larger bureau will translate into more power. People will also be interested in having a more pleasant working environment, and larger budgets will lead toward a more pleasant environment. One will find the office atmosphere much more pleasant in a growing agency where there are opportunities for internal promotion than in a stagnant agency where there are no advancement opportunities, or, worse, a shrinking organization where some people will have to be let go. Again, this leads bureaucrats to want to maximize their budgets.

The factors mentioned above are all reasons why individuals in a bureaucracy will personally gain from increasing their bureau's budget, regardless of what the bureau does. Another factor that draws less on self-interest is that people are likely to be drawn to those jobs that they believe are important. People who work for the EPA are likely to be stronger believers in environmental protection than the typical individual. People who work for the Consumer Product Safety Commission are more likely than the typical individual to believe that government regulation of consumer products can benefit consumers. Bureaucrats will be motivated to push for larger budgets because they believe in the benefits of their bureaus, and the fact that their own personal self-interest lies in larger bureau budgets only helps their enthusiasm for larger budgets. All of this is coupled with the fact that there is no bottom line where profits and losses can be weighed to evaluate the bureau's output.

Niskanen also noted that bureaus bargain with the legislature for their budgets but that bureaus have a big advantage in the bargaining process. The bureau is the expert in one particular area, while the legislature must oversee many areas. Furthermore, the bureau has detailed information about the actual costs of producing its output, and it can selectively make this information available to the legislature in such a way as to enhance its opportunity to get a larger budget. The bottom line is that bureaus receive larger than optimal budgets.

Because there is no clear profit indicator in a government bureau, bureaus may not be as well organized at pursuing their stated goals as are private sector firms. For example, it may not be entirely clear what the bureau's goals are. In managing public lands, for instance, the government has a number of constituencies. Some people want wilderness preserved, some people want recreational opportunities like hiking, hunting, and fishing that may conflict with preservation, and logging companies and oil companies want to utilize the resources on public lands. Ranchers want to graze their herds on the same lands that conservationists want to preserve for natural wildlife. Because the public lands are owned by the government and not by any specific individuals, the bureaus that oversee them will not have a clear mandate regarding how the lands should be used. This lack of a clear indicator of success, like profits in a market, makes it hard to evaluate the performance of bureaus.

Because of this difficulty, individuals within a bureaucracy will be less under the control of those in charge than would be the case in a private firm. Lower level bureaucrats can pursue their own agendas with much more freedom than if there was a clear bottom line with which they could be evaluated. The result is likely to be that some individuals within the same bureau could be pursuing different goals. For all of these reasons, those who have studied bureaucracy agree that the incentive structure is not conducive to efficiency, as is the case for profit-making firms.[10]

If government must be pressed into service in some area, then there may be no alternative to the reduced incentives for efficient behavior inherent in bureaucracy. The point is not to argue that bureaucracies should never exist but, rather, that one must take into account that if a bureaucracy is established to deal with a problem, the incentives will be such that the bureau will do less than an ideal job. That may be better than nothing, but in many cases, the market offers alternatives that preserve the incentives for efficient behavior.

POLITICAL INFLUENCES AND SPECIAL INTERESTS

The concept of planning evokes the image of experts in an area designing public policies to produce optimal results through coordinated action. But government planning always has a political foundation. The government does not get involved in activities unless there is some demand registered through the political process, either through a consensus of constituents or through specific special interests. Once the government does decide to get involved, political influences will be felt every step of the way, from the design of the government program to its day-to-day operation.

Because of the nature of the political process, special interests will have an undue influence over the type of legislation that is passed and over the implementation of that legislation once it becomes law. The general public has little knowledge about most government programs. Individuals realize that public policy will not be affected regardless of their opinions. An individual might think that the federal government should lessen its maintenance of navigable waterways, reduce farm price supports, and become less involved in international affairs, but these opinions will have little impact on public policy.

The typical citizen will be far better off understanding the details of private consumption alternatives, such as the features of various automobiles and the relative quality differences among restaurants. These items can make a big difference in the quality of the individual's meals and transportation, whereas the individual's information about government policy, while perhaps interesting, will minimally affect the individual's quality of life, not because the outcomes of government policies are unimportant to the individual but because one individual's opinions will not have much effect on the government's policies.[11]

Therefore, most individuals know relatively little about most government policies. However, some individuals have a special interest in being informed about certain policies. While the typical citizen will know little about the government's programs to dredge the channels of navigable waterways, those who ship over those waterways will have a big incentive to become informed, and they will have a big incentive to become actively involved in trying to influence public policy. Likewise, while most people will be relatively uninformed about the government's farm price support programs, farmers will be well informed and motivated to try to influence the government to create policies more favorable to them. In general, most people will be poorly informed about most public policy, while special interests will be well informed and will have a big incentive to try to influence the government's actions.

In the world of politics, making decisions that generate the most political support is not necessarily the same thing as making decisions in the public interest. Most voters know little about most of the decisions elected officials make, but those who are directly affected have an incentive to become well informed and politically active regarding those issues that directly affect them. Most people know little about the government's programs to support the incomes of tobacco farmers, but tobacco farmers know a great deal about those programs and work hard to keep their subsidies coming. Is it an anomaly that while the U.S. Surgeon General rails against smoking, the U.S. Department of Agriculture pays tobacco farmers to grow tobacco, or is this representative of the way in which government actually works? Programs such as these must be understood in terms of public policy being determined by the special interests who are most directly affected, rather than in terms of public policy being made to further the public interest.[12]

The nature of the political process produces government policies that favor special interests, rather than the general public interest.[13] When considering how the government might ideally become involved in public policy, therefore, one must always consider that special interests likely will have a substantial influence over the government's policies. Even after public policies are put in place, they can be modified by special interests engaging in the political process, so even if good government programs are established, without constant vigilance they can always go bad. The nature of the democratic political process is that anyone can lobby to make changes, and those who have a large special interest in programs will do so.

THE CHICAGO THEORY OF REGULATION

When firms and individuals in the private sector behave in ways that seem counter to the public interest, a common remedy is to pass regulations to control the undesirable behavior. The intuitive appeal of regulation is straightforward: if someone is not doing what the general public thinks they should, then the government will pass a law to make them. For example, if people are concerned that monopoly utility suppliers will charge too much for their services, the government can pass regulations requiring that they charge fair prices. If people are concerned that manufacturers are polluting the environment, the government can pass laws requiring that they stop. If people are concerned that manufacturers are producing unsafe products, then the government can require that their products be tested and certified as safe.

This intuitive appeal of regulation relies on the regulations actually doing what they are intended to do and depends upon those who are enforcing the regulations to do so in a manner that furthers the public interest. Rather than assume that regulations will work as intended, some economists have examined the incentive structure in the regulatory process and have concluded that, often, regulation will tend to favor the regulated industry rather than the general public who should be protected by regulation. This theory is often associated with economists at the University of Chicago — and with George Stigler, who was an economics professor there — so it has come to be known as the Chicago theory of regulation.[14]

Like the theories of bureaucracy and special interest politics discussed above, the Chicago theory of regulation recognizes the incentives that regulators face. They deal with the industries they regulate on a day-to-day basis, but they rarely interact with the general public. Much of the information the regulatory agency will have from which to make their decisions will come from the regulated industry. The industry has an incentive to present information in a way that is favorable to their point of view and to persuade regulators to make decisions that favor them. The general public, however, will have little input into the regulatory process. While those in the regulated industry make their living there and, therefore, have an incentive to be involved in the regulatory process, most of the general public will work in other areas and will have little incentive to become active participants in the regulatory process. As a result, the regulatory agency will have a natural inclination to favor the industry it regulates.

Public service commissions who regulate the rates of electric utilities, telephone companies, and so forth are charged with regulating in the public interest, but large input from the regulated industries, coupled with relatively little input from the general public, leads to decisions favoring the industries. Most people have little idea how to contact their public service commissions and would have little incentive to become involved. The likelihood of affecting the commission's decision is small, and there is little for the individual consumer to gain. One could save perhaps a few dollars off one's bill. The regulated firm has a few dollars on everyone's bill at stake, which will be millions of dollars. Therefore, there is a much bigger incentive for the firm to get involved in trying to regulate the commission.

The same principle applies to any other type of regulation. Consumers want safe products and have a Consumer Products Safety Commission to help obtain them. However, most people have little involvement with the commission, giving firms whose products are under review undue influence in the process. Likewise, banks and savings and loans are regulated to make sure their portfolios do not leave taxpayers with undue risk because of federal deposit insurance. That system appeared to be working well until its spectacular (and costly) breakdown in the late 1980s. As the facts are revealed, it is clear that the regulated firms had substantial influence over the regulatory process, even to the point of being able to use the political process to overrule regulators who found some institutions to be risky. Because consumers have little incentive to be informed those in the regulated industry can control the regulatory process.

Because politics are inevitably involved in regulation, the regulatory process is never going to work as well as it would in an ideal setting where regulators act solely in the public interest. This is not to say that regulation never would be warranted, but rather to say that it would be simplistic to assume that if a regulation were passed with the intention of producing some desirable result, the desirable result would automatically follow as a result of the regulation.

INCENTIVES IN MARKETS

Those who have studied the way in which resources are allocated in the public sector have found that there are a number of reasons why government solutions will not work as well in practice as in theory when the solutions are planned. The problem is that the individ-ual incentives of those who work in the government often do not lead them toward acting in the public interest. Human nature leads people to consider their own self-interests in any decision, so, realistically, we are asking too much of individuals in government if we ask them to act in the public interest when such actions would be in opposition to their own self-interests. This incentive problem is an important reason why government regulation, government bureaucracy, and even majority rule politics tends not to allocate resources optimally.

Those who have studied private sector resource allocation have found related problems in the operation of markets. People who are following their own self-interests sometimes undertake actions that harm others. Problems that arise in market allocation of resources occur because sometimes people who are engaged in market activities use resources that are not allocated through markets. Air pollution, for example, is a result of no market for air. Operators of steel mills pay wages for the labor they use, they pay for the coal and iron ore that make up their raw materials, and they pay for most of the resources they use, which gives them an incentive to take account of the cost of using the resources. However, because there is no market for air, they create air pollution with no incentive to take account of the effects of air pollution on others.

At this point, a traditional analysis of the problem recommends that the government create regulations to curb the pollution. Regulations could require certain types of pollution control equipment, limit the amount of pollution a firm could create, or even close down the offend-ing businesses. As seen above, regulations can create their own prob-lems, and an alternative solution would be to try to create property rights in clean air and give firms an incentive to take account of the environmental costs they are imposing on others in the best way they see fit. If firms can be charged directly for the amount of pollution they create, they have an incentive to find the cheapest way to reduce their pollution.

When government regulations require a certain solution, firms are precluded from finding ways to reduce their emissions more cheaply and have no incentive to reduce pollution any more than the govern-ment's regulations require. If firms were given rights to emit certain limited amounts of pollution and if these pollution rights were marketable, firms that can create more valuable output per unit of pollution would have an incentive to buy pollution rights from firms that create less economic value per unit of pollution, which can help clean the environment and allocate resources more efficiently. Market solutions for environmental problems will be discussed in more detail in Chapter 4, but, in general, market solutions to quality-of-life issues give individuals an incentive to allocate resources efficiently, whereas regulations — even when they work exactly as planned — only give individuals an incentive to meet the letter of the law as cheaply as possible.

The fundamental principle behind the market mechanism is voluntary exchange; the fundamental principle behind government policies is coercion. Because nobody is forced to trade in markets, exchange takes place only when all parties to the exchange believe that they benefit. Thus, participants in exchanges have an incentive to make what they have to exchange be as valuable to others as possible. If all parties to a potential exchange do not agree that everyone benefits, then no exchange will take place. The government, however, enacts policies and then forces individuals to comply. Thus, whereas market participants want to create as much value for others as they can (because they get more in return that way), those who abide by government policies simply follow the regulations and have no incentive to consider the effects of their actions on others.

Even if those who are trying to comply with government regulations want to do what is in the public good, the nature of government regulations prevents them from evaluating the regulations in that way. Noncompliance can bring with it penalties, so when responding to a regulation, those being regulated must look to the letter of the law to see whether they are doing what they need to do to be legal, rather than looking at the public interest goal of the regulation. In markets, people have an incentive to do what is best for each other; with government regulation, they do not.

MARKETS AND PUBLIC POLICY

The dismal record of socialism, wherever it has been tried, coupled with the successes of market economies to increase the standard of living for individuals wherever markets have been allowed to thrive, shows the general superiority of markets to deliver a better quality of life than government planning. Those who support heavy government involvement in quality-of-life issues will correctly point out that the government has been heavily involved in most market economies and that the choice is not between government planning and markets, but rather a choice of how much to leave to markets and how much to assign to government.

It has been useful in this chapter to review the reasons why government planning does not work well to allocate resources and produce wealth, because some of those same reasons will cause government policies intended to improve the quality of life to work less well than their designers might hope. The problems with government planning can be summarized under two major headings: first, government planning does not give individuals an incentive to create wealth for others, whereas a market does; and, second, central planning is ill-equipped to take advantage of all of the decentralized information that exists in an economy. Markets give individuals an incentive to utilize this information to create as much value for others as possible.

Critics of the market system have argued that while markets may be good at producing goods and services for individual consumption, markets do not produce those things from which we all benefit and which enhance the quality of life. The remainder of this book examines a wide range of these quality-of-life issues to show how markets can be used to enhance the quality of life and how government involvement in these areas, while generally well-meaning, is sometimes counterproductive and actually lowers the quality of life. The general principles reviewed in this chapter will be applied to specific quality-of-life issues in the following chapters.

In the middle of the twentieth century, when there was an earnest debate about whether market economies or centrally planned economies would produce a higher standard of living for their citizens, scholars such as Mises,[15] Hayek, and Friedman[16] explained why markets work better than central planning. This book builds on their foundations and on the work of many scholars after them to show why the same principles that apply to the production of individually consumed goods and services also apply to issues that enhance our collective quality of life.

NOTES

1.   Karl Marx, *Capital* (New York: Modern Library, 1906, orig. 1867).

2.   Mises began writing about this problem in German in the 1920s, and some later English statements of his ideas can be found in Ludwig von Mises, *Socialism* (New Haven: Yale University Press, 1951) and Ludwig von Mises, *Planned Chaos* (Irving-on-Hudson, N.Y.: Foundation for Economic Education, 1947.

3.   Oskar Lange and Fred M. Taylor, *On the Economic Theory of Socialism* (Minneapolis: University of Minnesota Press, 1938).

4.   Friedrich A. Hayek, "The Use of Knowledge in Society," *American Economic Review* 35 (September 1945: 519–30. Hayek developed a more substantial critique of socialism in Friedrich A. Hayek, *The Road to Serfdom* (Chicago: University of Chicago Press, 1944).

5.   I have discussed the use of simplifying assumptions extensively in Randall G. Holcombe, *Economic Models and Methodology* (New York: Greenwood, 1989).

6.   This statement follows an insight from Ronald Coase, "The Problem of Social Cost," *Journal of Law & Economics* 3 (October 1960): 1–44.

7.   This lesson follows along the lines of James M. Buchanan, "Politics, Policy, and the Pigouvian Margins," *Economic* n.s. 29 (February 1962): 17–28, who notes that whenever a political decision is made with less than unanimous approval, the

majority imposes a cost on the minority. Thus, to use the economist's term, there is a built-in externality present in any majority rule decision.

8. Some studies that make comparisons between bureaucratic and market supply of similar outputs are James T. Bennett and Manual H. Johnson, "Tax Reduction without Sacrifice: Private Sector Production of Public Services," *Public Finance Quarterly* 8 (October 1980): 363–96; Kenneth W. Clarkson, "Some Implications of Property Rights in Hospital Management," *Journal of Law & Economics* 15 (October 1972): 363–84; Cotton M. Lindsay, "A Theory of Government Enterprise," *Journal of Political Economy* 84 (October 1976): 1061–77; H. E. Frech, III, "The Property Rights Theory of the Firm: Empirical Results from a Natural Experiment," *Journal of Political Economy* 84 (February 1976): 143–52; Roger D. Blair, Paul B. Ginsberg, and Ronald J. Vogel, "Blue Cross-Blue Shield Administration Costs: A Study of Non-Profit Health Insurers," *Economic Inquiry* 13 (June 1975): 237–51; David G. Davies, "The Efficiency of Public versus Private Firms: The Case of Australia's Two Airlines," *Journal of Law & Economics* 14 (April 1971): 149–65; David G. Davies, "Property Rights and Economic Efficiency — The Australian Airlines Revisited," *Journal of Law & Economics* 20 (April 1977): 223–26; W. Mark Crain and Asghar Zardkoohi, "A Test of the Property Rights Theory of the Firm: Water Utilities in the United States," *Journal of Law & Economics* 21 (October 1978): 395–408; and Roger Ahlbrandt, "Efficiency in the Provision of Fire Services," *Public Choice* 16 (Fall 1973): 1–15. Each of these studies concludes that profit-making businesses are more efficient than institutions that are unable to earn profit as a reward for doing a good job. I know of no study that shows the opposite. One must conclude that, without the profit motive, bureaucrats are not going to carry out their jobs as effectively as they would if their bureaus could earn profits for efficient service.

9. William A. Niskanen, *Bureaucracy and Representative Government* (Chicago: Aldine-Atherton, 1971). Niskanen earlier sketched his ideas in "The Peculiar Economics of Bureaucracy," *American Economic Review* 58 (May 1968): 293–305, and later refined some of his ideas in William A. Niskanen, "Bureaucrats and Politicians," *Journal of Law & Economics* 18 (December 1975): 617–43.

10. For examples, see Ludwig von Mises, *Bureaucracy* (New Haven: Yale University Press, 1944); Gordon Tullock, *Bureaucracy* (Washington, D.C.: Public Affairs Press, 1965); and Anthony Downs, *Inside Bureaucracy* (Boston: Little, Brown, 1967).

11. This idea was developed by Anthony Downs, *An Economic Theory of Democracy* (New York: Harper & Row, 1957).

12. The impact of special interests on public policy was explained in Downs, *An Economic Theory of Democracy*. More recent developments are described in Barry R. Weingast, Kenneth A. Shepsle, and Christopher Johnsen, "The Political Economy of Benefits and Costs: A Neoclassical Approach to Distributive Politics," *Journal of Political Economy* 89 (August 1981): 642–64; and Randall G. Holcombe, *An Economic Analysis of Democracy* (Carbondale: Southern Illinois University Press, 1985).

13. For an academic discussion of this special interest model of politics, see Weingast, Shepsle, and Johnsen, "The Political Economy of Benefits and Costs," pp. 642–64; and Holcombe, *An Economic Analysis of Democracy*.

14. The clearest statement of this theory of regulation can be found in George J. Stigler, "The Theory of Economic Regulation," *Bell Journal of Economics and Management Science* 2 (Spring 1971): 3–21. For extensions of the Chicago view in articles by other Chicago professors, see Richard A. Posner, "Theories of Economic Regulation," *Bell Journal of Economics and Management Science* 5 (Autumn 1974): 335–58; and Sam Peltzman, "Toward a More General Theory of Regulation," *Journal of Law & Economics* 19 (August 1976): 211–40.

15. In addition to earlier works cited, Ludwig von Mises, *Human Action*, 3rd rev. ed. (Chicago: Henry Regnery, 1966) deals with the efficiency of markets in a more general way.

16. For examples, see Milton Friedman, *Capitalism and Freedom* (Chicago: University of Chicago Press, 1962); and Milton Friedman and Rose Friedman, *Free to Choose* (New York: Harcourt Brace Jovanovich, 1980).

3

Protecting Future Resources

Critics of the market system sometimes argue that it exploits future generations by using resources that should rightfully belong to future generations in order to produce more goods that we can consume now. They say that under the market system non-renewable resources are used up, and there is no incentive to preserve wealth for our descendants. In fact, the opposite is true. The market system provides substantial incentives to preserve resources for future generations, whereas entrusting resources to government stewardship creates the incentive to utilize resources now at the expense of potential future users. The fundamental principle is: if someone owns a resource in a market economy, the owner has an incentive to maintain and enhance its value because the resource can be sold any time the owner wants. If the government determines how the resource will be allocated, then nobody has a clear ownership interest. Anyone who wants to use the resource has an incentive to compete through the political process to gain its use. Anyone who is successful at gaining access to a resource through the political process has little incentive to maintain or enhance its value because the individual will not own the resource but will only have won the right to use it until someone else is successful at using the political process to gain access.

The problem with government ownership of a resource is that nobody actually has clear ownership rights, and no assignment of rights can be assumed to be permanent. What politics grants, politics can later take away. However, a private owner has every incentive to maintain and increase the value of a resource because he or she has the right to sell it for its market value.

The industrial revolution has brought with it a better quality of life with every generation. The twentieth century has seen dramatic increases in income, in the health of the population, and in the average life span, while, at the same time, the average work week has been shortened and most jobs have become less burdensome and safer. This is especially true of developed nations with market economies. It is less true — and sometimes not true — for centrally planned economies and in nations that erect barriers to markets and commerce. Quite clearly, nations that have encouraged markets and free trade have seen improvements in their quality of life, and this is especially evident when comparing market economies with centrally planned economies.

After World War II, Germany was divided into East Germany, with a centrally planned economy, and West Germany, with a market economy. The quality of life in West Germany was better by almost any measure than in East Germany. Incomes were higher, working conditions were better, the environment was cleaner, and, even in cultural and aesthetic areas, West Germany had a higher quality of life than East Germany. In the hostile environment of the Cold War, one might have imagined the economically stronger West Germany taking over East Germany by force, but the superiority of the quality of life in West Germany became so apparent to those in East Germany that East Germany chose to abandon her governmentally planned system in favor of the market system of the West. The West was able to win the Cold War without firing a shot because of the demonstrated superiority in the quality of life under a market system.

Would those who lived under a governmentally planned economy be willing to give up their system if they thought that, despite the apparent higher quality of life in the West, markets were mortgaging their futures to pay for the present? That is unlikely. Those who used to live under government planning recognize that the market system provides a better quality of life, both now and in the future. The problems of government planning in the allocation of resources have been played out around the world. Compare centrally planned North Korea with market-oriented South Korea. Look at the decline in the quality of life that followed Castro's creation of a centrally planned economy in Cuba.

These examples can illustrate the point, but they do not prove the case. Perhaps capitalist economies really are mortgaging their futures in order to enhance the present standard of living. Perhaps the developed nations of the world enjoy their high standards of living because they are exploiting less developed nations. The case can be illustrated by examples, but it must be made by understanding how markets provide incentives to protect resources for future generations.

REPRESENTATION OF THE UNBORN
IN POLITICS AND MARKETS

One criticism sometimes made against market economies is that, while they are good at producing goods and services for current consumption, they do so by exploiting future generations. By emphasizing the bottom line, no account is taken of the well-being of our heirs who are unable to lay any claim to the resources being used by the current generation. The solution, according to this view, is to use government to protect resources for future generations. This criticism is wrong in the way it depicts both markets and government. In fact, government allocation of resources gives no voice to future generations, whereas market allocation does.

When resources are allocated by government, they are subject to political control. That means that some interest groups will be competing with others to determine how resources will be used. For example, environmentalists may compete with loggers to protect governmentally owned timber lands. One group wants logging on those lands; the other does not. First, neither group can win an unconditional victory as long as the government owns the land. Environmentalists may temporarily stop the logging, but because whether logging is to be allowed is a political decision, loggers can continue lobbying to have the decision reversed. Environmentalists may temporarily prevent offshore oil drilling, but oil drillers can continue to lobby to have the decision reversed. Political victories are never permanent — they are always temporary. With government ownership, there is no way to prevent those with political power from using it to gain access to publicly owned resources. The public interest is irrelevant. Political power will be the determining factor.

Second, when political decisions are made, future generations do not get to vote. Some individuals might claim to represent the interests of future generations, but if they do, it would be only through their own altruism. They get no personal gain from representing the unborn. Oil drillers might want to develop energy resources on public lands, whereas environmentalists might like a pristine environment for hiking and other activities that bring them closer to nature. This would be self-interest. Would future generations be better off with more natural environment or with more developed energy resources to run their televisions and air conditioners and to provide their transportation? The answer is not clear cut, and, undoubtedly, when considering the interests of future generations, some natural resources should be preserved and some should be developed. Because the unborn do not get to vote, they will have no say in how resources will be used. Some groups will work against others in the political process, and, if any of the groups claim to represent future generations, they have no personal incentive to do so.

The market system, in contrast, provides a direct way for the preferences of future generations to be taken into account. Resources that are preserved for the future and that will have value to future generations can eventually be sold to them. Because of markets, people have an incentive today to create and preserve resources that will be valuable to the unborn. Why would a timber company plant trees today that will not mature until after the company owners have died? Why would the owner of oil reserves save the oil for the use of people who

have not yet been born? The timber, oil, and other resources that will
have value to future generations have a market value now, based on
the expected prices that future generations will pay for them. The
resource owner can sell the resources rather than use them, and the
next owner might also keep them for years before selling them rather
than using them, until finally, the resources are bought and used by
people who were not even alive when the original decision to preserve
the resources was made.[1]

There are two key points to recognize. First, in markets, individuals
will find it in their own self-interests to preserve resources for future
generations, because they can personally benefit from selling valuable
resources to others. Because resources can be passed on from generation to generation, the unborn do have a say in today's markets. The
same is not true in politics. While some people might altruistically
think of future generations when they engage in political activity, they
derive no personal benefit from doing so. The unborn are actually
represented better in markets than they are in politics.

Second, political victories can never be permanent. Because a
political victory today has made the government decide to preserve
resources for the future does not prevent the losers in this year's
political battle from trying again next year. Government preservation
of resources must be a constant battle, whereas if resources are
privately owned, the owner can decide to preserve resources uni-
laterally — and has the incentive to do so if those resources promise to
be more valuable to future generations than to those in the present.
Markets are inherently better at protecting future resources than are
governments.

TRADING WITH THE UNBORN

When markets for valuable resources exist, people do not need to
consume the resources they own to benefit from them. If they preserve
the value of the resources, they can sell them, so there is an incentive
to conserve any resources that will have value to future generations.
Resources can be preserved for endless generations, with each
generation preserving the resources with the expectation of selling
them to future generations. Individuals can, in effect, trade with the
unborn. They produce and conserve goods now for use by future
generations with the expectation that in the future they can sell the
results of their efforts.

The typical roofing shingle lasts 20 years, and because Americans
move frequently, this is much longer than the typical American will live
in a house. Why would anyone reroof a house with shingles that will
last longer than the person expects to stay in the house? Why would
people not use less expensive shingles that would last, say, five years,
or just put tarpaper on their roofs instead of shingles? The obvious

answer is that when they move, they can sell the house and get more money for a house that has a roof in good condition. Thus, a homeowner has an incentive to keep the house in good condition for the next owner.

This same principle applies to any resource allocated through the market. If a person has a lake on his property, why should he not throw his trash in the lake? Over the years, the lake will become polluted and less desirable, but the owner might expect to die before the lake becomes too polluted. However, because the individual can sell his property, he has an incentive to keep it in good condition because he will get more money for property containing a clean lake than a polluted lake. People have an incentive to preserve resources for people they do not know, or who are not even born yet, because those people will pay the current owner more for a more valuable resource. If the lake was owned "in common," or owned by the government, then the individual would have less of an incentive not to use the lake as an easy way of disposing of his trash, because the individual would have no way to profit directly from maintaining the lake in good condition.

Markets enable future generations to use their future economic power now to give the current generation an incentive to preserve resources for them. Governments allocate resources through the political process, and future generations get no vote in today's elections. People may vote with future generations in mind, but, then again, they may not. They certainly do not have the same personal incentive to take account of the demands of future generations as they would if resources were privately owned and allocated through markets. The best way to preserve resources for the future is to assign ownership rights to private individuals and to allow individuals to profit from their preservation of resources.

MARKETS AND THE RATE OF INTEREST

Those who defer consuming resources are rewarded by earning a return for not consuming. This is the role played by interest in a market economy. Assume that the interest rate is 5 percent.[2] An individual could consume her entire income in the present, leaving next year's income to finance next year's consumption. However, if she saves $1 this year with a 5 percent interest rate, she could consume 5 percent more for that dollar next year than this year. There is a reward for deferring consumption.

This reward can add up substantially. Saving $1 this year will yield $1.05 next year, but if saved for two years, it will earn another 5 percent, yielding $1.1025. If saved for five years, the dollar will grow to $1.28. After 10 years, the dollar would have grown to $1.63, and, after 20 years, the dollar would have grown to $2.66. If one thinks in terms of saving now to enhance one's children's (or grandchildren's) consumption, a dollar saved today will grow to $11.51 in 50 years, and

$132.39 in 100 years. The power of compound interest can provide an incentive to defer consumption.

By deferring consumption one sets aside resources to be available for the use of others. Rather than buying a car, for example, one could save that money, which would make it available to investors to borrow and then could use the resources that might have been used to build the car to invest instead in the productivity of the economy. This investment benefits those in the future. People who defer consumption benefit others because they make resources available to enhance future consumption. The market provides a reward for deferring consumption by allowing savers to earn interest on deferred consumption. The return from saving provides an incentive to sacrifice a little now in return for getting more later, and the resulting investment allows growth, which makes everyone better off.

MALTHUS AND WHERE HE WENT WRONG

Thomas Malthus's dismal vision of the future was described in Chapter 1. As Malthus saw it, rising incomes would allow more population growth, and the growth rate of the population would outstrip the growth in food production, keeping most of the population at a subsistence level, barely able to produce enough to keep themselves fed. If incomes ever rose, this would only enable more population growth, which would again drive the population's standard of living down to subsistence.[3] Malthus saw no escape from this bleak scenario, and his dismal projections were what originally gave economics the title of the dismal science.

With hindsight, we can see that for much of the world, Malthus's dismal projections were wrong. In some countries around the world today, the subsistence level of existence Malthus described still exists, but in Western Europe, North America, and the Orient, the standard of living is rising far more rapidly than the population. In the United States, less than 5 percent of the population produces enough food to feed the rest, leaving most of the workforce free to produce other goods and services. If Malthus had been correct, everyone would have had to work just to produce enough food to keep the population from starving. The difference between those parts of the world that have escaped the Malthusian specter and those that have not is, in a word, markets.

Since the dawn of the industrial revolution, the wealthiest nations in the world have had market economies. The economic growth produced by markets has given each generation a higher quality of life than the generation before. The reasons draw directly from material that has already been described in this chapter.

In order for the quality of life to increase from one generation to the next, people in the current generation must put off current consumption in order to invest for the future. If one generation consumes absolutely everything they can, the next generation will be left with nothing to provide themselves with the necessities of life. They will have no capital goods, no tools, no stock of knowledge — nothing. Why is it that one generation will forego some of their potential consumption in order to help later generations? Why does one generation invest to provide capital goods for their heirs, why do they develop a stock of knowledge and invest in an educational system to pass that knowledge on? As already described, markets give the current generation the mechanism to trade with the unborn, and the ability to earn interest gives them an incentive to do so.

When Malthus described Britain's emerging market economy during the industrial revolution, he failed to recognize the incentives that were in place to create a self-interest for each generation to provide for the future. By setting a little aside in the present in exchange for the return offered by the rate of interest, future generations would find a world that provided them with a higher standard of living than ever before. The result is that in economies that have relied on markets, the quality of life is undeniably higher than in economies that have not. There are subsistence level economies in existence in the last decade of the twentieth century, but those economies are run by dictators rather than markets.

The same mechanisms that have provided a wealth of goods and services in contemporary economies can also provide an increasing quality of life for future generations if those things that are important to the quality of life are allocated through the market mechanism. People will be much more diligent in protecting resources for future generations if they have the direct incentives that markets provide. A look at the nations of Eastern Europe and the Soviet Union after the fall of communism shows that government control of resources has resulted in much more environmental damage and much lower production of goods and services than in market economies. The reason is straightforward: when the government controls resources, the resources are allocated by political mechanisms that provide no direct incentives to preserve anything for the future. Markets do provide direct incentives to provide for the future. The ability to earn interest means that saving today can provide people with more in the future than they give up now, and the existence of markets for natural resources and durable goods provides the ability to trade with future generations. In essence, future generations are able to bid for the conservation of current resources because of the incentives contained in markets.

Malthus was wrong. Much of the world has prospered and lifted itself well above the subsistence level. It is important to see not only that Malthus's predictions did not come to pass but also why they did not come to pass. In those economies where markets provided incentives to save and invest, resources were conserved, and each generation enjoyed a higher standard of living than the generation before. In economies that attempted to use government planning to increase the standard of living for future generations, both the plans and the economies eventually collapsed. Government decision-making and central planning do not provide a mechanism for taking account of the interests of future generations. Markets provide those incentives. Centuries of observation since Malthus's day show that this is true in the production of goods and services, and when one understands why it is true, one sees that the same principles apply to the quality-of-life issues discussed here. In order to protect future resources and enhance the quality of life for future generations, the current generation should make more use of markets. However, all too often the current generation is turning to government planning. This will have the same detrimental effect on the overall quality of life as it has had on the production of goods and services in the centrally planned economies of the twentieth century.

THE POPULATION BOMB

Population growth is indirectly related to public policy and the quality of life because some people view overcrowding as a negative factor in the quality of life and some people might argue that all of the issues covered here are essentially irrelevant because population growth will eventually overburden the ability of the Earth's finite resources to support humanity. The issue is serious, but the details are beyond the scope of this study. It is worth noting, however, that in developed economies where income is high and almost all children survive into adulthood, birthrates have fallen dramatically to the point where some countries have birthrates that barely sustain their present population levels. Birthrates are highest in poor countries with high infant mortality.

In the United States, population growth has slowed throughout the twentieth century, and the United States is now growing at less than 1 percent per year. A number of developed nations have declining population growth rates that are now less than 0.25 percent per year, including Germany, Denmark, Italy, the United Kingdom, Belgium, and Ireland. In contrast, low income economies have average population growth rates of about 2.5 percent per year. For example, Kenya has a population growth rate of 3.5 percent per year, Pakistan has a 2.7 percent population growth rate, and Zaire has a 3 percent rate of growth in its population.[4]

The adoption of markets and the creation of a higher material standard of living are associated with lower birthrates, which will reduce the population problem. In the United States, the birthrate per 1,000 population was 28.4 in 1917 and had fallen to 16.2 by 1989.[5] In developed economies, population growth has continued to decline as those economies have become wealthier, and both birthrates and population growth rates are significantly higher in less developed economies than they are in developed economies. There is a clear relationship between quality of life and population growth — a higher quality of life means slower population growth.

Whatever one's opinion about the problem of overpopulation, the quality-of-life solutions recommended here would have the by-product of reducing population growth. If it were the other way, one would have to consider whether an increased quality of life was worth the cost in terms of faster population growth. This is much the same issue Malthus wrestled with. However, increasing quality of life carries with it slower population growth and perhaps even a halt to population growth. The population issue is only indirectly relevant here, but those in favor of halting population growth should see yet another reason for supporting the ideas presented in this book.

INNOVATION AND INCREASING PRODUCTIVITY

The most important reason why the standard of living has increased in much of the world is that innovation has led to increasing productivity in virtually every area. Imagine how well off you would be if you had to produce all of the goods and services you consume, given all you know about producing them. If you had to grow your own food, build your own house, make your own car, make your own television, and so forth, most people — even the poorest people in countries like the United States — would be considerably worse off. But innovation and increasing productivity have enabled the economy to produce lots of goods and services for everybody.

Assembly line production has made people take automobile ownership for granted. (In Florida, there are more registered automobiles than people.) The same increases in productivity that have occurred in manufacturing have also occurred in agriculture, and the advances in electronics in the last half of the twentieth century boggle the mind. Advances have also been made in areas of environmental protection and resource conservation. New technologies are available to protect the environment without sacrificing the material standard of living. While some complain about environmental damage in market economies, the environment is in much better condition in market economies than in centrally planned economies where government planners determined what they believed to be the optimal mix of production and environmental protection.

The increasing economic productivity that has raised the standard of living has also produced some undesirable environmental by-products. Some are a result of the increasing population that can be supported by a more productive economy. A few families can dispose of their raw sewage into a river with no negative environmental consequences, but when a large city does the same thing, the river cannot handle the volume and environmental damage results. When settlements were small enough that the environment could absorb the by-products of civilization, one would not expect anyone to worry about them, but now that they have become a problem, technology and innovation is being applied to preserve the environment and natural resources, just as it has been applied to the production of goods and services.

Economic development can work to preserve resources and enhance the environment, assuming that the proper incentives are provided. This means having clearly defined property rights over resources in the same way that property rights are clearly defined over the products of manufacture.

PROPERTY RIGHTS AND THE PROTECTION OF RESOURCES

As noted earlier in the chapter, individuals have an incentive to preserve resources for the future if they expect there to be future markets for those resources. The same is true for energy resources, environmental amenities, and anything else that can enhance the quality of life for future generations. The solution is to provide clearly defined property rights.

If manufacturing firms are allowed to produce pollution-causing smoke as a by-product of their production without having to bear the costs of their activities, then they have no incentive to clean up their emissions. Even worse, competitive forces work against their taking account of environmental damage, because if one firm incurs costs while trying to maintain a clean environment, other firms that do not incur those costs will be at a competitive advantage. With no property rights over the environment, firms may produce too much environmental damage.

A common solution is to use government regulation to force firms to clean up their acts. This can produce short-term benefits, but the long-term problem is that the government does not have the incentive to see that the environment is being protected at the lowest possible cost or that the best technology is being used. Furthermore, the incentives do not exist for polluting firms to develop better technology. If property rights are assigned to the environment and firms are charged for their environmental damage, they have the incentive to cause less damage now and to find better, cheaper, and more productive technologies for environmental protection in the future.

The next chapter discusses in more detail how markets can provide incentives to preserve the environment and protect resources for future generations. It is important to recognize that the protection of future resources means using the best environmental technology today and providing the incentives to develop better technology in the future. Enhancing the quality of life depends on taking care of and preserving resources and producing goods and services that enhance the standard of living. Markets provide the incentive to coordinate these two aspects of the quality of life.

THE PAST AND THE FUTURE

History provides reasons for being optimistic about protecting future resources and enhancing the quality of life. Two centuries ago, Malthus painted a dismal picture of the future of mankind and foresaw a world in which most people would be relegated to a standard of living barely at the subsistence level. In parts of the world that have allowed markets to work, those predictions have not come true; in areas of the world where economic activity has been centrally planned, those predictions are closer to being true. Areas that have been plagued by starvation and famine over the past two centuries have not been areas that have allowed markets to allocate resources.

In Europe and in North America, the quality of life has been better in each generation than it was in the past for centuries. In the Pacific rim, the market economies of Japan and South Korea have provided incredible increases in the quality of life for their citizens. Hong Kong has become a wealthy enclave surrounded by a much poorer China, and it is no coincidence that Hong Kong has relied on markets for its prosperity, while China has fallen behind by relying on government planning. The historical evidence shows that markets work to produce a high standard of living and superior quality of life.

While every generation has done better than the previous generation in market economies, the same cannot be said for economies run by government planning. After three decades of central planning, the Cuban standard of living has fallen dramatically, and the collapse of the centrally planned economies of Eastern Europe has shown likewise. In addition to low standards of living caused by unproductive economies, government planning has also produced a great deal of environmental damage. However, while all this evidence against government planning to enhance the quality of life exists throughout the world, in the United States, the government is increasingly called upon to enhance the quality of life. Why should it work any better in the United States than it has in the rest of the world?

Government is called upon because of the problems that are perceived to be the result of market activities, and this will continue because market decisions are not always perfect. If property rights are clearly defined, however, market decisions do tend to correct the mistakes of the past, and the evidence shows that this is not the case for mistakes made by government planners. The most productive course of action is to find and implement market solutions to problems as they arise rather than turning over increasingly more to the government.

While there is reason for optimism about the future, one would hesitate to be complacent because of the past record of government planning. What if the current attempts to use government to improve the quality of life are faulty? Eventually, the evidence of faulty planning would become apparent, and faulty methods could be replaced by more successful ones. However, the experience of Eastern Europe and the Soviet Union suggests that the evidence would have to be overwhelming before it would be sufficient to induce change. The Soviet Union turned to government economic planning 70 years before the economy collapsed, and they began searching for a different course. Four decades after the Soviet Union was established, reputable economists were willing to argue that central planning was superior to markets in the allocation of resources. If the current turn toward government planning to enhance the quality of life is as faulty as central economic planning was, a similar turn of events would suggest that the problems will not be generally recognized until the middle of the twenty-first century and then only after planning to improve the quality of life has made such a mess of things that there will be no avoiding a direct confrontation with the evidence.

Facts do not speak for themselves; they require interpretation. The fact is that market economies have produced unparalleled well-being and an unmatched quality of life for their citizens. The fact is that problems remain. The environment is being damaged; poorly qualified individuals are producing inferior quality output; many people receive substandard health care; the market for recreational drugs is destroying individuals and communities. The list could go on. Because the market has not solved these problems, one alternative is to use government. Another alternative is to design market mechanisms that can attack these problems the same way they have been used to produce goods and services.

A fair evaluation of these alternatives will compare the market mechanisms that can exist with government policies that can be implemented. The next several chapters look at a number of public policy areas in which the government has become actively involved. They look at the problems with government policies and the ways in which viable market alternatives can be used.

NOTES

1.   See Richard L. Stroup and John A. Baden, *Natural Resources: Bureaucratic Myths and Environmental Management* (San Francisco: Pacific Institute for Public Policy Research, 1983) for a discussion of these concepts.

2.   This discussion abstracts from inflation, so the interest rate here represents a real rate of return. Although it might be interesting to analyze investments in an

inflationary environment, assuming inflation away detracts little from the current discussion and keeps the focus on the chapter's subject matter, which is how markets help to allocate resources over time.

3.   In more technical terms, Malthus anticipated that population would grow exponentially, while the food supply would grow only linearly, which would forever mean that the standard of living could not grow above subsistence. See Thomas Robert Malthus, *An Essay on Population* (New York: E. P. Dutton, 1914, orig. 1798).

4.   These figures are taken from the World Bank, *World Development Report 1992: Development and Environment* (Oxford: Oxford University Press, 1992). Statistics on population growth in less developed economies exclude India, with an annual population growth rate of 1.7 percent, and China, with a 1.3 percent growth rate.

5.   The 1917 statistic is from B. R. Mitchell, *International Historical Statistics in the Americas and Australasia* (London: Macmillan, 1983) and the 1989 statistic is from the *Statistical Abstract of the United States*, 1991 edition. Mitchell's statistics on the United States give birthrates for whites only before 1917 and show the white birthrate declining from 29.2 to 27.9 from 1909 to 1917. The birthrate in the United States has been steadily declining throughout the twentieth century.

4

Protecting the Environment

One area in which the government has become increasingly involved is trying to enhance the quality of life is environmental protection. There are several overlapping but distinct aspects of environmental protection that have come under the government's environmental policies. One aspect of environmental protection is controlling the by-products of economic production and consumption. Air and water pollution, ozone depletion, and global warming fall under this heading. Another aspect is protecting natural areas from the encroachment of civilization. Preservation of deserts, forests, reefs, and wetlands are examples. Yet another aspect is the protection of endangered plant and animal species. Most certainly, environmental protection is important to the quality of life, but many people argue that, in the area of environmental protection, markets are inadequate, and government action is necessary. This chapter illustrates how complete markets provide incentives to protect the environment and explains why governmental control over environmental resources is likely to be counterproductive.

THE SOURCE OF ENVIRONMENTAL PROBLEMS

The previous two chapters have shown how private ownership of resources provides incentives to maintain resources in the way that would maximize their future value. This does not mean that with complete private ownership no environmental damage would take place but, rather, that private owners would have the incentive to take full account of the environmental costs of their actions. Would the elimination of all environmental pollution be desirable? No. Some environmental damage is worth the cost, because more would have to be given up to reduce the environmental damage than would be gained in return.

Air pollution could be reduced significantly if everyone were required to ride bicycles for transportation rather than ride in cars.

However, even the most strident environmentalists ride in cars, recognizing that the environmental harm that takes place through the air pollution produced is more than compensated for by the convenience of automobile transportation. Similarly, air pollution could be reduced if farmers gave up using tractors, but the costs in terms of reduced food production would be so great that nobody in the environmental movement has yet suggested giving up farm machinery. There is an optimal amount of pollution, and people will reduce pollution and environmental damage to the optimal level only if they have an incentive to account fully for the environmental costs they impose.

Complete private ownership of all resources would take care of the problem of environmental damage because everyone would have an incentive to fully account for the environmental harm they cause. There would still be some environmental degradation, such as when farmers use machinery to till the soil, but the environmental harm would always be outweighed by the benefits. The problem is that in the real world, private ownership is not complete, so people do not have sufficient incentives to take account of the costs they impose on the environment. Some air pollution would be optimal, as just noted, and if the air were privately owned, the owners would have an incentive to protect the value of their air by not allowing too much pollution. The problem is that private ownership rights are not clearly defined over many environmental resources, such as air, water, and wild animals, so the incentives do not exist to maintain their value.

Consider two questions that sound similar, yet are very different: "Why is there air pollution?" and "Why is there too much air pollution?" There is air pollution because some of the activities people find desirable create pollution. Pollution is a by-product of production, and production makes people better off, so it is reasonable to weigh the costs of the pollution against the benefits and to produce the optimal amount of pollution. There is too much air pollution because, in many cases, people have little incentive to consider the costs that their polluting activities impose on others. Whenever people drive cars, they impose pollution costs on others, yet they have little incentive to consider those costs in their decision on whether to drive. The solution is to give people an incentive to consider the costs that their behavior places on others.

REGULATORY INCENTIVES
VERSUS PRIVATE PROPERTY

One way to create an incentive for people to take account of the costs they impose on others is to create a regulation making it costly for them to do otherwise. Another way is to create a private ownership system whereby people have an incentive to protect the value of their own property. With private ownership, people always have an incentive to consider the full costs of their actions. With regulatory solutions, the solution is, at best, only likely to be approximately optimal, and it will need enforcement from some government authority.

As a result of air pollution caused by automobiles, the federal government requires cars to have catalytic converters that reduce the pollution. This regulatory solution will, at best, be approximately efficient, because it fails to discriminate among high-cost polluters and low-cost polluters. Catalytic converters are costly because they are expensive to install and because they reduce gasoline mileage. A catalytic converter in a car that is rarely driven and that is located in a low population area, such as North Dakota, will be very costly relative to the amount of environmental harm it mitigates. Conversely, it might be optimal to have more stringent pollution control on taxi cabs driven almost all day in New York City. Yet, the same regulatory restrictions apply to both. In all likelihood, the car in North Dakota creates too little pollution in the sense that the costs of pollution control for that car exceed the benefits of reduced pollution.

The drawback to regulatory restrictions is that the individuals involved do not have an incentive to control environmental damage but only to meet the letter of the law (or avoid being caught in violation). People have no incentive to maintain their catalytic converters or to make sure they are working efficiently, thereby requiring others to police the regulated individuals. In many parts of the country, inspections to test for excess exhaust emissions are required. Furthermore, there is only an incentive to meet the letter of the law, and there is no benefit to the individual for going further. Nobody has an incentive to install pollution control equipment beyond what is mandated by the government. In contrast, when people bear the full costs of their activities, they have an incentive to reduce environmental harm whenever the benefits of doing so exceed the costs. The challenge, then, is to find some way to create private incentives to reduce environmental harm.[1]

MARKETS IN POLLUTION RIGHTS

Markets can be created in pollution rights that allow individuals to create environmental harm only if they own the right to do so and if they allow individuals to sell the rights to others at a market-determined price. Markets for pollution rights are working on a limited basis already and could be greatly extended. Consider how such markets can work.[2]

Markets in pollution rights can be established by giving polluters in an area rights to continue creating the amount of pollution they are currently generating or by allowing them to sell the rights to others. Consider first creating such a market for industrial polluters. A firm obtaining pollution rights can continue to pollute as in the past, but because the rights are valuable, if the firm can reduce its pollution, it can sell the pollution rights it would no longer need to some other firm. This gives all firms an incentive to reduce pollution in any way they can (including reducing production), as long as the benefits exceed the costs. New firms that would like to produce in the area covered by the marketable rights could do so only if they could buy the rights from an existing firm. This gives value to the pollution rights, and it also provides an incentive for them to go to those who value them the most.

The advantages are considerable compared to alternative systems.[3] If pollution is controlled by regulating existing firms and by preventing new manufacturing concerns from entering the area, existing firms face all the incentive problems discussed above. They have an incentive only to meet the letter of the law, and they have no incentive to search for ways to reduce their pollution below what is legally mandated. With marketable rights, firms always have an incentive to discover cost effective ways to reduce pollution. Furthermore, if regulation produced a prohibition on new polluters, it would give established industries an advantage over new entrants that would, over time, take away some of the market forces that push more efficient firms to displace less efficient firms. If new firms cannot be established because of pollution control restrictions, existing polluters might continue to produce long after efficiency conditions would have pushed them out of the market if new competitors had been allowed.

Marketable rights can also be used to reduce pollution in an area. One way would be to require new polluters to buy the rights to more than one unit of pollution for each unit of pollution the new firm would produce. For example, if a new firm wanted to enter the area and would produce some air pollution, it would have to buy the rights to two units of pollution from existing firms for each one unit of pollution it wanted to produce. Another way would be to allow less pollution over time from existing rights. Thus, one unit of pollution this year would be reduced to nine-tenths of one unit in two years. This would reduce pollutants by 10 percent when the reduction took effect.

Another advantage of marketable rights is that people who desired clean air could buy them and not use them. Thus, if an environmental group wanted to reduce the amount of pollution in an area with marketable rights, the group could buy pollution rights with the intention of not using them, which would result in an improvement in the air quality. With existing regulations, there is no way for those who want a cleaner environment to enter into a market arrangement to buy one.

Marketable pollution rights will work better than regulation because they give all individuals an incentive to use their specific knowledge to reduce pollution. Regulatory solutions apply the ideas of regulators and cast regulators in an adversarial position against polluters. The polluters themselves may have good ideas about how pollution could be reduced, but they will be reluctant to suggest their ideas because implementation is likely to cost them money. Marketable rights put everyone on the same side, because reducing pollution benefits those who cause pollution. As noted in Chapter 2, Friedrich Hayek has explained how markets give every individual an incentive to apply any knowledge they have for the benefit of others, and marketable pollution rights can implement this important principle.[4]

Marketable pollution rights could be established for virtually any type of pollution. The concept could be applied to automobiles as well as industrial polluters and could apply to water pollution as well as air pollution. Some monitoring would be necessary, but no more than is required under regulatory control. The big advantage of marketable rights is that the system gives individuals the incentive to reduce pollution as much as they can, as long as it is cost effective to do so. Individuals have an incentive to use their creativity to devise pollution control methods because they will be the direct beneficiaries. With regulatory control, individuals have no incentive to help the environment, but have an incentive only to comply with the regulation.

In 1990, the Clean Air Act was amended to create marketable pollution rights for sulfur dioxide emissions by electric utilities. The Environmental Protection Agency (EPA) issued 5.3 million marketable permits, each allowing the emission of one ton of sulfur dioxide a year, to 110 polluters. Beginning in 1995, the polluters must have permits for all of their sulfur dioxide emissions or face substantial fines. Firms that want to emit more sulfur dioxide can buy permits from other firms, while those that are successful at reducing their own pollution can profit from selling their permits. In 1994, the permits were selling for about $240, meaning that any firm that could reduce its emissions by a ton for less than $240 has an incentive to do so in order to sell the right. Marketable pollution rights are not just a good idea in theory, they are already being used as a method of efficient pollution control.

COMMON LAW REMEDIES AS ALTERNATIVES TO REGULATION

One long-standing remedy to environmental problems is the law of nuisance. Although environmental regulations spell out in specific detail how pollution must be controlled and what environmentally damaging activities are allowed, the law of nuisance is much more flexible. Based on the notion of property rights rather than regulation, the law of nuisance makes it illegal for some individuals to use their property in such a way as to create a nuisance to others. What actually constitutes a nuisance is a matter for courts to decide, and the decision will be based on precedents from earlier nuisance cases. As the common law evolves, if individuals desire more environmental protection, then the law of nuisance will evolve to produce more stringent standards, thus providing a legal, but non-regulatory, remedy for environmental harm.[5]

The law of nuisance has the apparent disadvantage that, to be relieved of the environmental harm, the harmed party must sue the party causing the damage. This disadvantage is more apparent than real, because when environmental harm is controlled through regulation, often those who are harmed must approach the regulators to stop the harm, and often those causing the damage will argue that what they are doing is legal. In fact, they may be right. In a 1981 case, the EPA supported the right of a chemical company to put toxic wastes in a landfill, which a nearby community argued was harmful. The EPA said that the landfill was legal, but the community then took action in court, claiming that the landfill was a public nuisance. The chemical company lost in court.[6]

In this particular case, the law of nuisance stopped environmental harm that the EPA claimed was legal, but the case had larger implications. Once regulatory standards are passed for environmental protection, firms causing environmental harm need only meet those standards, and they can use the standards as a defense for their activities. Firms meeting regulatory standards have been judged as being in compliance with the law because they met the standards, whereas under the law of nuisance, a more general standard applies, and the general principle is that individuals are not allowed to harm the property rights of others, rather than that individuals must merely meet regulatory standards.[7]

In the United States, the law of nuisance and the principle of protecting private property through legal action is not nearly as developed as it might be because of the reliance on regulatory standards to determine acceptable behavior. If there were fewer regulatory standards, there would be better-defined common law standards for determining when the activities of individuals are causing environmental harm. This might prompt visions of everyone suing everyone else in the absence of regulation, but, as in other areas of law, once the law is defined by the courts, people have an incentive to follow it to avoid lawsuits. The common law provides a clear alternative to the regulatory protection of the environment.[8]

PROTECTING ENDANGERED SPECIES

The protection of endangered species has much in common with the problem of environmental pollution, because in both cases the underlying problem is a lack of clearly defined property rights. Why is it that eagles, elephants, and Florida panthers are endangered while chickens, horses, and dogs are not? The answer is that the endangered species are not owned by anybody while the non-endangered species are privately owned.

In the nineteenth century, buffalo were hunted nearly to extinction in the Western United States, while, at the same time, the cattle population in the west was growing. This was happening even though the number of cattle being slaughtered was greater than the number of buffalo killed, and the number of slaughtered cattle was growing. Why, when more cattle were being consumed than buffalo, was the cattle population growing while the buffalo population was rapidly declining? The answer: cattle were privately owned; buffalo were not.

Buffalo roamed the ranges of the old west with nobody having ownership rights over them. An individual who did not kill a buffalo would have nothing to gain from allowing the animal to live. If an individual did not kill a buffalo, it would roam the range until another individual killed it. Thus, the individual is faced with the choice of killing the buffalo for whatever advantages it might have to offer versus allowing it to go and giving the benefit of killing the buffalo to someone else. Because buffalo were not privately owned, it would cost the individual nothing to kill the buffalo, and the only way an individual could claim ownership rights over a buffalo would be to kill it.

Contrast this situation with the private ownership rights of cattle. Because cattle were privately owned, individuals had an incentive not to slaughter their cattle immediately but rather to maintain a herd of cattle and slaughter them in such a way as to maximize the value of the herd. This would require keeping enough cattle to maintain a breeding stock and enough breeding cattle to increase the size of the herd. Cattle had value to their owners both alive and after slaughter, so owners would slaughter cattle only when the value of the products of the cattle exceeded their value in maintaining the herd. With buffalo the animals had no value to individuals unless they were killed. Thus, hunting of buffalo continued without anyone considering the costs of killing an animal — only the benefits were considered. Killing cattle, however, involved weighing both the benefits and the costs.

Because of private ownership, incentives existed for owners of cattle to maximize the present value of all present and future cattle, which resulted in an increase in the number of cattle. Because they were not privately owned, nobody had an incentive to consider the future value of buffalo. Thus, they were slaughtered almost to extinction. Private ownership made the difference.

Similar problems exist today. In Africa, the elephant population has been dramatically reduced because of poaching; elephants are not privately owned. In Kenya, trade in ivory is illegal, and elephants are not allowed to be hunted. Ivory remains valuable, however, and from the beginning to the end of the 1980s, the elephant population declined from about 65,000 to 19,000 as a result of poaching. In Zimbabwe, however, where trade in ivory is legal and profits from ivory and elephant hides go to local communities, the elephant population rose from

30,000 to 40,000 during the same period.[9] The case of Kenya's policy versus Zimbabwe's is instructive. Where hunting elephants is illegal, and nobody has the right to own this valuable resource, the elephant population has plummeted. In Zimbabwe, where hunting is legal, and profits go to local residents, the elephant population is growing.

There is a direct parallel between Africa's elephants in the late twentieth century and American buffalo in the late nineteenth century. When specific individuals can profit from the products of elephants both in the present and future, those individuals have an incentive to protect the resource to maximize the present value of the total future stream of benefits. Killing all of the elephants now would be foolish and short-sighted because it would eliminate any future profit opportunity. Furthermore, those in the local communities have every incentive to protect elephants against poachers because any elephant taken by poachers is an elephant stolen from the local residents who could profit from it.

Contrast this with the situation in Kenya where nobody can legally profit from the elephants. Poachers are pursued by government wardens, but no individual owner stands to lose anything from the elephants killed by poachers. Thus, game wardens protect elephants because it is their job rather than because a poached elephant is an elephant stolen from them. The incentives are not as strong, because wardens do not profit from stopping poachers. They might profit if the poachers were able to bribe game wardens not to notice when poaching took place. This is not to say that game wardens are corrupt, but merely that the possibility for them to profit from corruption is there. In Zimbabwe, in contrast, there are no incentives for corruption because the local owners of elephants lose the full value of an elephant every time one is poached. In Zimbabwe, where local residents can profit directly from trade in ivory and other elephant products, the residents have an incentive to protect the elephants and to manage the elephant population so that it remains in perpetuity. In Kenya, where hunting is illegal and no individual can legally profit from preserving the life of an elephant, nobody has an incentive to protect elephants, and their populations are declining.

Prohibitions to protect endangered species, whether the prohibition is against hunting or against activities that destroy a species' habitat, are enacted with good intentions but create incentives that lead toward harming the species. If incentives can be created for profiting from the existence of an endangered species, then individuals find it in their own self-interest to maintain the species. For example, as ranching spread through the United States, many wild animals were killed by ranchers because they competed with the ranchers' domesticated animals. Some animals were predators while others simply competed for the same food supply. Ranchers could profit from their own herds, but not from wild animals. The nuisance was not entirely from the animals, either. Hunters would trespass on private lands to hunt the wild animals, much like the poachers of African elephants. This has changed because ranchers have begun leasing hunting rights to their lands. By leasing hunting rights, land owners can profit from native species, so they have an incentive to make sure that their populations remain large enough to make their property attractive for hunting. Native species can, thus, become an asset and not a liability through the profitable opportunities of private ownership.[10]

The best way to protect endangered species is to make it profitable for specific individuals to see that specific populations of animals survive. This takes place with private ownership. Saying that these species are so valuable that they are the heritage of everyone and should not be privately owned is idealistic but unworkable because something owned by us all is no different from something owned by nobody, which means that nobody has the incentive to see that it is preserved. Private ownership creates the incentives to preserve scarce and valuable resources, whatever they are, including endangered species. Good intentions, such as existed in Kenya to save the elephants, do not necessarily produce good results. The challenge is to create market arrangements that give individuals the incentive to protect endangered wildlife.

PRESERVATION OF THE NATIVE HABITAT

One hazard that civilization creates for the environment is the encroachment of development upon the native habitat. Development alters the ecosystem by displacing native vegetation and by removing the habitat of native animals. One of the goals of environmental protection is the preservation of these native habitats. The most common way to preserve the habitats is through government ownership. Government ownership of land has been continually expanded so that, at the end of the twentieth century, the federal government owns more than one-third of the land in the United States.[11] Government ownership of land creates the same kinds of problems as the common ownership of other resources: nobody has the incentive to take care of the property in such a way as to maximize its value. Private ownership can create those incentives.

Some of the reasoning of the previous section can be directly extended to this section. If, through hunting rights, land owners have an incentive to preserve the native species of animals, they also have an incentive to preserve the habitats in which those native species live. Hunters are not the only ones who value native species, of course. Bird watchers want to preserve native species and their environments. Private owners, such as the Audubon Society, buy lands specifically for preservation of both the flora and the fauna. Individuals who value

environmental preservation contribute to organizations such as
Audubon and the Nature Conservancy, who then use those contributions to buy land to be preserved. Environmental preservation is
demonstrably valuable because, through organizations like these,
people voluntarily pay money to purchase land to be preserved.

The natural habitat is also preserved in the many parks and
national forests owned by the government. Whereas private owners
have the incentive to manage their property in such a way as to maximize its value, those who manage government lands have nothing to
gain personally from maintaining the value of the property. Rather,
they are responsible to the political process and subject to political
pressures. Government land will be managed according to the political
pressures that potentially competing users can exert.

Should the government sell timber rights to allow loggers to harvest
trees in the national forests? Should the government allow oil
exploration in national parks? Should roads, restaurants, and lodging
be built in national parks to allow more accessibility while recognizing
the environmental damage this construction creates? If the goal is
really environmental preservation, perhaps people should not even be
allowed in. Private owners facing these questions have the incentive to
act in a way that maximizes the value of their property. The government responds to whomever exerts the most political pressure.

The Audubon Society strongly opposes oil exploration in national
parks and wildlife refuges. It is easy to understand why. The Society's
goal is the preservation of natural habitats, and it has nothing to gain
by allowing the federal government to sell mineral rights to property
that they want preserved. Oil companies argue that they can take
advantage of mineral resources on federal lands while doing minimal
damage to the environment, and the benefits of the energy resources
outweigh the minimal environmental costs involved. Disputes like this
are difficult to resolve to the mutual satisfaction of both parties
because neither party has anything to gain by yielding to the other.

The situation is different on the Audubon Society's privately owned
Rainey Preserve in Louisiana, however. The Audubon Society initially
rejected attempts by oil companies to explore its preserve, but the
companies were able to convince Audubon that they would do minimal
damage to the environment and that the Audubon Society stood to gain
considerable revenues from selling the mineral rights. The result was
that the Audubon Society has allowed petroleum extraction in the
Rainey Preserve under mutually agreed-upon conditions. During
some times of the year, activity must cease in deference to the wildlife in the preserve, and care is taken to hold the environmental
damage to a minimum. In exchange, the Audubon Society can use the
revenues from the mineral rights to buy other environmentally
sensitive properties.[12]

This example illustrates how private ownership provides incentives for all parties to cooperate in order to use property to maximize its value. Because it is a private owner, the Audubon Society could weigh the costs and benefits of oil exploration on its property and decide that the new land that could be purchased with the royalties was worth more than the environmental damage caused by the exploration. Parties with competing interests were able to engage in a mutually beneficial agreement. Meanwhile, the Audubon Society remains strongly opposed to oil exploration on federal land. The Society has nothing to gain from exploration there.

Should oil companies be allowed to extract petroleum from federal lands? Should timber companies be allowed to harvest trees in national forests? The answer, undoubtedly, would depend upon the specific case, but with government ownership, the true costs and benefits are not measured against each other. The Audubon Society will allow oil exploration on its property if the benefits exceed the costs, but the government will allow exploration on its property if the political pressure of the oil companies exceeds that of the environmentalists. Private ownership is a better way to preserve the environment.

The argument clearly extends to the existing national parks and other federal lands. The U.S. government does not have the same incentives to manage parks to maximize their value as would a private owner, and the competing goals of different users would undoubtedly be managed more effectively under private ownership. The Gallatin National Forest in Montana, for example, hosts thousands of campers, hunters, and others each year. In 1988, the U.S. Forest Service collected fees of less than $200,000 from users, yet spent over $2 million maintaining and administering the forest. Considering those costs, the use of the area is clearly underpriced.[13] If prices were charged to cover costs, fewer people would use the area, and the environment would be less burdened by human intrusion.

Surely it is desirable to use federal lands for hunting, fishing, and other recreation, but at the same time these individuals impose on the natural environment. In these areas intended to preserve nature what is the optimal amount of human activity? A private owner has the incentive to use the area optimally, whereas the government has no such incentive. If the users of the Gallatin National Forest were charged fees high enough to cover the maintenance costs of the forest, use would be reduced, further preserving the natural environment. If the national parks were owned by environmental organizations like the Sierra Club, the Audubon Society, and the Nature Conservancy, they would have better incentives for environmental preservation than when they are owned by the government.

While environmental organizations work to preserve environmentally sensitive lands, they also have the incentive to allow development of land if its value as developed land exceeds its value in a natural state. With government ownership, there is no incentive to consider the economic value of alternative uses of land. The Nature Conservancy is a private organization that actively purchases environmentally sensitive land with money contributed by its members. In furthering its goal of environmental preservation, the Nature Conservancy routinely will swap land it owns for land that is more environmentally valuable. If urban growth moves out to land owned by the Nature Conservancy, for example, the land becomes more valuable as developable real estate. If the Nature Conservancy can swap this land for a larger tract of more environmentally important land elsewhere, it will do so in order to further its goals of environmental preservation. Both parties will benefit, and the environment will be better preserved as a result. With government ownership, there is no profit motive, and such a swap would be unlikely to take place.

WHAT IS A NATURAL ENVIRONMENT?

Preservation of the natural environment is clearly desirable from an economic standpoint because people voluntarily contribute their own money to private organizations that preserve the environment. The question then arises as to how much human involvement there should be in managing the environment. Is it desirable to eliminate all human involvement in the environment?

One thing that too few people realize is that there is almost nowhere in the environment that has not been significantly affected by human involvement for thousands of years. Long before Europeans discovered America, there was a native population that had a significant impact on the environment through their use of fire and through their hunting and farming activities. Humans are, in fact, a part of the environment.

For thousands of years, the native population in the Everglades used controlled burns to eliminate dead vegetation and make the Everglades a healthier place for both plants and animals to thrive. When the government took over management of the Everglades and eliminated the controlled burns, decayed vegetation built up to the point that when it burned it caused mass destruction of the natural habitat. Similarly, for thousands of years, hunting by Native Americans has been a part of the balance of nature on the continent. With the population of natural predators, such as wolves, being controlled, if the population of prey, such as deer, is not controlled also, their population will expand until they damage and destroy vegetation in their search for food, and, rather than being hunted, much of the population will starve.

For thousands of years, human hunters have augmented natural predators in controlling the populations of some species, and the natural environment has not been untouched by human hands since then. For thousands of years, humans have used fire in a controlled way. It stands to reason that human involvement should be a part of maintaining an ecosystem. Private owners have an incentive to manage property in a way that maximizes its value, whereas the government does not.

The principle of private ownership to enhance environmental protection draws upon Hayek's principle of effectively using information, discussed earlier in the chapter.[14] Private owners have an incentive to manage their property to maximize its value, and those who know the property best are in the best position to use their specific knowledge of the property to protect it. Hierarchical organizations implement their policies from the top, and those at the top will be less familiar with specific ecosystems than the local population. Those closer to the ecosystem have more of a familiarity with past human impacts on the ecosystem and will be less likely to allow harm as a result of neglect. Humans have been a part of almost every ecosystem for thousands of years, and many ecosystems will collapse without some human involvement to maintain them. The challenge is finding the optimal involvement, and private owners have more of an incentive than bureaucratic managers.

POLITICAL VERSUS ECONOMIC CONTROL

These arguments are not meant to imply that the government is incapable of caring for the environment but rather that there is an important difference between political and economic control of any property and that the incentives in private ownership are better suited to environmental protection or any other goal that involves maintaining the value of property. One of the most important differences is that political control of property is never permanent, and it requires continual exercise of political influence. Private ownership allows relatively permanent control over property.

Consider again the issue of whether oil exploration should be allowed in a wildlife preserve. If the wildlife preserve is privately owned, the owner can decide the issue, and there is not much an oil company can do to impose its will on the property owner. If the preserve is owned by the government, the issue is always decided based on the relative political power of those who want oil exploration and those who do not. If the environmentalists win and exploration is not allowed on government property, those who want to explore can always reenter the political process at a later date. They can influence the political process through lobbying and campaign contributions.

A political decision can always be reversed, so a political victory is never permanent. An organization wanting to preserve an environmentally sensitive piece of property through the market mechanism can buy it and leave it untouched forever. An organization wanting to preserve an environmentally sensitive piece of property through government action must continually work against competing interests through the political process. The market provides a much more secure method of pursuing the goal of environmental preservation than does the government.

What implications do these ideas have for purposes of public policy? While some resources are firmly under governmental control, they are not in any meaningful sense owned by everyone in common, but are controlled by special interest groups through the political process. From a political standpoint, one way to institute private ownership would be to vest ownership with those groups who now are de facto owners because they control the political decisions that determine how the resources are used. If private ownership really is more efficient, then there would be some way to distribute resources that would make everyone better off. This view is undoubtedly idealistic, however, because if government decided to divest itself of natural resources, surely there would be large interest groups who would claim to be the rightful owners, and surely substantial costs would be incurred by these groups to prove their claims to ownership.[15]

CONCLUSION

Protection of the environment is a goal that virtually everyone believes is worthwhile and would enhance the quality of life. The disagreement comes in deciding how to implement policies to achieve the goal. Even when specific goals are agreed upon, the most effective methods for achieving those goals are often not agreed upon and to many people are counterintuitive. Consider protection of endangered elephant populations in Africa. The obvious approach makes killing elephants illegal, but laws do not enforce themselves, and the experience with that approach in Kenya has shown that it does not work. People must have the incentive to protect endangered species. In Zimbabwe, where local residents profit from the hunting of elephants, they have an incentive to protect the elephant population. Even as the elephant population in Kenya declines, Zimbabwe's elephant population is growing.

The idea that environmental resources belong to everybody and that they are too valuable to be privately owned has a nice ring to it, but something that is not privately owned and supposedly belongs to everybody, in fact, belongs to nobody. With common ownership, nobody has an incentive to take care of resources and maintain their value. With private ownership, the owner has the incentive to protect the value of the resource.

Government control of resources means political control. Ideally, governments should manage resources for the common good, but, in reality, political pressures have significant impacts on the allocation of resources, and government-controlled resources are managed to benefit those who have political power.[16] The idea that public ownership will preserve the environment for future generations while private ownership will squander resources for short-term profits is exactly backward. Because political control is never permanent, those who have the current political power to control resources have every incentive to use them for short-term benefits because, in the future, someone else may have more political power and may be able to wrest control of the resource. Private owners, in contrast, have an incentive to maximize the value of resources now and in the future because private owners can profit from resources that will be valuable in the future, whereas there are no direct current benefits accruing from public property.

The bureaucratic mindset for managing the environment comes from a biased perspective of individual behavior. It begins with the idea that individuals in the private sector will not act to protect the environment and follows with the idea that those in the public sector will act in the public interest. In reality, the people who work in the private sector are no better or worse than those who work in the public sector. They do face different incentives, and those differences may make them act differently. The challenge, then, is to give everyone an incentive to protect the environment, as long as the benefits of environmental protection are worth the costs. In fact, where private ownership exists, private owners have more of an incentive to protect the environment than their public sector counterparts.[17]

Real environmental problems exist, and the defense of private ownership as a way of dealing with environmental problems does not imply that there is no role for government. The government enforces laws and protects property rights, and the protection of the environment through the use of markets can take place only as long as there are markets that accurately value environmental amenities and only as long as individuals can be protected from the environmental damage done by others. This suggests that private property rights be strengthened and that individuals be given legal recourse when they are harmed by the actions of others. Marketable pollution rights and the application of nuisance laws, rather than environmental regulations, move in this direction.

Protection of the environment is important to enhance the quality of life, and there are real challenges involved in designing laws and institutions that will effectively protect the environment. Regulation and public ownership are moves in the wrong direction because they remove individual incentives to care about the quality of the environment. Those who are regulated have an interest only in complying with the standards so as not to violate the law. Marketable pollution rights are more effective at controlling pollution than regulatory standards. When environmental resources are publicly owned, nobody can directly profit from enhancing their value. The Nature Conservancy and the

Audubon Society have greater incentives to protect the environmentally sensitive lands they own than the U.S. Park Service has to protect
the national parks that nobody really owns. With private ownership
and clearly defined property rights, owners have an incentive to
maintain the environmental quality of their property.

The challenge lies in designing institutions that assign property
rights to environmental amenities to give individuals a direct personal
interest in enhancing the quality of the environment. Devising effective
solutions is not always easy, but, unfortunately, experience has shown
that too often well-intentioned initiatives turn out to be counterproductive and harm the environment they were intended to protect.
Central planning does not work any better at protecting the environment than it does at producing goods and services. This chapter
illustrates that the same general principles that have proven
successful at enhancing the material well-being of individuals can also
be used to protect the environment.

NOTES

1.   James M. Buchanan and Gordon Tullock, "Polluters' Profits and Political Response:
Direct Controls Versus Taxes," *American Economic Review* 65 (March 1975): 139–47 note that
firms might prefer regulatory control of environmental harm to alternative methods of control
because regulatory control will cost the firms less. Gene E. Mumy, "Long-Run Efficiency and
Property Rights Sharing for Pollution Control," *Public Choice* 35 (1980): 59–74 considers the
political feasibility of various methods of pollution control. The real challenge is not only to find
methods that in theory can reduce environmental harm but also to ensure that those methods are
politically viable.

2.   Erhard F. Joeres and Martin David, Eds., *Buying a Better Environment: Cost-Effective
Regulation through Permit Trading* (Madison: University of Wisconsin Press, 1983) cover the
theory of marketable pollution rights in detail.

3.   James J. Opaluch and Richard M. Kashmanian, "Assessing the Viability of Marketable
Permit Systems: An Application to Hazardous Waste Management," *Land Economics* 61 (August
1985): 263–71 simulate markets for hazardous pollutants and estimate that there would be a 50
percent savings from instituting marketable rights. See also Allen V. Kneese, *Economics and the
Environment* (New York: Penguin Books, 1977) who recommends the use of markets to control
environmental problems.

4.   See Friedrich A. Hayek, "The Use of Knowledge in Society," *American Economic
Review* 35 (September 1945): 519–30 for an insightful discussion.

5.   An extensive body of literature discusses the evolution of the common law to create
efficient legal rules. See, for example, Richard A. Posner, *Economic Analysis of Law* (Boston:
Little Brown, 1972); Randall G. Holcombe, *Public Finance and the Political Process* (Carbondale:
Southern Illinois University Press, 1983), Chap. 9; Paul H. Rubin, "Why is the Common Law
Efficient?" *Journal of Legal Studies* 6 (January 1977): 51–63; and George L. Priest, "The
Common Law Process and the Selection of Efficient Rules," *Journal of Legal Studies* 6 (January
1977): 65–82.

6.   This case is discussed in Roger E. Meiners and Bruce Yandle, "Common Law Solution
for Water Pollution: The Path Not Taken," Political Economy Research Center Working Paper 92-
6, Bozeman, Montana; and in Roger E. Meiners and Bruce Yandle, "Constitutional Choice for the
Control of Water Pollution," *Constitutional Political Economy* 3 (Fall 1992): 359–80.

7.   Meiners and Yandle, "Common Law Solutions" discusses other cases in which the meeting of regulatory standards has been accepted as a defense for causing a nuisance.

8.   See Bruce Yandle, *The Political Limits of Environmental Regulation: Tracking the Unicorn* (New York: Quorum Books, 1989).

9.   See Terry L. Anderson and Donald R. Leal, *Free Market Environmentalism* (San Francisco: Pacific Research Institute for Public Policy, 1991), pp. 65–68 for a discussion of these ideas.

10.   Anderson and Leal, *Free Market Environmentalism*, pp. 68–71 discuss this idea.

11.   This figure is from Anderson and Leal, *Free Market Environmentalism*, p. 38.

12.   This case is described by Anderson and Leal, *Free Market Environmentalism*, p. 64.

13.   There is also the possibility that costs are too high because the government is not constrained to make a profit. These figures are from Anderson and Leal, *Free Market Environmentalism*, p. 64.

14.   See Hayek, "The Use of Knowledge in Society."

15.   See Thomas E. Borcherding, "Natural Resources and Transgenerational Equity," in *Economics and the Environment: A Reconciliation*, ed. Walter E. Block (Vancouver, B.C.: Fraser Institute, 1990), Chap. 2. The idea that those competing for benefits will incur socially wasteful costs falls under the general heading of rent seeking and is discussed at length in James M. Buchanan, Robert D. Tollison, and Gordon Tullock, *Toward a Theory of the Rent-Seeking Society* (College Station: Texas A&M University Press, 1980).

16.   Yandle, *The Political Limits of Environmental Regulation* discusses the incentives of those in government from the perspective of an insider.

17.   See Terry Anderson, "The Market Process and Environmental Amenities," in *Economics and the Environment: A Reconciliation*, ed. Walter E. Block (Vancouver, B.C.: Fraser Institute, 1989), Chap. 4. Several case studies emphasizing this theme are found in John Baden and Richard L. Stroup, Eds., *Bureaucracy vs. Environment: The Environmental Costs of Bureaucratic Governance* (Ann Arbor: University of Michigan Press, 1981).

5

Growth Management and Land Use

Land use planning is one of the well established methods by which governments work to try to enhance the quality of life. In the United States, land use planning began in earnest early in the twentieth century with the establishment of municipal zoning laws. The primary purpose of zoning regulations, both then and now, has been to preserve residential neighborhoods in the face of urban expansion. Essentially, the premise is that growth imposes costs on individuals, and zoning regulations provide a mechanism for protecting individuals from bearing the costs of others' activities.

In the latter part of the twentieth century, the expansion of automobile travel created more growth-related costs, both real and imagined, and simple zoning regulations no longer seemed to provide sufficient growth management. New development added to traffic congestion, automobile travel facilitated urban sprawl, and developers dumped the costs of their new developments onto old residents. Suburban development created the demand for more comprehensive growth management. Some states, such as California, have attacked the issue on a local basis and have a host of local ordinances restricting growth. Other states, such as Oregon and Florida, have statewide growth management laws that attempt to undertake comprehensive land use planning. Is this type of land use planning necessary, or even desirable? Does it enhance the quality of life? This chapter considers these questions.

Conceptually, there is a great deal of similarity between the growth management issues discussed in this chapter and the environmental issues discussed in Chapter 4. Environmental issues deal with the natural environment whereas growth management deals with the man-made environment. However, in both cases, problems arise when individuals undertake activities for their own benefit without fully accounting for the costs imposed on others. Nobody wants new subdivisions farther from the center of a city to create more traffic congestion just as nobody wants manufacturers upstream to dump industrial effluents into the river to create pollution downstream. The river is part of the natural environment whereas the roadway is a part of the man-made environment. However, in both cases problems arise when users do not fully account for the costs they impose on others. The problems are similar, and so are the solutions.

THE CONCEPT OF GROWTH MANAGEMENT

The potential for problems to arise because land use decisions of some individuals create harm to others is obvious, but the decision to deal with those problems by imposing land use regulations is also fraught with problems. Foremost among the potential problems of regulation is that of political control, so the results of land use regulation are not necessarily what some omniscient benevolent dictator would decide but are the results of political struggles that favor those who have political power. Another potential problem is that desirable land use is partly a matter of opinion. Some people prefer to live in a bustling city where the population density is high and there are lots of nearby urban amenities such as restaurants, entertainment, and shopping. Other people prefer suburban living, with single family homes and big yards, even if it means having to drive some distance to reach commercial establishments. Centralized growth management necessarily creates an environment where some people can use the political process to push their views of desirable development on others.

If all land use decisions were to be made by the owner of the land, subject to the proviso that one person's land use could not create a nuisance to another, the property owner would have an incentive to develop the property to maximize its value. This ought to be desirable, as long as some people's activities to enhance the values of their property did not harm the values of other people's property. When the government becomes involved in dictating land use decisions, the way in which property is used is transformed from a private decision to a collective decision. Some people obtain the legal right through the political system to dictate how other people can use their property.

The problems created by the political determination of land use are similar to those discussed in Chapter 4 about the environment. Essentially, everyone has some say about land use decisions through the political process, but nobody has the final authority to make the decision. Those with the most political power will see more decisions going their way. However, while the landowner has an incentive to see that the property is used so as to maximize its value, those who participate in the political process have no incentive to consider the value of the land because that value accrues to the owner. Those involved in the political process of deciding land use will consider the spillover effects that affect people other than the property owner but have no incentive to make decisions that will maintain the value of the property.

Because growth management legislation transfers some of the right to make land use decisions into the political process it is of necessity redistributional. The property owner loses some rights, which are transferred into common ownership through politics. The redistributional aspects of growth management legislation are apt to play a large role in determining actual land use policies as people get involved in the decision-making process for their own personal benefit rather than for the common good.[1]

Consider two examples. First, if growth restrictions prevent as many new homes from being built this restriction on the supply of housing will increase the value of existing homes. Thus, existing homeowners have an incentive to oppose new growth for their own financial benefit. Increases in housing prices can provide some benefits to homeowners but clearly hurt renters, who will pay more in rent. Thus, growth restrictions help homeowners and hurt renters. Because homeowners tend to be financially better off than renters, growth restrictions redistribute from the poor to the rich. Homeowners are more likely to be active participants in the political process, and the redistributive element in growth management creates incentives that can harm the public interest. Growth restrictions will be considered further below.

A second example illustrates the redistributive element with a specific case. A Tallahassee attorney wrote an article in the local newspaper opposing development on the nearby Wakulla River. The natural beauty of the river belongs to everyone, he argued, and developers should not be allowed to damage the environment for their own personal gain. He was using the growth management laws to try to prevent development on the river. A few weeks later, the attorney's house was featured in the homes section of the same newspaper. You guessed it — the attorney's home was built on the Wakulla River and had a nice view of the undeveloped banks on either side. The attorney had his house on the river, and he was trying to use the growth management process to prevent others to do what he had done. One way to protect his view would have been to have purchased the nearby property, but with growth management legislation he could use the political process to control how others could use their property without having to buy it.

If non-owners can make decisions about how property owners can use their property, they do not have an incentive to consider all the costs and benefits but can use the political process to transfer some of the benefits of the property to themselves. Before analyzing more specifically the political decision-making process that accompanies growth management, the next section looks at how markets would be expected to work in making land use decisions.

MARKETS AND LAND USE DECISIONS

One would be hard-pressed to find many examples of large-scale developments that have been primarily the result of private land use decisions rather than government influence. The government is heavily involved in land use decisions ranging from zoning laws, which began early in the century, to road location decisions, which influence development decisions. There are relatively large planned cities such as Reston, Virginia, and Columbia, Maryland, but these overcome some of the problems of private land use decisions because a single developer planned them to begin with. In these cases, the developer has an incentive to solve problems of conflicting use in a way that many different property owners, all wanting to develop their own properties, might not.

Perhaps the best example of large-scale development in the United States that is relatively free of government land use planning is Houston, Texas — the largest U.S. city that has no zoning laws. The absence of zoning laws leaves land owners free to develop their property as they see fit, so Houston provides a good case for examining the effectiveness of zoning laws. How is land use in Houston different from land use in cities that use zoning?

In an extensive study of land use decisions in Houston, Bernard Siegan found that there is little that differentiates land use patterns in Houston from land use patterns in cities that use zoning.[2] Houston has residential neighborhoods that are separated from business districts, and industry is located away from both residential and commercial areas. One of the main differences that Siegan found is that, without zoning ordinances to specify the minimum sizes of lots, setbacks from the road, and so forth, lot sizes for houses in Houston tended to be smaller than average, resulting in more compact residential developments of detached homes. This is consistent with the idea that zoning ordinances are used to the advantage of the well-to-do in an attempt to keep what they consider to be undesirable neighbors away.[3]

Siegan's findings suggest that zoning ordinances do not make much difference in the process of land use planning, and some reflection on the process by which land use decisions are made in the market helps to show why this is the case. One might be concerned that without zoning laws some entrepreneur might decide to tear down the house next door and build a gas station, but gas stations are unlikely to locate on residential streets. Residential streets have relatively little traffic, and gas stations, like other businesses, depend upon having convenient locations with lots of traffic in order to help generate business. Thus, gas stations, convenience stores, and retail businesses will be located on major thoroughfares with heavy traffic, regardless of zoning restrictions. They will fare better if they are located near busy intersections with convenient access. In short, retail businesses prefer to locate in places that would be undesirable as residential neighborhoods.

While people prefer to shop at convenient locations on well travelled roads, they want to live on quiet streets without much traffic, which would be undesirable for business. Thus, there are natural economic factors that will segregate commercial and residential users of land. Industrial users, in contrast, want to be near major transportation arteries like railroads, waterways, and interstate highways, but because they do not need to be conveniently located to commercial areas, they will locate away from the center of commercial activity, where property is less expensive. The factors that attract one industrial user will attract others, so industrial areas will develop naturally, without the government establishing industrial parks or restricting locational decisions through zoning.

Market forces will cause commercial areas to develop on heavily travelled roads and at major highway intersections. Market forces will locate residences in areas with less traffic without resorting to zoning. Government management is not necessary for efficient land use decisions. There is an invisible hand at work guiding private land use decisions to be efficient, just as the invisible hand guides other market activities.

ADDITIONAL LEGAL MECHANISMS

The legal system provides additional ways to promote efficiency in land use decisions without government planning. One mechanism discussed in Chapter 4 is the law of nuisance. If one person's use of property creates a nuisance for nearby users, then the well-established doctrine of nuisance can be used as a remedy. The widespread use of zoning has reduced the reliance on the law of nuisance because zoning determinations make those decisions instead. For example, if a developer wants to build a convenience store in an area zoned for multifamily homes, the developer will apply for a zoning change, and the issue will be debated as a matter of zoning. Without zoning, the issue would be whether that use of property would constitute a nuisance to its neighbors.

A second legal mechanism that is used extensively in Houston and elsewhere is the restrictive covenant. A developer who builds a residential subdivision can provide some assurance to those who buy homes that a gas station will not be built next door by placing a restrictive covenant on all of the lots in the subdivision requiring that they be limited to residential use. Covenants are often much more restrictive than zoning ordinances and might require that houses in a subdivision have a minimum amount of floor space, that the lots be a minimum size, that no trucks are allowed to be parked in the driveway, and might even require that a homeowner get the approval of a subdivision architectural board before making any additions or even before changing the exterior color of the house.

In this way, restrictive covenants can take the place of zoning laws and can preserve the residential character of neighborhoods as long as the residents desire to do so. The major difference is that restrictive covenants can be changed with the approval of those property owners who are covered by them and need not be battled out in the political process. Thus, local owners retain control of land use decisions over their property. There may come a time in which urban development makes a residential area more profitable to be redeveloped as a shopping center. With restrictive covenants, it is up to the property owners to decide whereas, with zoning, it becomes a political decision.

MORE COMPREHENSIVE GROWTH MANAGEMENT

Zoning decisions are made by local governments, which seems plausible because most of the effects of land use decisions will be felt by local populations. However, local zoning regulations have been criticized as being too weak to be effective for several reasons. First, local political decisions are subject to manipulation by those who have local political power, which is likely to include owners of major landholdings. Thus, landowners may be able to use their political power to change zoning to match their development preferences. Zoning might be ineffective, then, because developers have the political power to manipulate local political decisions.[4]

Other problems might arise because zoning is not comprehensive enough to control all of the adverse impacts of the land use decisions of private individuals. Developments in other jurisdictions can add to the traffic, can impact the environment, and can burden public services in distant areas. Thus, there might be the demand for more comprehensive growth management. On the surface, one can hardly object to having managed growth rather than haphazard, unplanned, uncoordinated growth. The concept of growth management has a nice ring to it. In practice, that implies that those who manage growth can more effectively make land use decisions than the people who own the property, and this may not be true. Again, Hayek's principles regarding the use of knowledge come into play. Individuals who are aware of local circumstances and local opportunities may be in a better position to make land use decisions than central planners who are designing an overall plan.[5]

Land use decisions are never unplanned. Rather, individual owners make plans for their own property, and if they believe they have ideas that can enhance the value of the property of others, in a market system they can buy the property and use the knowledge they have. Thus, market-driven development is able to use the knowledge of every individual. Centrally planned growth management is specifically designed to deny individuals opportunities to use their own plans, substituting instead the central plan. Knowledge of local opportunities is replaced by the wisdom of central planning. Whether this improves land use decisions depends on whether the central planner can make better land use decisions than those with better information about local conditions. The previous section illustrated the logic of market-driven land use decisions, showing that market incentives produce logical and coherent land use plans. Can central planning do better? One way to examine this question is to look at cases where comprehensive growth management has been implemented.

Oregon and Florida have passed comprehensive statewide growth management laws. Oregon's growth management legislation was passed in 1973, while Florida's was passed in 1985.[6] Florida's legislation was broadly based on Oregon's, and the next several sections will use Florida's growth management legislation as a case study to illustrate the operation of comprehensive government land use planning.

GROWTH MANAGEMENT IN FLORIDA

Florida's growth management laws require each local government to draw up a local comprehensive plan, which must comply with the provisions of the law. The local comprehensive plans are then submitted to Florida's Department of Community Affairs, which decides whether the plans are in compliance. If the department decides they are not, they are sent back to the local government to be modified and brought into compliance. Local governments can lose state funds if they do not have plans deemed in compliance, so local governments have an incentive to comply with the state laws. After they are drawn up, the plans can be modified as often as twice a year, which provides some flexibility in the plans. Revised plans must also be approved by the state. Because all local plans must be approved at the state level, the state government has extensive control over all land use decisions in Florida.

Perhaps the most significant provision of Florida's growth management law is the concurrency requirement, which states that infrastructure must be in place concurrent with the development it is to serve. As a practical matter, this concurrency requirement applies mainly to roads, although other infrastructure is covered by the law. With regard to roads, the concurrency requirement is implemented as follows. Roads are assigned a target level of service in the local comprehensive plan, which specifies how much traffic congestion is allowed on the road. If new development would cause the level of service on a road to fall below the level specified in the plan, then the development could not take place until the infrastructure was improved to provide the target level of service. Development is not allowed unless adequate infrastructure is there to serve it.

Florida's growth management laws do not specify how infrastructure is to be provided to meet the concurrency requirement. Government is not required to provide infrastructure, and in some cases it may not be feasible for developers to provide it. For example, there might be a congested road in a developed area, and a proposed subdivision on the perimeter of the area might generate additional traffic on that road, which could be several miles away. If the road is already too congested according to the level of service specified in the local comprehensive plan and the new subdivision would add traffic, the development would not be allowed according to the concurrency rule.

Without funding for infrastructure, development is not allowed, but the law makes no provision for infrastructure funding. This was in part a conscious choice. One of the big factors generating support for growth management legislation in Florida was traffic congestion. Even though a solution was not proposed, one line of reasoning was that by making it illegal to develop in congested areas, affected individuals would be forced to find a solution. In fact, a partial solution has been found. In response to the pressures produced by the concurrency requirement, Florida's legislature modified the Growth Management Act in 1993 to allow local comprehensive plans to create concurrency areas. Development within a concurrency area may be allowed to take place even if roads are already too congested if the developer contributes money toward relieving traffic congestion within the area. Political pressures have begun to weaken what was once viewed as the strongest component of Florida's Growth Management Act.

The concurrency requirement is explicitly stated in Florida's Growth Management Act, but a number of other goals are mentioned in passing, and one that has proven to be the most significant is that the local comprehensive plans are supposed to discourage the proliferation of urban sprawl. Urban sprawl was not defined in the legislation, but subsequently has been defined by Florida's Department of Community Affairs. Many plans have been rejected by the department because it ruled that they did not do enough to discourage the proliferation of urban sprawl. Another requirement is that plans must make provisions for affordable housing. The implications of growth management for affordable housing will be discussed at greater length in Chapter 6.

Oregon's growth management legislation works by dividing all land into areas and defining acceptable use, development, and population density within those areas. Central cities are urban service areas, where high-density development is permitted. An urban expansion area surrounds the urban service area to allow for growth, and areas beyond the urban expansion area must have very low densities. While the Florida law does not require this type of partitioning, in practice Florida has followed the Oregon model. A land use map is drawn up, and certain types of uses with certain types of densities are allowed in each area. In Florida, some low-density areas are restricted to one house per 20 acres or even less. In practice, growth management in Oregon and in Florida amounts to a type of state-wide zoning.

THE PHILOSOPHY OF GROWTH MANAGEMENT: RESTRICT DEVELOPMENT

In the abstract, the concepts of managed and coordinated development seem desirable. In practice, growth management is actually legislation that limits what people are allowed to do with their property. It does not in any way encourage any type of development but does discourage development because it erects additional barriers in the development process. New development must comply with the local comprehensive plan. In Florida it must satisfy the concurrency requirement, and proposed developments can be challenged on the grounds that they are not in compliance with growth management law. Growth management opens no new development opportunities to anyone, but does close off development opportunities. If someone's property lies outside the area designated for development, it cannot be developed. The type of development allowed is specified, much as in zoning laws, but is subject to state rather than local oversight.

In practice, the philosophy of growth management is to restrict development. Rather than allow a property owner to decide when and how a parcel will be developed, the state determines whether development is allowed and, if so, what type of development can take place. Are the effects of this type of restriction desirable? Much of the remainder of this chapter examines that question. First, it is crucial to recognize that the way growth management works in practice is by restricting what people can do with their property. It affords nobody more development opportunities but affords many property owners less.

URBAN SPRAWL

One of the primary goals of growth management restrictions has been to try to control urban sprawl. Urban sprawl, according to its critics, is unaesthetic, is inefficient, creates traffic congestion, and is harmful to the environment. The creation of urban service areas and clear urban boundaries in the comprehensive planning process shows the way in which the battle against urban sprawl has been implemented in both Oregon and Florida. Development is allowed in urban areas to encourage urban infill and is not allowed beyond the urban boundary.

Much of the fight against urban sprawl in Florida has been a matter of policy rather than legislation. The original growth management legislation stated that local plans should discourage the proliferation of urban sprawl, but the legislation did not define urban sprawl. As a result, Florida's Department of Community Affairs, which is charged with judging whether local plans are in compliance with the state growth management law, defined urban sprawl and has rejected many local plans because they did not meet the department's policy.[7]

One of the policies that has been used to fight urban sprawl in Florida is informally known as the 120 percent rule. The rule is not written down anywhere but is well-known as a guideline for determining an acceptable amount of developable area in a local comprehensive plan. The University of Florida projects population growth in all areas of the state, and the 120 percent rule specifies that a local comprehensive plan cannot allow more development than would be required to accommodate 120 percent of the area's projected population. To take an actual example from Leon County, in which Tallahassee is located, the originally submitted plan would have allowed residential development in an area north of town and in an area south of town. Both areas are adjacent to already-developed areas. If both approved areas were fully developed, they could accommodate more than 120 percent of the projected population, so the plan was rejected. To comply, the land-use map had to be redrawn with less developable area to meet the 120 percent rule.

Enforcement of this 120 percent rule has the obvious effect of restricting the supply of developable land, and a reduction in the supply will raise land prices, which will make housing more expensive. Surely more expensive housing will be detrimental to most people. This point is relevant to Chapter 6, which addresses housing and homelessness. Perhaps, however, this restriction brings with it other benefits. Florida's Department of Community Affairs published a detailed explanation of its view of urban sprawl in order to make clear to local governments the kind of development it was trying to prevent. Urban sprawl is characterized by leapfrog development, strip or ribbon development, or low-density single-dimensional development. Each of these concepts will be examined to judge whether the costs of restricting development have offsetting benefits.[8]

LEAPFROG DEVELOPMENT

Leapfrog development occurs when new development is located away from an existing urban area, bypassing vacant parcels located closer to the urban area that are suitable for development. Leapfrog development occurs because developers choose to develop less expensive land farther away from an urban area rather than more costly land closer in. Leapfrog development entails some costs because it is more expensive to extend infrastructure to the leapfrogged area and because it creates more traffic and longer commutes into the urban area. Further, it may cause environmental damage.

This view of leapfrog development overlooks many of the benefits of this type of development, primarily because it views the new development as a static outcome rather than as part of a dynamic growth process. At the outset, it is clear that the people purchasing homes in the leapfrog development view it to be a better opportunity than living closer in to the urban area. The main reason is undoubtedly that land prices will be lower, so housing will be more affordable. It is not unreasonable for people to decide that they will accept longer commutes in exchange for more comfortable, lower-priced housing. A caveat must be noted here. Because it will be costly to extend infrastructure, the leapfrog development must pay its true infrastructure costs in order for the development to be truly cost-effective. Thus, it is the responsibility of the local governments to see that the costs of water, sewer, roads, and so forth are charged to the development. Otherwise, inefficient leapfrog development can take place to take advantage of the government subsidy.

If the new development does pay its share of the costs, however, the leapfrog development produces benefits for those who choose to live there. Furthermore, over the long run leapfrog development produces excellent areas for commercial development and results in more efficient development patterns overall. Why would land closer in to the urban area be more costly than land farther out? The obvious answer is its development potential. However, commercial developers will be reluctant to place new commercial developments on the outskirts of an urban area. Commercial areas benefit from a central location, making them more easily accessible to more people. How can such prime commercial development areas be created? Leapfrog development creates them.

When a new development leapfrogs over undeveloped land, the undeveloped land becomes an ideal location for commercial development. Now, it will be surrounded by other development, making it a central location ideal for commercial activity. If leapfrog development is prohibited, ideal commercial locations like this will not be created. Leapfrog development is actually a vital part of development in growing areas. This is not to say that leapfrog development is always good, but rather to observe that often it is beneficial. Despite the potential benefits, the official policy of Florida is to oppose leapfrog development as a matter of official policy in all cases, rather than consider its merits on a case-by-case basis.

STRIP OR RIBBON DEVELOPMENT

Strip or ribbon development occurs when high amounts of commercial, retail, and office development occur in a linear pattern along both sides of major arterial roadways. Critics of this type of development argue that it reduces the efficiency of the roadway in moving traffic because much traffic will be on the road to gain access to the businesses. Although Florida officially opposes this type of development and rejects local comprehensive plans that permit it, strip or ribbon development is an example of an efficient development pattern.

Businesses like to locate on busy roads because they rely on traffic for their business. By placing them on major roads, it makes access easier for customers and actually reduces traffic overall. This type of development also creates natural locations for residential development between the ribbons of commercial development that follow the major roads. By locating residences between the ribbons, it is possible to create residential streets with relatively little traffic yet make them conveniently located to commercial activities on the nearby thoroughfares.

In many situations, strip or ribbon development has caused problems because of poor planning. The problem is not the development itself but that insufficient rights-of-way were obtained for the major roads, and that too many curb cuts were allowed, which create congestion as people enter and leave businesses. Strip or ribbon development does not have to allow every business to have a driveway every 50 feet along major roads. With planning, access lanes can be built to permit the smooth merging of traffic entering and leaving businesses. This type of development does not have to be unsightly if the right-of-way is made wide enough for landscaped buffers between the road and the businesses. This requires governments to plan ahead to secure rights-of-way for major thoroughfares in order to avoid problems that often arise with strip or ribbon development. The development pattern itself is efficient. Busy thoroughfares are the best locations for commercial establishments. Problems occur when governments do not effectively manage the roads that afford access to those establishments.

If government owns the roads, then government has the responsibility for managing its property, the same way that private owners have the responsibility for managing theirs. This can involve controlling access and preventing spillover costs (which might include unsightly development). This does not imply that governments dictate land use adjacent to its roads but merely that it prevents land use decisions from creating costs in excess of benefits. Government control of spillover costs on its roads is analagous to government control of pollution into rivers it owns, but government can control spillover costs from neighboring properties without controlling land use decisions.

LOW-DENSITY, SINGLE-DIMENSIONAL DEVELOPMENT

This type of development is typified by the large residential subdivision. Houses have relatively large lots, and those who live there must drive everywhere because the only thing nearby is other houses. Often, this type of development is the result of zoning laws that do not permit mixed use of property. At the outset, there are two possible suggestions for overcoming the problems of low-density, single-dimensional development. First, allow leapfrog development, which creates a perfect opportunity for commercial development to be interspersed with residences. Second, allow strip or ribbon development, which puts commercial establishments adjacent to residential areas.

Single-dimensional development is more likely to occur when leapfrogging is not permitted. Nobody wants to put their commercial establishments on the perimeter of an urban area, so without leapfrogging, new development on the perimeter is primarily residential while commercial developers look for more central locations. Unwittingly, the types of development opposed by those who fight urban sprawl actually help to create some of its worst features.

Low-density development is claimed to be undesirable because it contributes to sprawl, it extends commuting distances, and it harms the environment. In fact, low-density development is likely to help the environment because it creates a lower ratio of paved to unpaved areas. In dense urban areas, buildings, roads, and parking lots take up a great percentage of the land, leaving little of the natural environment to absorb pollutants. Air pollution and water runoff problems will be more severe. If people live in subdivisions with yards and trees the natural environment absorbs some of the negative by-products of civilization, so smaller amounts of polluted water and air will have to escape the area. The environmental costs of suburban living are offset by environmental benefits.

The biggest argument in favor of low-density development is people like it. Normally, crowded living conditions are associated with a lower standard of living, and by allowing individuals more space, their standard of living rises. Ironically, many of the advocates of more compact development patterns live in nice homes with big yards. They want other people to live in crowded apartments. Low-density living patterns mean more room and a higher standard of living. Every urban area has apartments available for those who prefer that lifestyle, but many people choose (and more people aspire to) their own detached homes indicating that this is a desirable feature of development.

WHAT IS SO BAD ABOUT URBAN SPRAWL?

Urban sprawl has a bad ring to it. Just saying it produces a knee-jerk negative reaction. Before we decide we are against it, though, we should be clear about what it is and why we do not like it. Florida's Department of Community Affairs made an effort to do that by laying out a clear definition of urban sprawl.

When urban sprawl is examined it can be seen as a desirable development process. Leapfrog development looks inefficient until it is

seen as part of a long-term development process that creates opportunities for centrally located commercial areas. The worst aspects of strip
or ribbon development are the results of poor planning for highway use.
This strip or ribbon development locates commercial establishments on
heavily travelled roads, which is desirable, and locates residential
areas away from heavily travelled roads, which is also desirable.
Single-dimensioned development is often the result of government
planning through zoning or through trying to prevent leapfrogging and
ribbon development. Low-density development is a sign of a high
standard of living. In short, once a working definition of urban sprawl
is developed it can be seen as a healthy and efficient development
process.

This does not imply that all instances of these development processes are efficient but that they can be. However, the comprehensive
growth management policies in Oregon and in Florida, the states that
have gone the farthest, oppose them as a matter of policy. Despite their
intentions, the actual effects of comprehensive growth management
will undoubtedly be harmful. Unfortunately, it is likely that most
observers will not see that this harm is caused by growth management
legislation. They will be thinking that things would be worse without
the legislation and will consider additional legislation to help solve the
problems caused by the initial legislation. While growth management
sounds desirable, a careful analysis of actual growth management
policies illustrates that they are counterproductive.

CENTRALIZED VERSUS DECENTRALIZED DEVELOPMENT

The specific policies discussed above form part of a more general
vision of the way in which development takes place. Growth management legislation is written under the premise that development takes
place by having suburban areas spread out from a central urban core.
People work in the central cities, commuting from the suburbs. In fact,
this characterization of development is not an accurate portrayal of
actual commuting patterns. In Los Angeles, for example, only 3 percent
of the total workforce works downtown. There are 19 major activity
centers in the Los Angeles area, but even these areas account for only
17.5 percent of the area's total employment. Most people live and work
in the suburbs, and the average commute for individuals in the Los
Angeles area is 20 minutes.[9]

If left to its own devices, development will occur in a decentralized
manner, which efficiently allocates land use by making different types
of activities conveniently located to one another. Rather than having a
centralized city where everyone commutes, decentralized growth provides nodes of development, allowing people to live close to the node
where they work and allowing a more efficient pattern of two-way

traffic during peak periods as people travel between nodes. Decentralized development, with many activity centers rather than one central urban core, allows the best of both worlds because it keeps commuting distances in large population areas short but allows the amenities of suburban living. Growth management as it is actually practiced works against this type of efficient development whereas natural market forces promote it.

Some individuals might prefer to live in a community like New York City where there is a central urban core and a high population density. Others might prefer suburban living. Decentralized land use decision making gives communities more control over the types of development they will have, thereby allowing differences among communities and allowing individuals to choose the type of area they prefer. Centralized growth management imposes the same model of development on everyone. After some analysis, that model is not even efficient in the way that it allocates land. Things might be different in some abstract ideal world of great land use planners, but in the real world of growth management and land use planning, the plans cause more problems than they solve.

THE GOVERNMENT'S RESPONSIBILITY: MANAGE ITS RESOURCES

Is there a role for the government in growth management and land use planning? Yes. The government's responsibility is to manage the resources it controls and, with regard to growth management, one big component is the roads. People associate urban sprawl with transportation problems, and many of these problems arise because the government has not effectively managed and controlled access to its roads. In congested commercial areas, traffic is clogged because of too many access points to highways, and insufficient rights-of-way were planned to handle the traffic load. The government can control access by limiting the number of allowable curb cuts and requiring access lanes or separate access roads rather than direct access to thoroughfares.

Often, the problem is lack of adequate foresight by those who design and administer the roads. In some cases, it might have been difficult to foresee future traffic congestion, but anyone who drives in an urban area can cite instances of problems that should have been foreseen and of problems that will begin to manifest themselves in a few years. If planners cannot manage these resources over which they have relatively direct control, one should be leery of turning over the whole land use process to planners.

A parallel can be drawn between publicly owned natural resources (rivers) and publicly owned man-made resources (roads). Just as the government controls access to waterways by managing who can discharge into them and often who can withdraw how much water the government is responsible for controlling access to roads by making them efficient movers of traffic and providers of access. Having land adjacent to a road does not necessarily provide the right of access, as interstate highways show by example. Advance planning is required, however, because it is difficult to take away one's access to adjacent roadways once it has been granted. Optimal access arrangments for roadways must be planned when the road is built.

Perhaps private roads would provide one way to deal with the optimal access issue, but as long as the government owns the roads, it is responsible for controlling their use in the same way that it is responsible for its natural resources. By controlling access and by determining where new roads will be built there is ample room for the government to manage growth without directly controlling the land use decisions of private property owners.

CONCLUSION

Land use decisions have a large impact on the quality of life, and a natural temptation exists to manage and coordinate land use decisions rather than allow individuals to do whatever they want with their land. Upon examination of the issues, two factors should dampen one's enthusiasm for centralized growth management. First, an invisible hand of the market guides property owners to develop their property resulting in efficient land use patterns without government interference. Second, when government land use planning is examined, land use decisions made under the name of growth management are inefficient and will more likely hinder rather than help the development process.

The invisible hand of the market can be aided by the law of nuisance, which provides a mechanism for preventing nearby property owners from undertaking activities that harm the property values of their neighbors. In addition, restrictive covenants can be used to protect individuals and their neighborhoods from unwanted encroachments. The law of nuisance would undoubtedly be more effective if there were not so many government regulations regarding land use already, and the use of restrictive covenants is widespread despite government regulations, such as zoning, that provide similar functions.

Growth management and land use planning are issues that appeal to those who are relatively well off. They see additional development as eroding their quality of life and want laws to do something about it. As this chapter has suggested, those laws are often counterproductive. Lower-income people are more interested in the related issues of homelessness and affordable housing. The next chapter considers these issues, building upon the lessons of growth management discussed here.

NOTES

1.   See Randall G. Holcombe, "Growth Management in Florida: Lessons for the National Economy," *Cato Journal* 10 (Spring/Summer 1990): 109–25 for additional discussion of the distributional aspects of growth management legislation.

2.   See Bernard H. Siegan, *Land Use Without Zoning* (Lexington, Mass.: D. C. Heath, 1972); Bernard H. Siegan, "Nonzoning in Houston," *Journal of Law & Economics* 13 (April 1970): 71–147.

3.   See Richard F. Babcock, *The Zoning Game: Municipal Practices and Policies* (Madison: University of Wisconsin Press, 1966) for a discussion of actual zoning practices.

4.   Babcock, *The Zoning Game* discusses the local politics of zoning.

5.   Friedrich A. Hayek, "The Use of Knowledge in Society," *American Economic Review* 35 (September 1945): 519–30 provides the foundation for these ideas.

6.   The Oregon legislation is described by Kelly Ross, "Sixteen Years of Statewide Zoning: The Oregon Case," in *Private Property Rights, Land-Use Policy, and Growth Management,* ed. John W. Cooper (Tallahassee, Fla.: Montpelier Books, 1990); the Florida legislation is overviewed by Randall G. Holcombe, "Growth Management in Florida," in *Private Property Rights, Land-Use Policy, and Growth Management,* ed. John W. Cooper (Tallahassee, Fla.: Montpelier Books, 1990).

7.   Because Florida's Department of Community Affairs went well beyond the letter of the law in defining and enforcing its urban sprawl policy, many critics of the department have accused it of creating its own rules rather than following the statutes. The department has stood its ground, however, in pursuing its anti-sprawl policy.

8.   Florida Department of Community Affairs, *Technical Memo* 4, No. 4 (undated, but released in 1989).

9.   These figures are from Peter Gordon and Harry Richardson, "You Can't Get There From Here," *Reason* (August/September 1989): 34–37.

6

Housing and Homelessness

Homelessness was hardly recognized until the 1980s, when it was catapulted into national attention. In a decade in which many Americans were experiencing increasing prosperity, an increasingly visible minority had no place to live. While every individual case is different the fundamental causes of homelessness can be broken down into two categories. The first category encompasses those who are mentally ill or who are dependent on drugs or alcohol to the extent that they are not capable of becoming a part of mainstream society. The second category encompasses those who cannot afford housing. The first category makes up the bulk of the homeless while the second attracts most of the news coverage and public sympathy. Both groups could be helped by improved public policies addressing housing problems, but, ironically, public policies, in general, have worked to create homelessness.

This chapter begins with the premise that homeless people would prefer to have a place to live if housing were free. The primary factor that keeps them homeless is insufficient incomes. If their incomes were sufficient or if housing prices were lower they would not choose to be homeless. One way government policy has addressed housing problems is to enter the housing market directly, either by providing housing for low-income individuals at subsidized rates or by subsidizing rent payments for qualified individuals. Government housing programs, which have had their share of problems, will be considered later in the chapter. The chapter considers affordable housing more directly and looks into the way that the government's involvement in housing affects prices. Many government regulations and programs make housing more expensive, which puts housing out of the financial reach of more people. The next section picks up where the previous chapter left off by considering the effect of growth management legislation on affordable housing.

GROWTH MANAGEMENT AND HOUSING PRICES

Florida's growth management legislation addresses affordable housing by requiring that all local comprehensive plans contain provisions for affordable housing. Good intentions do not necessarily produce good results, however, so it is worth considering how growth management legislation affects housing prices. As Chapter 5 illustrated, growth management legislation restricts the amount of development that can take place. It does not enable anyone to undertake more real estate development than they could have done without the legislation, but it does prevent people from developing property they might have developed in the absence of growth management legislation. Whatever its other effects, growth management legislation reduces the amount of real estate development.

A reduction in development means that less new housing will be created. Housing prices are determined by the laws of supply and demand, and a reduction in the supply of housing will increase its price. Thus, by restricting the amount of housing that is being added to the housing stock, growth management will increase the price of housing and make housing less affordable. Laws can say whatever legislators want them to, but despite a provision in Florida's growth management legislation requiring localities to provide for affordable housing, the fact that the legislation restricts the amount of new housing that will be constructed will have the opposite effect and will make all housing more expensive. Growth management works against the goal of affordable housing.

DISTRIBUTIONAL IMPACTS OF GROWTH MANAGEMENT

Why, if growth management makes housing less affordable, would anyone be in favor of it? The answer is that, like any policy that causes some prices to rise, some people will benefit from it. The proponents of growth management are upper-income people who are interested in general quality-of-life issues because they are already dealing successfully with some of the basic issues like how to provide food, clothing, and shelter for their families. Most proponents of growth management own their own homes, so increases in housing prices will leave them relatively unaffected. If they decide to sell their houses, they can benefit from the higher prices.

In general, growth management favors those who own property that is already developed or property that is allowed to be developed under the laws. Owners of existing commercial and business property will benefit from growth management because the laws will prevent new developers from creating as much new commercial real estate. The reduction in competition will increase the rent on existing commercial property. By restricting development, growth management means more wealth and higher income for many people.

Who loses because of growth management? New residents who will have to pay more for housing bear some of the costs as do people who are prevented from moving to an area because of high costs. Growth management also harms renters because as property values go up so do rents. Landlords and homeowners are higher-income people while renters are usually lower-income people. Therefore, growth management favors the rich over the poor.

In the long run, everybody will bear the costs of growth management. The children of rich people will find that when they reach the age where they want to rent an apartment or buy a house, those costs will be greater because of growth management legislation. If the conclusions of Chapter 5 are correct, growth management legislation encourages inefficient development patterns, which ends up hurting everybody. In the short run, however, the benefits of growth management legislation will go to upper-income people, and the costs will be borne more heavily by lower-income people and, in particular, renters. The rise in property values will create an increase in rents, which further harms the goal of affordable housing.

BUILDING CODES AND ZONING

While large-scale growth management is relatively rare, other types of restrictions on development also increase the costs of housing. Building codes require that certain criteria are met for new construction. Building inspectors make sure that the code is met. The inspection process itself is costly, both to taxpayers and to builders, but codes also may be inflexible and often benefit building professionals more than those who live in the completed buildings.

In Chicago, electrical wires must pass through metal conduit to meet the local building code whereas in Washington, D.C. this is not necessary. Some localities permit PVC plumbing; others do not. PVC is a plastic plumbing material that is easy to install, especially when compared to the more traditional copper pipe. One can easily see why plumbers would work hard to prevent PVC plumbing because do-it-yourselfers could more readily displace professional plumbers. Even in new construction, the extra effort involved to install copper rather than PVC translates into more income for plumbers — and higher housing prices. If wiring is deemed safe in Washington, D.C., without having to pass through metal conduit, why is it not also safe in Chicago?

Differences in building codes from one location to another also help to give local contractors an advantage because they are familiar with the specific local regulations. This additional market power helps keep up the wages of local workers and adds to housing prices. One might argue that quality standards are necessary to make sure that buyers do not purchase substandard homes out of ignorance. The role of building codes, in this view, is to protect the consumer. Consumers could be better protected without government building codes, however. Building codes are among the quality standards to which the discussion of the next chapter applies.

There are ways to get around building codes, and one is to live in a mobile home. In most states, mobile homes are considered vehicles rather than houses from a legal perspective, and building codes do not apply. This creates a kind of a safety valve because people who cannot afford the quality of housing required by the building codes can live in a mobile home. One of the drawbacks to living in a mobile home, however, is that many places restrict where they can be located through the use of zoning laws.

As noted in Chapter 5, the main impetus for adopting zoning laws was the preservation of residential neighborhoods near areas of business growth. Residential neighborhood preservation has always been at the foundation of zoning laws, and zoning laws typically specify much more than just the way in which a property is to be used. Zoning laws can specify minimum lot sizes, minimum house sizes, how much a house has to be set back from the street and from adjoining lots, and perhaps even who is allowed to live in a residence.[1] All of these factors are designed to preserve a high quality of life for people who live in the zoned area, but they contribute to higher housing prices by preventing the construction of less expensive housing units.

People who want to live in nice neighborhoods with large yards and large houses ought to have the right to do so if they can afford it. However, zoning laws use the political process to specify the types of housing other people can build on their property. Chapter 5 illustrated how one's interests can be protected through the use of restrictive covenants in lieu of (or in addition to) zoning. Zoning has the undesirable side effect that it can prevent more affordable housing from being built even when everyone in the area desires it. Building codes and zoning are two examples of government involvement in housing markets that make housing more expensive without demonstrably producing offsetting benefits.

URBAN RENEWAL

Few programs work against the goal of affordable housing as obviously as urban renewal. Whereas zoning laws preserve the residential neighborhoods of those who are relatively well off, urban renewal destroys the residential neighborhoods of those who are relatively poor. Sometimes government housing has been built to replace the housing that has been destroyed through urban renewal, but often the government destroys housing and replaces it with sports facilities, convention centers, or commercial buildings. Neighborhoods that once provided homes for the poor become new territory for the middle and upper classes. As Jerome Rothenberg noted several decades ago,

Projects have substantial lead time, usually destroy more units than they construct, and usually replace very low quality units with very high quality units. . . . The result is a regressive income redistribution, with lower-income groups who consume at the lower end of the housing stock suffering most, and higher-income groups who consume at the affected higher end of the housing stock benefitting most.[2]

Urban renewal is intended to improve the area it renews, but people who live in the area to be renewed often object to renewal projects because, despite what appears to be substandard living conditions, those who live there do not think urban renewal benefits them.[3] Living conditions are not as good in the slums as in the suburbs, but rents are low. The systematic elimination of the low rent district does push some people into better housing, often at a higher cost, but it also pushes some people into homelessness. Urban renewal, as a national public policy, began with the Housing Act of 1949 and accelerated as a part of the increase in all social programs in the 1960s.[4] After results did not live up to promises, urban renewal as a term is heard less often, but urban renewal policies continue as governments push to take over central city areas for public projects.

Urban renewal provides yet another example of a public program that works against affordable housing. By destroying inexpensive housing, it raises housing costs for the group that can least afford it.[5]

WHAT CREATES AFFORDABLE HOUSING?

The single factor that creates the most confusion in discussions of affordable housing is a confounding of construction costs with housing prices. In areas where there is an ample supply of developable land, there will be a close correspondence, but housing prices are determined by the laws of supply and demand, not by construction costs. One cannot build affordable housing, in the sense that the characteristics of the building will determine whether or not it is affordable. One can only build housing units with particular characteristics. The market for housing will determine the price of housing based on supply and demand.

The San Francisco area is known for its high housing prices and understandably so. It is surrounded on three sides by water, and little developable land is left. With a relatively fixed supply of land, demanders of housing units are left to bid up the price. An informal comparison of housing prices in the early 1990s suggests that a 900 square foot house in the San Francisco area costs roughly about what a 4,000 square foot house would cost in Tallahassee, Florida. San Francisco has relatively little developable land whereas Tallahassee is surrounded by undeveloped land.

Tallahassee's relatively affordable housing could change, however, if Florida's growth management regulations prove to be effective in restricting growth. While Tallahassee has room to grow, a legislated barrier of undevelopable land because of growth restrictions could prove to be as effective as the San Francisco Bay at shutting off the supply of housing and pushing housing prices up. In the 1950s, California's housing prices were near the national average. By the 1980s they had skyrocketed to well above the national average as a result of growth restrictions, both legislated and natural.

Housing prices are determined by supply and demand. Affordable housing is produced by increasing the number of housing units relative to demand. If more housing is built, housing prices will be lower than if there are restrictions on the building of housing units. In short, the best way to encourage affordable housing is to encourage real estate development.

RENT CONTROL AND AFFORDABLE HOUSING

Rent control provides another example of the democratic political process working against affordable housing. Rent control typically is a political response to rising rents, and rising rents often are a result of government policy restricting housing. The scenario plays this way. People want to protect their quality of life and view growth restrictions as a way to do so. Growth restrictions cause real estate prices to rise which makes rents rise. Since renters are a larger voting block than landlords, there will be political pressure to institute rent controls. A rent control guarantees that rents will not go up as long as the renter stays in the apartment or guarantees that rents will not go up faster than some legally mandated maximum. Therefore, the longer the renter stays in the apartment the lower the rent is compared to the rent that would be charged in a free market. The rent control law gives the renter a bargain.

Were this the end of the story, rent controls would simply transfer income from the landlord to the tenant, making the tenant better off at the landlord's expense. However, like so much in public policy, there are secondary effects that work to make the situation worse. By keeping housing prices artificially low, rent control increases the demand for housing, but, at the same time, artificially low housing prices reduce the housing supply. Because housing is a durable good, the effects of rent control will take some time to show up. At first, rent control merely appears to produce more affordable housing, but over the longer run the supply of housing is reduced for two reasons. First, because it is less profitable to own rental housing less new rental housing will be built. Second, the lower profitability of rental housing will reduce the supply of existing housing as current landlords convert their buildings from rental housing or simply let them deteriorate until they are no longer fit for habitation.

Rent control laws are often accompanied by laws restricting the ability of apartment owners to convert their buildings. Otherwise, they might turn them into condominiums and sell them or they might convert them into offices or some other non-housing use. If they are unable to convert their buildings, landlords have little incentive to maintain them. Because renters are paying below the market value they will not want to leave their apartments, so landlords do not need to maintain them in order to maintain their flow of income, which is fixed by the rent control law. Often, the opposite is true, and if an apartment becomes vacant, the landlord can raise the rent for the new tenant. Rent controls create an adversarial relationship between landlords and tenants.

Without rent controls landlords want to keep their tenants happy because they want their tenants to stay. Vacant apartments generate no income, and it is less costly to continue renting to a stable group of long-term tenants than to continue turning the apartments over. Similarly, tenants do not want to be evicted and do not want landlords to raise the rent to try to force them out, so they want to remain on good terms with the landlord. In the absence of rent controls, the landlord and tenant engage in voluntary exchange and want to remain on good terms so they can continue to exchange for their mutual benefits.

With rent controls, the tenant has a right to stay in the apartment paying less than the landlord would like to collect. Landlords have an incentive to try to encourage tenants to move while tenants may benefit from imposing costs on landlords. For example, ordinances may require that landlords maintain their rent-controlled buildings and that renters in buildings with maintenance problems become entitled to rent reductions. In some cases this has led to incidents such as renters reporting plumbing problems but not letting repair people into their apartments to fix the reported problems. Then the renters argue that they are entitled to reduced rents. In any case, the landlord cannot evict the tenants.

Some landlord-tenant problems may be tenant-induced while others may be primarily the fault of landlords. The point is that rent controls move the landlord-tenant relationship from one of cooperation to one of conflict. Because of inflation, controlled rents become less and less able to cover even maintenance expenses on buildings. Eventually, the landlord will no longer find it profitable to maintain the property, and it will be abandoned. This story has been played out countless times in New York City where, ironically, in a city that has a substantial homeless population there are multitudes of apartment buildings that are abandoned because their owners no longer find it worthwhile to maintain them. Rent controls have destroyed a substantial part of the existing housing stock and at the same time, have discouraged people from adding new housing to it.[6]

The stated intention of rent control is to maintain the availability of affordable housing, but its actual results are just the opposite. While the original tenants and their heirs can remain in their rent-controlled apartments at below-market rents, rent controls reduce the availability of affordable housing for people without housing. By reducing both the supply of housing and the turnover of existing housing, rent controls contribute to the problem of homelessness.[7]

GOVERNMENT PROVISION OF HOUSING

One solution often used to deal with housing problems is to have the government provide housing. Nowhere in the United States has the government been more aggressive at providing housing than in New York City where, in 1986, the city government owned 9 percent of the total housing stock and 70 percent of the housing in central Harlem.[8] The city's ownership of the housing stock is a direct result of rent controls. Because many buildings have been under rent control since World War II, the rents became inadequate to maintain the buildings, and many buildings were abandoned beginning in the 1970s. The city has taken over abandoned buildings, renovated them, and has become the new landlord. The government in New York City sympathizes strongly with tenants to the extent that it appears that the city has a deliberate policy of forcing landlords into abandoning their buildings so that the city can take over. This environment is clearly not conducive to the ownership of rental housing. Construction of new rental housing is discouraged so that more than 60 percent of New York's housing stock is over 60 years old.[9]

Government-owned housing, in New York and elsewhere, has seen its share of problems. Housing is poorly maintained and often abused by its tenants. Streets and parks attract criminal activity to such an extent that parents are afraid to let their children play outside. Much of the blame lies in the nature of public ownership. In housing, as with other resources, saying that something is publicly owned means that nobody really has an ownership interest, so nobody has an incentive to take care of the property. With privately-owned apartments — in free markets without rent controls — the landlord wants to maintain the property and attract responsible tenants in order to enhance the value of the property. Tenants, in turn, have an incentive to take care of the property in order to keep from being evicted. Nobody has similar incentives in public housing with the result that too often it begins deteriorating as soon as it is occupied.

One solution for this problem is to give the responsibility for management to the people who have the biggest stake in the outcome — the tenants. Perhaps the biggest problem with public housing has been that while much attention has been paid to designing the physical layout of the housing little attention has been given to designing effective governing institutions for the housing units once they have been completed. If it is not feasible to privatize public housing giving management responsibility to those who live in the housing has been proven to be an effective way of improving the quality of life in government-owned housing.[10]

HOMELESSNESS AND MENTAL ILLNESS

One reason why homelessness is more visible in the late twentieth century than it was in the middle of the century is that many people who now are homeless would have been placed in mental institutions decades ago. Deinstitutionalization began in the middle 1950s. In 1955 there were 559,000 patients in mental hospitals in the United States. Twenty years later the population in mental hospitals had fallen to about 140,000.[11] At one time, mental hospitals were used to provide long-term shelter for the mentally ill. Mental hospitals still provide treatment, but community-based programs now serve the deinstitutionalized mentally ill, and most former mental patients have been released to live with their families.

Ideally, a combination of family care and community-based social services would take care of the large population of individuals who formerly would have been institutionalized. In reality, many are now homeless and lack either the motivation or the ability, or both, to become a part of mainstream society. A significant percentage suffer from alcohol or drug abuse. A 1987 study of the homeless in Los Angeles indicated that nearly half suffered a combination of alcoholism and mental illness and that over 60 percent were abusers of either alcohol or drugs.[12] How are these people able to survive? They do so through a combination of scavenging and begging, the assistance of organized charities, and government programs.

Through government programs and charities, help is often available that could improve the standard of living of the homeless, and often bring them out of homelessness. However, in many cases, the homeless do not take advantage of all of the benefits to which they would be entitled.[13] In many cases, they do not like the conditions that are imposed on them — they would rather sleep on the street than follow the rules of a shelter or would rather scavenge and ask strangers for money than deal with the welfare bureaucracy. We might conclude that this is their choice, but the mentally ill may not be able to make informed choices. They are able to survive, however, because a wealthy society has enough left over to sustain them. The government offers to provide more help in most cases but only for those who are willing and able to deal with its bureaucracy. Should there be a more substantial safety net?

THE SAFETY NET

Before the proliferation of welfare programs, families typically cared for other family members who could not care for themselves. The family was the safety net. Despite the drawbacks, this system indicated clearly who had the responsibility for caring for those who were unable to make it on their own. Yes, people without family members to support them could fall through the safety net, as still happens today with the government's safety net. Before the welfare state those without family to care for them would have to depend on voluntary charity.

People relying on family members or charity for their care would see that, first, their well-being was directly contingent upon others being willing to continue their support and, second, that they were imposing a burden on others. Both of these factors would give those who might be able to do so an incentive to care for themselves. Nobody wants to be a burden on others in their group, and nobody wants to depend upon an uncertain income from the generosity of others. These incentives are removed when government programs provide the safety net. Those programs are called entitlements and convey the impression that recipients are entitled to them. Recipients are not burdening anybody by accepting what they are entitled to and, in any event, have no direct contact with taxpayers in the same way as they would with family members. Furthermore, because the payments are entitlements, one would have less concern about being cut off from a payment stream to which one was entitled. Entitlements enable recipients to escape from the dependence of their families and live on their own, even if this might mean being homeless.[14] For some, freedom and homelessness is preferable to family dependence.

Undoubtedly most homeless people would choose to have a place of residence if residences were free. The problem is the cost of housing exceeds the individual's ability (or willingness) to pay. One solution is to increase people's incomes so they can afford housing. Another would be to lower housing costs. Problems of homelessness seem most visible and most publicized in wealthy areas. California and New York lead the nation, but rarely is there much notice paid to homelessness in poorer states like Arkansas and Mississippi. The latter states have problems with substandard housing, but substandard housing undoubtedly keeps some people housed rather than homeless. As noted earlier in this chapter, eradicating substandard housing in urban areas contributes to homelessness by eradicating low-cost housing that relatively poor people can afford.

Homelessness creates a downward spiral from which it may be difficult to recover. When a person loses a permanent place to live, the person loses the ability to give an indication of stability to potential employers. When looking for work one is much better off having a permanent address, a place to receive mail, and a place to shower. One's opportunities for improvement are greatly reduced if one becomes homeless. Thus, the best safety net against homelessness is affordable housing, but many government programs work against affordable housing by eradicating low-quality housing and by restricting the ability of developers to produce more housing.

CONCLUSION

Homelessness is becoming an increasingly serious problem in the United States, but housing policies in general work to create more homelessness. Homelessness occurs because people cannot (or choose not to) purchase housing on the incomes they receive. Thus, the homelessness problem could be reduced if housing were less expensive. The price of housing is determined by the laws of supply and demand. An increase in the demand for housing relative to its price will increase the cost of housing while an increase in the supply of housing relative to the demand will reduce the cost of housing. Since World War II, U.S. housing policy has been geared toward reducing the supply of housing and raising its cost. Urban renewal has destroyed more housing units than it has created, and has replaced low-quality, low-cost housing with housing of higher quality but also of higher cost. Growth management policies have restricted the amount of development that can take place, further reducing the supply of housing. Zoning restrictions and building codes have kept the cost of housing high. Where these policies have been most effective, pushing housing costs up the most, rent controls have been instituted, further reducing the supply of housing and reducing the turnover of rental properties. Rent control provides short-run benefits to those who already have housing but harms those who do not.

The homelessness problem would not be completely solved by changing housing policies because the homeless include people with mental illness and with drug and alcohol addictions who would have trouble fitting into mainstream society. However, if housing problems did not force some of them into homelessness, at least some of that group would not have left mainstream society. It is especially tragic when people who are poor but want to earn a living and live a normal life are forced into homelessness because of housing policies that price housing out of their reach. Seeing the problems of the homeless, the common response is that the government should do something, but the government already has done something. It has regulated the housing market, reduced the supply of housing, and forced developers to build more expensive housing all of which have contributed to the housing problem.

Chapter 5 indicated why the government's efforts at growth management and land use planning are misguided and do not enhance the quality of life. What about government regulations to improve the quality of housing? Reflecting on this question, Chapter 7 considers the general subject of quality standards regulation.

NOTES

1. Auburn, Alabama's, zoning law prohibits unrelated people from living together in houses zoned for single-family use. Auburn is a college town, and this restriction was designed to prevent groups of college students from renting and living in houses in single-family neighborhoods.

2. Jerome Rothenberg, *Economic Evaluation of Urban Renewal* (Washington, D.C.: Brookings Institution, 1967), p. 15. Chester W. Hartman, "The Housing of Relocated Families," in *Urban Renewal: People, Politics, and Planning,* ed. Jewel Bellush and Murray Hausknecht (Garden City, N.Y.: Anchor Books, 1967), pp. 315–53 notes that families relocated as a result of urban renewal move into better housing but at a higher price.

3. William Worthy, *The Rape of Our Neighborhoods: And How Communities are Resisting Take-Overs by Colleges, Hospitals, Churches, Businesses, and Public Agencies* (New York: William Morrow, 1976) in a book whose title is long but descriptive explains factors behind neighborhood resistance to urban renewal.

4. See Scott Greer, *Urban Renewal and American Cities* (Indianapolis: Bobbs-Merrill, 1965) for an early history of urban renewal.

5. Martin Anderson, "The Federal Bulldozer," in *Urban Renewal: The Record and the Controversy,* ed. James Q. Wilson (Cambridge, Mass.: MIT Press, 1966), Chap. 9 estimates that in the 1950s urban renewal destroyed approximately 126,000 housing units and built only 28,000 in their place.

6. See Milton Friedman and Rose Friedman, *Free to Choose* (New York: Harcourt Brace Jovanovich, 1980) for a discussion of rent controls and their effect on the New York City housing stock.

7. Public policies that cause homelessness are discussed in detail by William Tucker, *The Excluded Americans: Homelessness and Housing Policies* (Washington, D.C.: Regnery Gateway, 1990).

8. These statistics are from Tucker, *The Excluded Americans,* p. 312.

9. Information about the New York housing market comes from Tucker, *The Excluded Americans* which gives an excellent account of the negative effects of rent controls.

10. Success stories of tenant management of public housing are reported in David Osborne and Ted Gaebler, *Reinventing Government: How the Entrepreneurial Spirit is Transforming the Public Sector* (Reading, Mass.: Addison-Wesley, 1992). See also, Elinor Ostrom, *Crafting Institutions for Self-Governing Irrigation Systems* (San Francisco: Institute for Contemporary Studies, 1992) who discusses principles for establishing self-governing systems to oversee publicly-owned facilities. While Ostrom's principles are directed toward irrigation systems, they would provide excellent guidance for running public housing. Some theoretical foundation and case studies are found in Shui Yan Tang, *Institutions and Collective Action: Self-Governance in Irrigation* (San Francisco: Institute for Contemporary Studies, 1992).

11. See Ellen L. Bassuk and H. Richard Lamb, "Homelessness and the Implementation of Deinstitutionalization," in *The Mental Health Needs of the Homeless,* ed.

Ellen L. Bassuk (San Francisco: Jossey-Bass, 1986), pp. 7–14.

12.   These statistics are from Lisa Thomas, Mike Kelly, and Michel Cousineau, "Alcoholism and Substance Abuse," in *Under the Safety Net: The Health and Social Welfare of the Homeless in the United States*, ed. Philip W. Brickner, Linda Keen Sharer, Barbara A. Conanan, Marianne Savarese, and Brian C. Scanlan (New York: W. W. Norton, 1990), Chap. 13.

13.   Entitlement programs that could benefit the homeless are discussed by Rolando A. Thorne, Catherine Zandler, John B. Walker, Jr., Linda Keen Scharer, and Marisa Canto, "Entitlements," in *Under the Safety Net: The Health and Social Welfare of the Homeless in the United States*, ed. Philip W. Brickner, Linda Keen Sharer, Barbara A. Conanan, Marianne Savarese, and Brian C. Scanlan (New York: W. W. Norton, 1990), Chap. 20.

14.   See Charles Murray, *Losing Ground* (New York: Basic Books, 1984) for a discussion of welfare programs creating welfare dependency.

7

The Regulation of Quality Standards

At one time, the watchwords for consumer protection were caveat emptor — buyer beware! In twentieth century America that attitude has largely fallen by the wayside, as the seller has become increasingly responsible for the quality of products that are sold. Partly, this is a function of changing legal liability. More and more courts are finding producers liable for any injury that results from the use of their products regardless of whether the product was used responsibly by the buyer. Whether a person falls off a ladder or crashes a private airplane, it is likely that the courts will find the producer liable for damages resulting from the accident, even if the product was used recklessly and irresponsibly. However, there are other reasons why buyers have less reason to beware at the end of the twentieth century than they did at the end of the nineteenth century.

Sellers are increasingly willing to guarantee a purchaser's satisfaction, regardless of any legal liability. Many retailers allow customers to bring products back for a refund for any reason if the customer later regrets a purchase. In the late twentieth century many companies guarantee satisfaction by allowing returns for a full refund within 30 days of a purchase. They are not legally required to do so, but they provide such guarantees because the market demands them. The seller who offers such a guarantee can more than make up for the costs of a few returns by the additional sales to people who would otherwise be inclined to buy elsewhere. That such guarantees are becoming increasingly common in the market indicates that a guarantee of product quality is becoming more important.

Such guarantees make sense, too, for complex products like computers, VCRs, and so forth. One can look at a hammer and judge with accuracy how the hammer will perform and if it will do what he or she expects it to. It is harder to do the same with a computer, so it is more important for the manufacturer to offer a guarantee of satisfaction. Note that goods like hammers, clothing, and other easily judged goods are offered with money-back guarantees. The market offers these guarantees because consumers want them and are willing to pay for them.

Another reason why caveat emptor is less important as a buying principle is that the government has become increasingly involved in the regulation of product quality. The government inspects and regulates food, drugs, banks, and a host of other goods and services to guarantee their safety. The Food and Drug Administration, the Consumer Product Safety Commission, and the Federal Deposit Insurance Corporation are twentieth-century innovations of government that protect buyers; therefore, buyers have less reason to protect themselves.

The immediate question is: Why can't consumers protect their own interests? In many cases, there is a good reason why consumers may not be able to protect their own interests as well as an outside observer could. However, this does not necessarily mean there is a role for the government. If there is a demand for regulation of product quality the market can provide it. Before looking into how the market ensures product quality, this chapter examines why there is a demand for this regulation.

THE DEMAND FOR REGULATION

Many goods and services have a quality dimension to them that purchasers value but is difficult for purchasers to measure. For example, patrons of a restaurant are likely to desire a sanitary kitchen and careful handling of food to prevent spoilage that can lead to germs and disease, but, by themselves, the customers are unlikely to know whether these standards for kitchen sanitation are met. Few restaurant customers would choose to eat at a restaurant that handles food so carelessly that 1 percent of the restaurant patrons become ill, but it might be difficult for customers to identify restaurants that are this careless. If an individual ate at such a restaurant once a week, the person would become ill from the restaurant's food only once every two years on average and may well attribute the illness to something else. In short, it is easy for a customer to tell if the food tastes good; it is hard for a customer to tell if the food was prepared under sanitary conditions. Thus, customers are willing to pay for regulation, and the regulators certify that the food is being prepared under sanitary conditions.

Similar examples could go on without end. Airline passengers can tell about cabin comfort, the attentiveness of stewards and stewardesses, and (for frequent travelers) the ability of an airline to stay on schedule. They find it harder to judge whether aircraft have been adequately maintained and whether pilots are proficient, so they demand regulations to ensure that this important, but difficult-to-observe, dimension of quality meets their standards. Similarly, individuals with no training in medicine may find it hard to judge the qualifications of medical doctors, even after having visited one. Thus, there is a demand for regulation to ensure that the patient with relatively little knowledge will receive competent medical care.

These examples show that consumers value the regulation of quality standards when there are aspects of quality that are important to consumers but that are hard for consumers to detect. Regulators who are experts in the area they are regulating can examine the quality of goods and services and certify to consumers that quality standards are being met.

THE VALUE OF BRAND NAMES

One way in which quality standards can be enforced is through the use of brand names. Names such as McDonalds and Coca-Cola are valuable to their owners because people will pay a premium to have a McDonalds hamburger rather than just a generic hamburger, and people will pay a premium to have a Coca-Cola rather than just any cola drink. The brand name enables customers to identify the specific brand and choose it over its competitors.

If, for some reason, customers want to avoid a particular brand, the brand name enables purchasers to do that as well. Thus, even without regulation, McDonalds has an incentive to maintain sanitary kitchen conditions because if customers ever began to suspect that McDonalds did not have clean kitchens, they could easily avoid McDonalds and eat at other fast food restaurants. Nothing even has to be proven. A customer could simply say, "I think the last time I ate there the food made me ill, so I'll try another place." If only a few customers think this, and start talking to each other, soon a restaurant gets a bad reputation, and its brand name becomes a liability rather than an asset. Because firms desire to maintain their valuable brand names, they maintain product quality even with regard to quality aspects that consumers would find relatively difficult to detect themselves.

Another potential source of product quality information is present and former employees. If a few people who have worked at a firm document quality control problems, a firm's reputation can be harmed rapidly. Word of mouth can be effective. "I used to work there, but I wouldn't eat there. I've seen how they handle their food." Such a statement spreads: "I know someone who used to work there, and he wouldn't eat there because of the way they handle their food." Brand names give the owners of the brands an incentive to ensure that the firm's quality meets customer expectations.

ARE BRAND NAMES ENOUGH?

While brand names provide powerful incentives to ensure product quality, they may not always be sufficient. What about new firms that have no prior reputation? What about regional brand names that may not be readily identifiable to potential customers? Consider, for example, travelers who have a choice between eating at a McDonalds restaurant or at Mom and Pop's Local Restaurant about which they know nothing. Without regulation, they might be reluctant to try Mom and Pop's because they cannot be assured that an unknown brand name will meet their demands for product quality. In this example, brand name is not enough, and potential customers will desire regulations to assure them that quality standards are being met. More to the point, Mom and Pop's Local Restaurant will benefit from regulation because regulation is a way that customers unfamiliar with their brand name can be assured that Mom and Pop's meets generally accepted quality standards.

Customers want regulation to assure them that quality standards are being met. Firms want regulation to assure potential customers that they can buy from the firms without fear that they cut corners on quality in areas that are difficult for customers to observe.

THE MARKET FOR REGULATION

If regulation is valuable to both firms and their customers, then the market should produce this regulation without government intervention. Indeed, this is the case in areas that the government does not regulate already. If government regulations are in place, there is little incentive for private regulatory agencies to form, unless customers generally perceive that government standards are insufficient. However, where government regulations do not ensure the level of quality that consumers desire, private regulatory agencies will arise in the market, paid for directly by the regulated firms (and indirectly by the firm's customers in the price of the product). Most of the remainder of this chapter discusses two private sector regulatory agencies: Best Western motels and Underwriters Laboratories. The chapter concludes by noting other ways in which the market can assure product quality without government regulation.

BEST WESTERN

Best Western motels is a private sector regulatory agency. Best Western owns no motels, but allows motels to display the Best Western logo if the motels pay a fee to Best Western and if the motels meet the quality standards that Best Western specifies. This enables travelers who are unfamiliar with specific motels in an area to identify easily those motels that meet the quality standards Best Western specifies.[1]

Best Western has a 22-page booklet of rules and regulations with which Best Western motels must comply, as well as a 10-page booklet listing construction and refurbishing specifications for Best Western motels. Some examples of quality standards with which Best Western motels must comply include swimming pool standards; the width of motel hallways; the number, size, and location of parking spaces; soundproofing requirements for rooms; door and lock specifications; standards for flooring material and room furnishings; quality standards for television sets and reception; and much more. Smaller items, such as sheets, towels, and ice buckets, are also included in Best Western's regulations.

Although all Best Western motels must meet the Best Western standards, there are not standard Best Western motels because Best Western does not have standard motel designs, decors, and the like. Every motel is independently owned and is different, but all motels meet Best Western's quality standards. Best Western is not a franchise or a chain of motels but is an agency that regulates the quality of motels and certifies that motels meet its standards. All Best Western motels pay for the right to be regulated by Best Western, and Best Western inspects all motels at least twice a year to see that they are in compliance. Motels that do not maintain compliance with Best Western regulations lose the right to remain a Best Western motel.

Best Western does offer motels one service that is not regulatory in nature — a reservation service. This benefits the motels but provides another reason why all Best Western motels want the Best Western quality standards to be met. Customers will be reluctant to phone for a reservation at a Best Western motel in a distant location without assurance of quality, so the quality of one motel can affect the business of all others. The Best Western regulatory agency knows this and maintains quality standards so that its member motels will continue to pay Best Western for its regulatory activity.

Staying at a nice motel is a matter of comfort but probably not a matter of life and death. Just the same, it is difficult from looking at the exterior of a motel to tell the quality of the accommodations inside, so customers want something to help guide them. Sometimes brand names can provide this guidance, but for motel owners who do not own a large chain of motels, the brand name will provide no information to travelers. The regulation has obvious value because the motel owners are willing to pay to be regulated. As the Best Western example shows, when government regulations do not provide the level of quality assurance that customers want, the market for regulation will provide a private sector regulatory agency to do the job.

UNDERWRITERS LABORATORIES

Underwriters Laboratories is a firm that establishes standards for electrical equipment and then tests electrical equipment to see if it meets the standards. Equipment tested and approved in this manner by Underwriters Laboratories is then entitled to display the UL seal signifying that the equipment meets their standards. The firm was established in 1894 and incorporated as Underwriters Laboratories in 1901. Underwriters Laboratories earns its income through payments it receives from the firms whose products it tests.

As a private sector regulatory firm, Underwriters Laboratories has no power to force other firms to bring their products to it for testing. Rather, firms want to have their products tested and approved by Underwriters Laboratories so that the products can display the UL logo and are willing to pay Underwriters Laboratories for that privilege.[2] Apparently, firms believe that products that are UL approved are worth more, the evidence being that they voluntarily pay Underwriters Laboratories even though there is not a legal requirement to do so.

Underwriters Laboratories has attained enough of a reputation that some consumers will not buy products without UL approval. Many businesses, for example, have established as a policy that all electrical equipment they purchase must be UL approved, even though there is no legal requirement for such approval. These firms want regulation more stringent than the federal government mandates and are willing to pay for this regulation themselves. The process by which UL approval is granted is similar to the way that government regulation might take place.

Underwriters Laboratories publishes standards for various types of electrical devices, so information is readily available regarding what standards a product must meet to gain UL approval. The approval process begins when the firm that wants a product approved contacts Underwriters Laboratories and gives them information about the product. Underwriters Laboratories then tells the firm what standards the product must meet, how many product samples it will need to examine, and the cost of the testing. In exchange for the fee, Underwriters Laboratories tests the product to see if it complies and, if it does, licenses the firm to use the UL seal of approval on the product. After approval is granted, the firm contracts with Underwriters Laboratories to maintain compliance with the UL standards, and a follow-up procedure is established that gives Underwriters Laboratories the right to check the firm's products to make sure that they continue to comply with the standards. Follow-up procedures include both the terms under which Underwriters Laboratories can do future testing and procedures and testing with which a manufacturer must comply to guarantee that defective products are not sold. Under its contract, Underwriters Laboratories has the right to make up to four unannounced inspections of the production facility per year.

Underwriters Laboratories is a regulatory agency and nothing more. It designs and publishes regulations and tests products to see if they meet its regulations. Underwriters Laboratories makes money because the firms that bring products to it want their products to be regulated. The expense of the regulatory process is paid for because consumers are willing to pay more for products with the UL seal of approval. It is common knowledge that electrical devices are potentially lethal. Purchasers of electrical devices can take their chances, perhaps inspecting the devices themselves, or they can buy products with the UL seal and have some assurance that someone else with specific knowledge about electrical products has inspected them. Because getting UL approval is costly regulation is worth the cost to consumers who buy UL-approved products, and it is equally obvious that a private sector regulatory agency provides this regulation without government intervention.

This model of private sector regulation can apply to virtually every quality-related regulation the government imposes. For example, government health inspectors currently certify that restaurants meet the government's standards for sanitation and cleanliness. Without government regulation, there undoubtedly would be private health inspection firms that would establish standards and certify that restaurants meet those standards, in exchange for a fee. Restaurants so certified would be entitled to display the logo of the inspecting firm just as products now display the UL logo after approval. A private market for regulation would exist in the absence of government regulation if consumers were willing to pay the cost.

INSURANCE COMPANIES AS REGULATORS

The examples of Best Western and Underwriters Laboratories show how markets can produce the same type of regulation that is produced by the government. There are other mechanisms at work in the market that produce consumer assurance of product quality. For example, firms like Consumers Reports independently test and evaluate products and report results to their subscribers. Another example — the subject of this section — is the role insurance companies play as regulators of product quality.

The federal government has extensive regulations over the quality of private aircraft and over the qualifications of the pilots who fly them. These regulations form the basis for quality assurance demanded by insurance companies. Clearly, a company that insures a private aircraft has a financial incentive to make sure that the aircraft is maintained in airworthy condition and that the pilots who fly the aircraft are qualified. The federal government requires inspections and maintenance on aircraft and requires pilots to pass examinations to obtain a pilot's license. Insurance companies use these federal regulations as the basis for their quality control.

Aviation insurance policies state that they are issued with the understanding that the aircraft meets federal maintenance requirements and that the pilots meet federal requirements to fly the aircraft. If the aircraft has not been maintained or if the pilot does not meet federal qualifications insurance coverage will not be in effect. This provides an incentive to meet the minimum federal standards.

Apparently, federal standards for aircraft maintenance meet the market test but those for pilot standards do not. It is uncommon, and perhaps completely unheard of, for insurance companies to require aircraft owners to maintain aircraft at a higher level than federal standards dictate, but many aviation insurance policies require pilot qualifications in excess of the minimum required by federal regulations. For example, once licensed, pilots only need to pass a flight review every two years to keep their licenses current. For lower-performance aircraft, this is usually sufficient for insurance companies. However, for higher-performance aircraft (typically, turboprops and jets), insurance companies routinely require that pilots complete an approved refresher course every year in order to be insured. This is in excess of federal regulations.

In addition, many insurance policies will have minimum experience requirements for pilots. It will be difficult for helicopter pilots to get insurance unless they have more than 200 hours of experience flying helicopters, for example.[3] All policies will have some requirement that pilots have a minimum amount of experience flying that type of aircraft. It makes sense that an insurance company would not want to insure pilots on their first flight in a certain type of aircraft.

Because of federal regulation in the airline industry, insurance carriers are likely to let the federal government enforce their quality standards for airlines. Airline pilots are required to have recurrent training and must undergo both a physical exam and a flying exam every six months. In the absence of federal regulations, it is easy to see that aviation insurance companies would have much to say about quality control in an airline they insured. Meeting safety standards that lower risks enables the insurance company to charge lower premiums, so both the insurance carrier and the airline would benefit from regulation by the insurance company if there were no federal regulation.

Without federal regulation, the airline's insurance would be of much more interest to airline passengers as well. With the current extensive federal regulation, passengers believe the federal government is enforcing quality standards and have little incentive to check on their own. If there were no federal regulations, one possibility is that airlines would advertise their insurance coverage in the same way that motels advertise that they are a member of Best Western. Passengers would come to know the brand names, just as they know the brand names of McDonalds and Coca-Cola, and would want to fly on airlines with recognized insurance carriers who would also serve the function of quality regulators.

Contrast the potential for quality control through private insurance with the lack of quality control in public insurance. The savings and loan (S&L) collapse in the late 1980s and early 1990s occurred under a regime of federal regulation and federal insurance. Regulators were supposed to ensure that S&Ls were solvent, and the federal insurers were supposed to close down any S&Ls that were not. The sad history of the program showed that there was inadequate regulation and supervision and political interference with the business of regulating. This resulted in the collapse of the S&L industry and a complete depletion of the S&L insurance fund. A private insurance company would have gone bankrupt, which would have provided the incentive for the insurance company not to let the situation develop in the first place. With government regulation and insurance, the regulators simply asked Congress for more money and got it. When there is no bankruptcy and taxpayers foot the bill for any mistakes that are made, there is much less incentive to avoid mistakes.

This is not to say that private sector insurance is perfect, or that private sector insurance companies would make ideal private sector regulatory agencies. However, their incentives are in the right place, and when compared to the government's performance it is hard to argue that private firms would do worse.

The general point of this section is that there are a lot of potential private sector institutions for assuring quality control. In addition to private sector regulatory agencies like Best Western and Underwriters Laboratories, insurance companies and consumer organizations like Consumers Reports can provide information and assurance of product quality. If the government were not involved in regulating quality, there are lots of market institutions that would operate in place of government regulation.

WHY IS MARKET REGULATION NOT MORE PREVALENT?

Private sector regulatory agencies have a lot going for them. The regulatory firms need to be effective regulators because their profits depend on it. The regulated firms want to meet regulatory standards to attract customers, and customers want to be informed. Another advantage is that the regulated firms themselves pay for the regulation because it is in their interest to be certified as meeting quality standards, so taxpayers do not have to foot the bill. If market regulation is so great, why is there not more of it?

The simple answer is government regulation crowds out private regulation. Because the government uses tax dollars to finance its regulation firms in the regulated industry do not pay directly for regulation. Because of government standards, customers in an industry assume that government regulation is protecting them. In this situation, there is little incentive for firms to pay extra money to certify something that the government says it is already certifying. Government regulation of product quality effectively precludes market regulation.

The widespread regulatory actions of government stifle private regulation even in industries that are not regulated by government. If some type of problem arises in any industry, there is always the call for government to intervene and create regulations that deal with the problem, which implies that if an industry is not regulated, regulation is not needed. If it were needed, the government would already be regulating the industry. With this illusion of a government umbrella protecting everyone from harm, there is relatively little public demand for private regulation.

The rarity of private regulation is not a reason for wanting government regulation. Private regulation is rare because government regulation is so widespread, and if government regulation were cut back substantially private regulation would arise to take its place. The examples in this chapter illustrate how private regulation would work. Would it cost a lot of money to establish private agencies to replace the regulation government is already doing? No. In every comparison ever made, private firms produce more cheaply than government. The tax dollars saved from eliminating government regulation would be more than enough to pay for private regulation, and, with private regulation, the people who benefit from the regulation would be the people who pay for it.

If the government ceased its regulatory activity immediately, would private firms be established to replace all government regulation? Probably not. With regulatory firms like Best Western and Underwriters Laboratories, the firms that are regulated must pay the costs of regulation, which means they must be able to pass those costs on to customers in order to make the regulation worthwhile. Clearly, customers who stay in Best Western motels and buy UL-approved products are willing to pay the cost of the regulation. This establishes a market test for the value of regulation because products will be regulated only when the benefit to the consumer outweighs the cost of imposing monitoring and enforcing the regulation. With government regulation, the cost is placed on taxpayers in general, rather than directly on the beneficiaries of regulation. With no market test, it is possible that the costs of some government regulations outweigh the benefits. All private regulatory agencies produce benefits in excess of their costs in order to sell their services.

CONCLUSION

This chapter has explained how markets can provide for the regulation of quality standards without any government involvement. This concluding section argues that regulation through firms in the private market is likely to be superior to government regulation for two reasons. First, market firms have more of an incentive to be effective regulators. Second, individuals will be more likely to check the quality standards that are being regulated rather than assuming that the government is taking care of them.

Private regulatory agencies like Best Western and Underwriters Laboratories depend on the quality of their regulation for their profits. If the firms are lax and their names are not associated with higher quality products, then firms will no longer be willing to pay Best Western and Underwriters Laboratories to use their names. Why would a firm pay to be a Best Western motel if the Best Western name did nothing to distinguish the motel from other motels?

Government regulators do not have the same incentive to enforce their regulations. Government regulators will rarely have a personal knowledge of the customers of the firms they regulate, but they will be personally acquainted with the individuals working in the firms they regulate. As a result, they will have more of an inclination to let infractions in regulations go or to tell the regulated firms that they need to change their ways without using official channels to enforce the regulations. The type of quality that is being regulated is hard for consumers to detect, and if the firm is shut down for violating the regulations its owners and employees will obviously suffer. In case of infractions, the government regulator must decide whether to use enforcement and create hardship on the firm and its employees or to let the matter go and hope that the firm improves.[4]

The government will never lose profits from being a poor regulator; in fact, the opposite is likely to be true. If information that the government is doing a poor job of regulating an industry begins to circulate, typically there is a call for the government to do more regulation, which probably means bigger budgets for the regulatory agency. In 1991, news stories that the Federal Aviation Administration (FAA) allowed Aloha Airlines to continue flying aircraft that did not meet government standards for airworthiness were met with demands for more stringent FAA regulation. The FAA claimed to be strapped for funds and asked for more money so it could do a better job. Thus, lapses in regulation can actually benefit a government regulatory agency because of the knee-jerk reaction to ask the government to do more to take care of us when a government failure becomes apparent.

In contrast, if a private sector regulatory agency had the same lapse, its reputation would be damaged, its profits would decline, and it might be forced out of business. If, in place of the government, Aloha

Airlines had been regulated by a private company such a lapse in regulation would immediately lower the credibility of any airline regulated by that private company, which would cause other airlines to seek regulatory alternatives. The private regulator would lose business and profits. Thus, it would want to protect its reputation by not allowing a substandard airline to fly using its regulatory logo.

Note that if in this hypothetical situation the private regulatory company decided not to regulate the airline the airline would not automatically go out of business. It could continue to fly, perhaps finding another regulatory agency or perhaps letting customers decide if they wanted to risk flying on an unregulated airline. Most customers probably would choose another air carrier certified as meeting safety standards, which is what provides an airline with the incentive to be regulated to begin with. However, unlike the FAA, which chooses to allow the airline to remain in business or not, the private regulatory agency simply decides whether it wants to certify the airline as meeting its quality standards. It is easier for the private regulator to quit certifying the quality of the airline than it is for the government to do so.

People who like absolute guarantees of safety will dislike the private regulation option because, as just noted, Aloha Airlines would be allowed to continue to fly even if nobody would guarantee that it met minimum quality standards. However, absolute guarantees are an illusion, and it is more likely that the airline would continue to fly in substandard conditions with government regulation than without. In this example, Aloha Airlines did continue to fly for years without meeting FAA standards, but because of government regulation, the public was misled into believing that the airline did meet those standards, and because of government regulation, the public had little incentive to check to see if the federal regulations were being enforced. All the while, Aloha continued to fly. Under private regulation, the regulatory firm would have dropped its certification, and airline passengers would have made sure that airlines actually met safety standards.

No form of regulation will be perfect, but regulation through market forces is superior to government regulation. Regulators have more of an incentive to do their jobs, and customers have more of an incentive to see that firms meet their quality standards.

The S&L crisis of the late 1980s and early 1990s is an example of many of the problems that arise with government regulation. In addition to inadequate supervision by the regulators and political interference with what should have been the business of insurance, many people mistakenly assumed the government was insuring them against loss, when, in fact, it was not. In today's society, one assumes that government regulation prevents firms from engaging in activities that are harmful to customers because government regulation is so pervasive, and in S&Ls, federal deposit insurance gave the impression that one could not lose money entrusted to an S&L. In at least some cases, that impression was false.

S&Ls were allowed to offer higher interest rate certificates of deposit that were not federally insured, along with lower interest rate certificates of deposit that were federally insured. When an S&L with uninsured deposits went bankrupt, depositors lost their savings. In 1990 a retired couple said on a television news program that they lost their life savings in a failed S&L. They mistakenly assumed that their deposits were insured, when, in fact, the deposits were in an uninsured account that paid higher interest. Their money was lost when the S&L went bankrupt. Was the couple really unaware that the higher interest they were earning came at the cost of foregoing federal deposit insurance? Their story is at least plausible.

One of the problems of widespread government regulation is that people assume that federal regulations protect them, especially in highly regulated industries like banking and airlines. Thus, believing that they are protected by the government, they have little incentive to check for themselves. Because there are no absolute guarantees it is desirable for people to have an incentive to collect information about the quality of goods and services they purchase. Without government regulation, private firms would benefit from providing this information to consumers. Private firms will pay to be subject to regulation, as do Best Western motels and the customers of Underwriters Laboratories, because consumers want this assurance of quality. Government regulation, using tax dollars, prevents private regulatory firms from being established. If government regulation were in some way better than private regulation, this might be justified, but as this chapter illustrates, this is not the case.

Market regulation will not be flawless, but experience shows that government regulation is not flawless either. However, looking at the incentives involved in each case, everyone involved — the regulated firms, the regulators, and the customers — have more of an incentive to act in ways that ensure that quality standards are met when private sector regulation is used rather than government regulation.

NOTES

1. See Randall G. Holcombe and Lora P. Holcombe, "The Market for Regulation," *Journal of Institutional and Theoretical Economics* 142 (1986): 684–96 for additional discussion of the ideas in this section.

2. While Underwriters Laboratories cannot force firms to submit their products, governments can pass laws requiring firms to do so under some circumstances. The National Electrical Code specifies that any device electrically connected to a telephone network must be UL certified, for example, and many local governments have adopted the National Electrical Code as a part of their statutes. In communities that have done so, there is a legal mandate to have products UL

certified. While it is likely that someone could hook up an uncertified device without being detected, this still gives firms a government-induced incentive to utilize the services of Underwriters Laboratories.

3.   This experience can come from training flights with an instructor who is insured. This amount of experience is costly, however, so that most civilian helicopter pilots were trained and received their initial experience in the military.

4.   This is an application of the Chicago theory of regulation, discussed in Chapter 2 and typified by George J. Stigler, "The Theory of Economic Regulation," *Bell Journal of Economics and Management Science* 2 (Spring 1971): 3–21.

8

The Regulation of Health Care

Few people disagree with the old adage that the most important thing people have is their health. Nothing affects the quality of life more. This is the first of two chapters that deal directly with public policies toward health. Chapter 9 focuses on health insurance and the rationale for public health policies and explains the factors underlying what is often called the health care crisis, building on ideas presented here. This chapter is a direct extension of Chapter 7 — it examines the regulation of quality standards as they apply to medicine. The two areas in which quality standards loom large in health care are the certification of medical professionals and the regulation of medicines and drugs. The arguments in this chapter follow directly from the conclusions of the last. There is no reason for the government to regulate quality standards for medicine and medical care. In the absence of government regulation, market regulatory agencies will be established to the degree that consumers demand them.

This chapter goes a step further than Chapter 7 because it describes how private regulation could be established in such a way that it would be superior to the government's regulation. Chapter 7 illustrated how private sector regulatory agencies like Best Western motels and Underwriters Laboratories work. The chapter argued that it would be possible to have such agencies anywhere that government regulation of product quality currently exists. This chapter singles out a particular area — medical care — to examine in more detail how private regulation could work and why the results of private regulation would be superior to government regulation.

Health care provides a good area for examination because, not only is it difficult for customers to evaluate the quality of health care they are receiving but also the quality of health care is vitally important to the quality of life. If a case can be made for doing away with government regulation of medical care, then a similar argument can be made in other areas that are not so crucial to the quality of life. The two areas considered in this chapter are the quality of physicians and the quality of medical drugs.

THE QUALITY OF PHYSICIANS

In the United States, the quality of medical doctors is regulated by state medical boards that specify educational standards that medical doctors must meet. In addition to internships and residency requirements, the National Board of Medical Examiners has established national standards for physician quality recognized by states. State standards include graduation from an American Medical Associaton (AMA) approved medical school. The entire process of physician certification is controlled by physicians, from the state boards to the AMA to the National Board of Medical Examiners. While there is a rigorous screening process for certifying the quality of physicians, once one is licensed to practice medicine, reexamination or recertification is not necessary. The implied assumption is that once someone has passed the screening process and is judged qualified to practice medicine, no further testing is necessary to assure that the person is still qualified.

In other areas, the government is more directly involved in setting standards and determining individual qualifications. Pilots who fly for commercial airlines must take proficiency examinations every six months, for example. Does it take more skill to fly an airliner than to perform open-heart surgery? The government monitors the quality of airline pilots much more closely than that of surgeons, but there are good arguments that consumers should demand more quality control over physicians. Pilot quality may be more directly observable by passengers than physician quality by patients, but in both cases a mistake could be life-threatening. One big difference is that a pilot's mistake that threatens the lives of passengers also threatens the life of the pilot, whereas a physician's mistake threatens only the patient's life. Pilots have more incentive to protect the safety of their passengers than physicians have to protect the safety of their patients.[1]

In some cases a group of physicians might negatively evaluate a peer, for example, when a hospital board of physicians decides that it will no longer allow a particular doctor to practice in the hospital. Even in these cases, however, the physician who has been negatively evaluated by his peers can continue to practice medicine (although not at that hospital) with no further checks or evaluation of the his or her competence.

The only quality control the government exercises over physicians is over their education, and here the control is only indirect. The government monitoring of physician quality is as much illusion as reality. When you visit a 60-year-old doctor, how valuable is it to you to know that the government certifies that this person was proficient more than three decades ago? The government's approval to practice medicine does not guarantee anything more than this.

While physician quality is nominally under state regulation, in practice, the AMA sets the standards for state regulation. Physicians cannot be licensed to practice medicine unless they graduate from an AMA-approved medical school. The AMA decides what schools will be approved and how many students each school can admit.[2] While it may appear desirable to allow only those who have graduated from approved schools to practice medicine, this, in effect, means that physicians control the conditions for entry into their own profession. They decide how many new physicians there will be and what an individual must do to become a physician. Recall that once they are admitted into the fraternity of practicing physicians they can continue to practice medicine with no further tests of their ability to practice.

Things have not always been this way. Prior to the 1830s, most states licensed their physicians through state medical societies, but in the 1830s and 1840s states abandoned their regulation of medical professionals. Some states dropped licensing altogether, while others retained licensing but allowed individuals to practice medicine without a license.[3] In response to reduced governmental regulation, the AMA was formed in 1847, and the Association of American Medical Colleges was formed in 1876. Both organizations certified physician quality, but they had the broader agenda of trying to force those practitioners who did not meet their standards out of the medical profession. One way to do so was through governmental restrictions, and they viewed state licensing examinations as a method of excluding those who did not meet AMA standards from practicing medicine.

State control of the practice of medicine had been all but abolished by the Civil War, but state certification was reintroduced in the late nineteenth century, and by 1893 medical examinations were required in 18 states as a prerequisite to practicing medicine, and another 17 states required a medical degree from a state-approved school.[4] While states nominally controlled the certification process, in practice it was the physicians themselves, through medical societies and the AMA, who determined who was certified to practice medicine. Differences among state regulations were reduced, first, by reciprocity agreements whereby doctors certified to practice medicine in one state would automatically be granted a license in others, and second, by the establishment of the National Board for Medical Examiners in 1915, which helped to standardize certification procedures among the states. While the certification of physicians nominally remains in state hands, it is the AMA that dictates who will be allowed to enter medical school, and who will be certified to practice medicine.

THE DOCTOR CARTEL

It is reasonable to ask why the regulation of physician quality would be structured in this way. Why not allow any qualified doctor to start a medical school, for example, the same way that any qualified pilot can start a flight school?[5] Then, why not test doctors periodically to see if they are still proficient, the same way that pilots are tested? Because physicians control the regulatory process, one should not be surprised to find that the regulations work to the benefit of those who are in charge of the regulations — the physicians.

In any industry, competition among sellers produces the lowest prices and gives sellers an incentive to provide the most quality for the money. Sellers would prefer higher prices and more profits, but competition prevents this. The solution, from the seller's standpoint, is to form a cartel. The AMA, by controlling the certification of medical schools and by limiting the number of students who can attend a medical school, closely controls entry into the medical profession and, therefore, increases the incomes of those who practice medicine.

The Organization of Petroleum Exporting Countries (OPEC) provides a good example of how cartels work. In 1973 OPEC declared an embargo on oil exports followed by an agreement among OPEC members to restrict their exports of oil. The result was a dramatic increase in the price of crude oil (from about $3 per barrel to about $12 per barrel) and a correspondingly dramatic increase in the profits of oil exporters. By restricting exports OPEC eventually was able to push the price of oil above $40 per barrel before the cartel weakened, and the price of oil fell.

By agreeing to reduce their exports, OPEC was able to push the price of oil substantially higher, but with more profits to be made from the sale of oil many exporting countries increased their exports and the cartel weakened. The ultimate strength of the cartel was because Saudi Arabia was by far the largest exporter and could exercise a great deal of influence over the cartel and the price of oil.

The point is that in order for a cartel to increase its profits it must restrict its output, but as OPEC shows, if profits go up cartel members have an incentive to cheat on the agreement and expand output to get more profits. The cartel then falls apart. Somehow, an enforcement mechanism needs to be put in place that will continue to restrict output, and physicians found that enforcement mechanism through state regulation. Although the physicians alone could not restrict the output of medical services, they could use their political clout to get state governments to restrict output. It then becomes illegal to cheat on the cartel.

Because the AMA controls the accreditation of medical schools and the number of students that can be accepted to them, it controls the number of people who can practice medicine. These limits place a strong barrier to entry into the medical profession, and, just as when OPEC restricts the amount of oil sold the price of oil goes up, when the AMA restricts the number of physicians practicing medicine the price of physician services goes up.

The way in which physician quality is regulated illustrates that it, in essence, creates a cartel of physicians by creating a barrier to entry. Medical schools have many more qualified applicants than they accept, illustrating the barrier to entry, and once physicians are certified, there is no recertification necessary to continue practicing medicine. An organization interested in the quality of all practicing doctors would periodically examine the skills of medical professionals — as is done with pilots — whereas an organization interested in creating a barrier to entry that keeps salaries of existing practitioners high would be interested in restricting entry into the profession but would not insist on recertification. The latter case applies to the regulation of the quality of physicians.

The restrictive effect is apparent when looking at the number of graduates from U.S. medical schools. In 1900, before widespread state restrictions, 5,214 individuals graduated from medical school. That number dipped to 3,047 by 1920. In 1950, there were only 5,553 individuals graduated from medical school — barely more than in 1900, despite an increase in the U.S. population from 76 million to 152 million. Thus, in 1900, there were 68 individuals graduated from medical school for every 1 million residents while by 1950 the number had dropped to 37 per million.[6] This reduction in the proportion of the population graduating from medical schools occurred as advances in medical technology were increasing the demand for physicians.

By 1980, there were 15,136 graduates from medical school, or about 66 per million population, which is close to the proportion from 1900. However, when one considers advances in medical technology and the increase in the share of income going to medical care, one would expect a larger percentage of the population to enter medical practice were it not for the barriers to entry created in the name of regulating product quality.

An examination of the regulatory process for physician quality currently enacted by state governments in the United States shows that it is geared more toward restricting entry into the practice of medicine and keeping physician salaries high than to assuring patients of high quality. Regulation restricts the number of individuals who can enter medical practice but does not regulate the quality of medical practice by physicians once they are licensed. A regulatory policy geared more toward quality control would demand continual recertification. Because physicians can practice for decades with no government monitoring of the quality of their work the government regulation of the quality of physicians is more illusory than real. Nevertheless, it does serve the purpose of benefiting doctors by keeping their incomes high.[7]

As the figures cited above show, in the later years of the twentieth century physicians have been less successful in limiting their numbers than earlier in the century, at least if the ratio of physicians to the total population is taken as a measure of the barrier to entry. Nevertheless, licensing practices and control of medical school admissions still restrict the number of individuals who are allowed to practice medicine. The evidence is that there are more qualified applicants to medical schools than there are spaces to accommodate them. There is a barrier to entry into the medical profession that has the effect of increasing the quality of entrants. However, there is no regulation of the quality of physicians among those who already have been licensed to practice medicine.

WHY REGULATE PHYSICIAN QUALITY?

One should not be surprised to find that regulation as it is currently undertaken in medicine gives most of its benefits to suppliers. It was the suppliers who originally designed the regulation, and one would not expect regulations to work against those who design them. Furthermore, in any industry there will be a tendency for regulators to favor those whom they regulate. Regulators have close contact with those whom they regulate but have only occasional contact with the general public, making it far easier for the regulators to see the point of view of the group they are supposed to control than the group that is supposed to benefit from the control. Because of the nature of physician regulation, it is not surprising that the regulation is geared more toward the interests of the physicians than their patients.[8]

If regulation were necessary to ensure the quality of physicians the current nature of medical regulation might be cause for alarm, but, as Chapter 7 illustrated, government regulation is not necessary to assure quality and may even be counterproductive. As things currently stand, those who use physician services believe that they are being protected by regulation, although the regulators do little in the way of monitoring physicians once they are licensed. If the current regulation were done away with, patients would no longer be able to rely on the government's quality standards, so they would have an incentive to obtain quality information on their own. Because the typical person will not have much knowledge about the qualifications of medical personnel, there will be a market for private sector regulatory agencies to fill the void. As explained in Chapter 7, firms such as Best Western, which regulates the quality of motels, and Underwriters Laboratories, which regulates the quality of electrical equipment, will have an incentive to certify the quality of physicians.

If the current government regulations were abandoned immediately, everyone could still assure themselves of the quality of care that now exists under government regulation by going only to an AMA-certified physician. Because the AMA already regulates the quality of physicians and because the AMA would continue to exist if all government regulation were eliminated the AMA standards would still exist for those who wanted them.

Under the current system of regulation, there is little incentive for alternate certification firms to enter the business because the government sanctions the AMA's regulatory system. However, without government assistance some people may want physicians who meet different standards. The opportunity for competing regulatory agencies would be created. One could imagine, for example, an organization called Best Western Doctors that had different standards for certification than the AMA. People could then choose the standard they wanted.

Some customers would prefer higher standards. For example, some individuals would undoubtedly choose a Best Western physician over an AMA physician if Best Western required their physicians to pass annual competency examinations. Some individuals might want lower standards along with the lower prices that would accompany lower standards. Firms made up of nurses might be established to give routine physical examinations, and if any problems were found they could refer the patient to a doctor. Often, an individual may feel ill but not go to a doctor — partly because of the expense and partly because of the long wait expected at the office. If a clinic were established with a reputation for seeing patients quickly for minor ailments patients might go there rather than self-treat their problems.

Walk-in clinics do currently exist, and with the artificially reduced supply of physicians, it is becoming more common (but still rare) to find clinics with no physician on the staff. They are often run by nurse practitioners. Other alternatives, such as chiropractors, treat some types of ailments as well. However, these alternatives to physician-run clinics and medical practices are at a disadvantage because, typically, state law prevents them from performing a full range of medical services. For a medical facility to give the full range of services, it must be staffed by a state-certified physician, and the medical cartel reduces competition. That is why when you go to a typical medical clinic unannounced, you wait a long time, but when you go to your local Super-Lube unannounced, they change the oil in your car right away and you do not wait. There is lots of competition in the oil change business, and quick lube places that are not really quick will lose business to those that are. However, because of the restrictions on entry into the medical profession, there is a lack of competition, causing high prices and customer inconvenience.

The lessons from this chapter and Chapter 7 show that there is no reason to regulate the quality of physicians. The AMA already exists to certify physician quality and would continue to do so without government regulation. However, if government regulation were eliminated, there would be a market for competing regulatory firms that would have different quality standards. One could always choose AMA quality but for minor ailments could opt for lower standards at a lower cost. While this may sound undesirable, remember that the most common alternative to the current medical system is self-treatment, and visiting an uncertified but experienced medical practitioner might be preferable. One could also seek higher quality than the AMA standards. Under the current system, there is little alternative to the government-certified quality standards, therefore, it is difficult to choose among various physicians who might be available.

The more widespread use of medical providers such as Health Maintenance Organizations further suggests that regulation may not provide as much information to patients as in the past. Health Maintenance Organizations have incentives to protect their brand names and to maintain the quality of those who practice within the organization, providing an additional avenue of quality assurance. Without government regulation, these organizations would have larger incentives to disseminate information on the quality of their practitioners.[9]

If government regulation were abandoned, doctors would surely have a greater incentive to advertise their qualifications and certifications. As it is, medical offices typically have small signs advertising the doctors' names, followed by M.D., and little else. Patients trust government regulation to look out for them. In a more unregulated environment, patients would have more of an incentive to find out about the qualifications of their physicians, which in turn would give physicians more of an incentive to stay qualified and to make information to that effect readily available to potential patients. In the absence of government regulation, physicians would have a much greater incentive to let their patients know what training they have had, how they were certified, and other relevant dimensions of quality.

THE REGULATION OF MEDICAL DRUGS

The same arguments that apply to the regulation of physicians also apply to the regulation of medical drugs. At the beginning of the twentieth century, government had little involvement in regulating the quality of medicines, but the Progressive Era around the turn of the century saw increasing government involvement in a number of areas, including the regulation of medicines.[10] The watershed event in regulating medicine came with the Food and Drug Act, passed in 1906.[11] The impetus for passage of the Food and Drug Act came from a number of sources including the popularization of the view that government should use its power to protect consumers; the reaction of the general public to muckraking journalism at the time, of which *The Jungle* by Upton Sinclair is the best known example; and from the increasing degree of medical knowledge that caused consumers to want more information to separate quack medicines from those that could be of some real benefit.

The main concern of the 1906 law was to ensure that products sold to the public were sanitary, but the reach of the Food and Drug Administration (FDA) was extended in 1938 with a law requiring the FDA to certify the safety of new drugs. In 1962 the law was further extended so that the FDA would have to certify that drugs are both safe and effective before they can be marketed.[12]

At first glance, one can hardly object; after all, nobody wants to take drugs that are not safe and effective. By requiring such certification before the drugs are marketed, however, some drugs are delayed from coming to the market, thus preventing people who could benefit from them from getting them, and other drugs that might be safe and effective are never marketed because the expense of certification is too great. All drugs cost more because the cost of the regulatory process is included in the cost of drugs. All things considered, the cost of regulating the quality of drugs may outweigh the benefits.[13]

Perhaps the easiest to understand of these costs of regulation is the delay caused by the requirement that a drug be certified as safe and effective. After the drug is developed, but before it can be marketed, it must go through tests to demonstrate its safety and effectiveness. Typically, a part of the testing procedure is a double-blind experiment on human subjects where doctors prescribe the uncertified drug in question to patients. Some of the patients get the actual drug while some get a placebo, and neither the prescribing doctors nor the patients know who is getting the real drug. The two groups of patients are compared to see if the drug was safe and effective for those who got the treatment. All of this takes time. Meanwhile, others who might like to try the drug are not allowed to do so. If the drug eventually proves to be safe and effective, it is apparent that after its development it was kept from some people who could have benefited from its use because it was not yet certified.

The cost of not marketing drugs that eventually prove to be safe and effective must be weighed against the benefits of not using unsafe or ineffective drugs to see if the law is beneficial. However, the law itself provides for no such weighting, and the FDA errs on the side of caution. If the FDA approves a drug that eventually proves to be harmful, it is much more likely to feel negative repercussions than if it delays the introduction of a drug that eventually proves beneficial. Furthermore, all drugs tend to have side effects of varying degrees, and the FDA approval of a drug as safe and effective gives those taking the drugs a complacency that would not exist without regulation. Now, someone taking medication believes it is safe and effective because the government says so. Without regulation, those taking drugs would have a greater incentive to find out more about the drugs themselves.

In addition to the lag in marketing drugs, some drugs that serve small markets will never be marketed because of the costs of certification. While the drug may already exist and its use for a particular rare disease may be known a manufacturer has little incentive to get FDA certification if only a handful of people will use the drug.

Yet another problem of much greater potential long-term significance is that the current regulations stifle the incentives for pharmaceutical innovation. A number of studies have documented the adverse effects of regulation on the development of new drugs.[14] Because of the expense and uncertainty involved in the certification process, smaller drug companies are excluded from innovative activity because it is too costly and too risky. This leaves the innovation to large multinational drug companies that can take the risk but are willing to do so only if the potential return can be expected to justify the initial expense. The net result has been to reduce the amount of innovative research taking place in drug development. Because of regulation over the past several decades, today's drugs are less effective than they would have been without regulation.

Some medical problems are widespread enough that there are potential profits from drugs to treat them, so regulation might only slow research and delay the marketing of drugs while certification takes place. However, for illnesses that are relatively rare, there will be little profit in developing drugs to treat them, and research that might have developed an effective drug in an unregulated environment will never occur because of the costs of certifying a drug.

In summary, government regulation of medical drugs has several negative consequences: it raises the cost of all drugs, it delays the introduction and use of beneficial drugs, it reduces the amount of innovation in the drug industry, and it prevents certain types of drugs from ever being introduced. In exchange for these costs, the government certifies that medical drugs are safe and effective. The policy experts who have evaluated the costs and benefits of drug regulation have almost uniformly concluded that the costs of the regulations are not worth their benefits.

WHY REGULATE MEDICAL DRUGS?

The reader who has followed the reasoning of this chapter and Chapter 7 will recognize that government regulation of medical drugs is not necessary because in the absence of government regulation, private sector regulators will certify the quality of medication, just as they do in other industries. Companies like Best Western and Underwriters

Laboratories can profit from providing information to consumers, and publications like *Consumer Reports*, which already evaluates medicines, would have an incentive to do more in-depth studies of those drugs now available only by prescription.

There are some differences between drug regulations and the regulation of physician quality considered earlier in the chapter. One big difference is that there already is a private organization, the AMA, that would immediately be in a position to certify the quality of physicians if government regulation were to disappear, whereas there is no comparable widespread organization that would fill the void in drug regulation if the government were to immediately pull out. All currently available drugs have already been certified as safe and effective by the FDA, though, and this would undoubtedly be advertised for those drugs. Consumers would only have less government-provided information about newly available drugs, and they would have a greater incentive to become informed.

Undoubtedly, one important source of information about the safety and effectiveness of drugs would be the same source most people on medication currently use: their doctors. Patients presume that their doctors know more about the drug he or she prescribes than just that it is FDA-certified. Doctors would continue to have the same incentives they now have to find out about the safety and effectiveness of drugs, and consumers who had little knowledge surely would want to take advantage of medical professionals who would be more knowledgeable.

Even before FDA regulation of medication, the AMA established a role for itself in providing information to patients — or perhaps more accurately — in separating patients from information so they would have to rely more on their doctors. The AMA had a policy at the turn of the century that drug companies would have to choose between advertising their products either to physicians or to the general public.[15] Physicians would not accept medicines advertised to the general public and discouraged drug companies from putting instructions for using drugs on drug packaging. This meant that patients would have to rely on physicians for information about the effects of drugs, dosage, and so forth. Physicians were able to insist on this policy because of the market power they held, as described earlier in the chapter.

When the FDA created separate categories for over-the-counter and prescription drugs, it merely codified the practice that the AMA had already insisted on. This practice produced substantial benefits to the AMA because the advertising by drug companies in the AMA's journal became a major source of AMA funds. The absence of instructions and information on prescription drugs, whether by an arrangement between the AMA and drug companies or through government action by the FDA, reduces competition and is harmful to consumers. Such arrangements would not have been able to sustain themselves were it not for the economic power of physicians produced by government regulation.

One might question this free-market approach to the regulation of medical drugs on the grounds that before the FDA drugs were unregulated. The FDA was created in response to shortcomings and abuses that occurred in the absence of regulation. Undeniably, many ineffective and even unsafe medications were being sold at the turn of the twentieth century. Addictive drugs were routinely available and used, making drug addicts out of individuals who were only looking for effective medication. Two factors must be considered before using the pre-FDA era as an example of unregulated drug markets. First, there was much less information and experience available regarding the use of drugs, and the same ignorance that plagued drug markets without regulation would have hampered regulation. In fact, regulation was demanded only in response to the accumulated information about the potential harmful effects of drugs. Second, the same forces that caused regulation to be demanded would have produced market substitutes had the government not become involved. One would not expect either government regulation or market-based regulatory and information-generating firms without a clear reason to demand their services.

As it happened, once the potential hazards of medical drugs became known, the government established the FDA in response, which lessened the demand for any market alternative. If the FDA had not been formed, the consumer demand for regulation would have produced private sector regulatory firms that would have offered their services to test and certify drugs. Very likely, following the Best Western and Underwriters Laboratories examples, the firms producing the drugs would have been the ones to pay for the regulation. The lack of private firms in this line of work is only the result of the FDA providing the regulation. The government is rarely reluctant to exercise its power anywhere it might perceive a demand, and it is not unrealistic to look at the government as being in competition with market firms to provide regulation. The government's big advantages are that it can establish regulation by legislative fiat and can use taxpayer money to finance its operation.

CONCLUSION

Chapter 7 illustrated that there is a market for regulation. If the government does not regulate firms in an area where the general public desires independent assurance of product quality then firms will arise in the market to certify the quality of products. The type of regulation in the market is likely to produce better information about product quality and give consumers better options to obtain both high quality and lower quality at a lower price; this would not be the case with government regulation. This chapter has applied the ideas of

Chapter 7 to two important areas of medical care: physician quality and drug quality. Those conclusions continue to hold. Without government regulation, patients would be able to assure themselves of the same physician quality that they now receive and would have better information and better options to obtain higher quality care when they desired or to get lower quality care at a lower price if they desired. Likewise with drugs, removal of regulation would result in more innovation, better drugs, more rapid availability of new drugs, and lower prices. Nominally, the reason for regulating these important areas of medical care is to increase the quality of life. However, regulation produces a lower quality of medical care and a lower quality of life, all things considered.

Without government regulation, information would be more readily available to allow consumers to make better informed choices. The lack of such information today is the direct result of the government's regulation. Without the illusion of government protection, medical practitioners and sellers of drugs and other medical supplies would have an incentive to supply consumers with information, and independent firms would have an incentive to verify that information. Would it not cost a lot of money to produce all this information? Yes, but it already costs a lot of money to regulate the medical profession. Surely it would be cheaper to have consumers pay for the information they want rather than have the government spend tax dollars to produce the information.

Would this system not leave some individuals who have difficulty collecting information vulnerable to shady unregulated practitioners? Yes it would, but that vulnerability already exists under the regulated system. While physicians and prescription drugs are regulated, folk healers, herbal remedies, and other possible treatments already lie outside the regulated system of medicine. Furthermore, there is a vast market for illegal drugs that can harm those who take them. No system is foolproof, and no system can protect everyone from everything, but a deregulated system would place the responsibility for gathering information and for obtaining medical treatment with the person who desires treatment. In a free society, individuals should have the free choice to accept options other than the government's approved options. A system in which the government certifies remedies as safe and effective takes away individual responsibility and accountability and lowers the incentives for individuals to seek information and make their own decisions. Ultimately, these are the incentives that police the market system and assure consumers of quality goods and services. Quality suffers when the government makes decisions in place of consumers whether in medical care or any other area.

These ideas about regulation in the medical industry will be controversial, to be sure, but they do not even address the fundamental problems with the way in which medical care is provided. The regulation of physicians and the resulting cartelized industry play large roles in what is often referred to as the health care crisis. The role of regulation in the health care crisis is not limited to the issues of price and quality discussed in this chapter, however. The market power of physicians has affected the market structure of the medical industry in ways that have had a much greater influence than simply increasing prices. Chapter 9 addresses these fundamental problems in the medical industry and discusses health insurance and public health policies.

NOTES

1.   The legal system provides some incentive through the possibility of malpractice suits, but physicians will be insured against this risk. However, insurance companies have an incentive to monitor the quality of their physician-clients. One should also recognize that physicians are likely to be more at-risk from their patients (mostly through the transmission of disease) than pilots are from their passengers. However, regulation nominally is intended to protect customers of the regulated businesses in both cases, not the service providers.

2.   Because regulation is nominally controlled by governments, it may overstate the case only slightly to say that the AMA regulates medicine. However, Frank D. Campion, *The AMA and U.S. Health Policy Since 1940* (Chicago: Chicago Review Press, 1984) — a book on which the AMA holds the copyright — explicitly states that maintaining medical standards is a function of the AMA. He notes

The AMA performs this function by being involved in developing and maintaining standards of professional education and training — and ultimately performance. Together with other organizations, the AMA plays a major part in the accreditation of medical schools, residency training programs, and the institutions that offer continuing education programs for physicians already in practice. The AMA participates in the Joint Commission on Accreditation of Hospitals; it is involved heavily in accrediting programs for the training of allied health professionals. (p. 47)

Thus, the AMA is directly involved in regulating not only its own profession but also related professions that have the potential to offer competing services independent of physician supervision.

3.   See Rosemary Stevens, *American Medicine and the Public Interest* (New Haven: Yale University Press, 1971) for a discussion of the history of the regulation of medical doctors in the United States.

4.   See Stevens, *American Medicine*, pp. 42–43.

5.   Any pilot with a current instructor's certificate can give flight lessons and have his or her students take the government examinations leading to a pilot's license. However, flight schools that meet more stringent requirements can establish accelerated programs. There is some advantage to having an accredited flight school, then, but it is not necessary to attend one to get a pilot's license.

6.   Statistics on the number of medical school graduates are from Campion, *The AMA and U.S. Health Policy Since 1940*. Population figures are from the U.S. Statistical Abstract.

7.   Campion, *The AMA and U.S. Health Policy Since 1940* considers the argument that AMA control of medical education is undertaken to further the economic interests of physicians but dismisses it. He states, "While undoubtedly responsive in some degree to the calls of self-interest, physicians are more strongly

motivated by their pride in being a doctor and their sense of professional responsibility." (p. 432).

8.   The idea that regulations benefit the regulated industry is explained more fully by George J. Stigler, "The Theory of Economic Regulation," *Bell Journal of Economics and Management Science* 2 (Spring 1971): 3–21.

9.   Shirley Svorny, "Should We Reconsider Licensing Physicians?" *Contemporary Policy Issues* 10 (January 1992): 31–38 discusses this issue.

10.   For a more general discussion of the government's increasing involvement beginning in the progressive era, see Robert Higgs, *Crisis and Leviathan: Critical Episodes in the Growth of American Government* (New York: Oxford University Press, 1987).

11.   A brief history of the Food and Drug Act is given in Melvin J. Hinich and Richard Staelin, *Consumer Protection Legislation and the U.S. Food Industry* (New York: Pergamon Press, 1980).

12.   Rita Ricardo Campbell, *Drug Lag: Federal Government Decision Making* (Stanford, Calif.: Hoover Institution Press, 1976) discusses historical developments in drug regulation. See also, Peter Temin, "The Origin of Compulsory Drug Prescriptions," *Journal of Law & Economics* 22 (April 1979): 91–105.

13.   Peter Temin, "Regulation and the Choice of Prescription Drugs," *American Economic Review* 70 (May 1980): 301–5 argues that the system may provide benefits to drug companies because they can limit their marketing for prescription drugs to physicians rather than having to market to the larger group of drug consumers.

14.   See, for example, Sam Peltzman, *Regulation of Pharmaceutical Innovation* (Washington, D.C.: American Enterprise Institute, 1974); Henry G. Grabowski, *Drug Regulation and Innovation: Empirical Evidence and Policy Options* (Washington, D.C.: American Enterprise Institute, 1976). See also the related articles, Sam Peltzman, "An Evaluation of Consumer Protection Legislation: The 1962 Drug Amendments," *Journal of Political Economy* 81 (September 1973): 1049–91; Henry G. Grabowski and John M. Vernon, "Consumer Protection Regulation in Ethical Drugs," *American Economic Review* 67 (February 1977): 359–64.

15.   See Paul Starr, *The Social Transformation of American Medicine* (New York: Basic Books, 1982), pp. 131–32 for a discussion.

9

Health Insurance and
Public Health

This chapter deals with the same general subject area as the previous one — health care — but from a different vantage point. Whereas the previous chapter noted that regulation in health care markets can lead to outcomes contrary to the stated intention of the regulation, this chapter considers the much broader issue of health care markets and the concept of public health policies in general. It is becoming increasingly frequent to find the words "health care" followed by the word "crisis."[1] The symptoms of the health care crisis are increasingly rising health care costs coupled with segments of the population that are receiving health care services below the standards enjoyed by the rest of the population. While the deregulation discussed in the previous chapter would help control costs it would not end the health care crisis. There are deeper problems. First, the definition of public health problems has been expanded to include what really are private health issues. Second, health insurance has eliminated many of the market forces that could act to control health care costs.[2] This chapter deals with both of those issues.

Some evidence of the health care crisis can be gleaned simply by looking at the trend of health care expenditures over a few decades. Health care expenditures from personal income, taken as a percent of GNP, have about tripled since 1950. In 1950, personal health care expenditures were about 3.1 percent of GNP and rose to 3.8 percent in 1960, 4.8 percent in 1970, 6.9 percent in 1980, and 9.1 percent by 1988.[3] Increasing expenditures as a percentage of income are not necessarily an indication of a crisis, of course. Income growth in general could lead to an increased demand for medical care. Technological advances in medicine could also contribute by providing better health care, leading to increased costs. However, the casual evidence obtained by users of the health care system suggests that costs appear to be rising out of control, and higher costs price medical services out of the reach of a portion of the uninsured population. As a result, hospitals must absorb more unreimbursed medical expenses, which in turn causes costs to rise even more for those who pay the bills.

An analysis of the health care delivery system shows that the structure of the health care market blunts incentives for cost containment. The delivery system itself must bear much responsibility for the increases in health care costs. This chapter argues that the monopoly power of physicians described in the previous chapter altered the method of payment for medical services to remove incentives from the medical markets. Some have argued that the current problems in health care are the result of a failure of the market in medicine and that government oversight would help the situation. This chapter argues the opposite. Those who criticize the current system as an example of market failure must recognize that the government already has a substantial involvement in the medical industry. In 1985, the government's share of health care spending in the United States was 42 percent.[4] There is already heavy government involvement in health care, which significantly limits the extent to which market forces can be effective.

PUBLIC VERSUS PRIVATE HEALTH

This analysis begins by considering why government should be involved in the health care industry at all. An important distinction exists between public health issues and private health issues, but that distinction has been obscured as public health policy has evolved. Public health policy now covers both the truly public health areas and private health problems that are publicly funded. Public health policies were originally established to stop the spread of communicable diseases and to prevent health problems caused by communal living. Malaria, smallpox, and polio are diseases that, because of their communicable nature, warrant a public health policy. Heart disease, however, is a problem that affects particular individuals, is not communicable, and is a private health problem rather than a public health problem.

Public health programs originated to control the negative medical side effects of individuals living together in large urban areas. In the United States, public health programs were originally the responsibility of local governments, and the federal government did not get involved directly until late in the nineteenth century. Periodic epidemics of cholera and typhoid fever spread through cities on the Mississippi River where large concentrations of people were attracted for commercial activities and used the river both as a source of water and as a dumping place for effluents. In addition, the constant influx of new individuals through these cities provided a vehicle for the introduction of communicable disease. The primary role of the federal government until 1878 was to quarantine ships and ports in order to control epidemics.[5] Local governments became responsible for ensuring that the water supply was not contaminated and that waste was disposed of in a sanitary manner. Before the twentieth century public health was more related to engineering than to medicine.[6]

In 1830, only five cities had health boards, but by 1900 every state had a state board of health. In 1878, the federal government established the Marine Hospital Service, which was renamed the U.S. Public Health Service in 1912. In the nineteenth century the emphasis was entirely on controlling the spread of communicable diseases. The scope of public health policy has continually expanded until today it extends from prenatal care to nursing homes for the elderly. At least part of the expansion of public health policy is because of its success in its original mission. The life-threatening communicable diseases that were originally the target of public health policies nearly have been eradicated in the United States, so public health departments would have to expand their scope if they were to survive.

True public health issues arise when the activities of one individual can affect the health of another. In part, this can occur with communicable diseases because the illness spreads from person to person. The general public has an interest in minimizing the extent to which everyone has communicable diseases, because controlling the disease in others lessens the chance that it will spread. Policies to deal with communicable diseases include widespread vaccination and the requirement that sewage be treated and not be allowed to contaminate water for household use. Advances in sanitation and drug technology in the twentieth century have turned public health problems from life-threatening events into minor nuisances.[7]

An effective public health program takes into account the differences between public health problems and private health problems. Public health problems, such as communicable diseases and environmental hazards, cannot be dealt with effectively by individual effort. Community-wide sanitation efforts and vaccination programs are in everyone's best interest because one person's communicable disease is a health threat to everyone else in the community. Private health problems, such as heart disease and cancer, may be widespread but do not call for the same kind of public health programs as communicable diseases. No matter how widespread those problems are those diseases do not pass from person to person.

If non-communicable diseases come from an environmental problem then there is a public health issue. The elimination of lead and asbestos from the environment is a legitimate public health goal because those substances have been linked to non-communicable health problems. However, other widespread non-communicable diseases are the result of individual choices made by those who become ill. The links between smoking and lung cancer and obesity and heart disease are examples.

If individuals choose behaviors that lead to disease should the public then have the responsibility of treating those diseases?

A free society ought to allow individuals to act as they please as long as their behavior does not harm others. The argument against smoking in public places is that the second-hand smoke can harm others. However, if individuals want to smoke in a private place, which will harm nobody but the smoker, that ought to be the individual's prerogative in a free society. Problems with this line of reasoning start to emerge when the public health system takes on responsibility for private health problems as well as public health problems. If smokers do not harm others with their smoking and obese people do not harm others with their overeating then their activities should be their choice. However, if they are more likely to become ill as a result and if the public health care system then takes care of them their behavior places a cost on everyone who pays to maintain the health care system.

There are two important consequences that arise from placing private health issues in the domain of public health policy. First, private health choices do have public consequences, which may lead to the demand for public regulation of private behavioral choices. Second, individuals themselves have less incentive to control their behavior in areas that can adversely affect their health. If a problem arises, the general public will absorb their health care costs.

Public health policy plays the legitimate and important role of minimizing communicable diseases and of controlling environmental problems that cause health problems. These public health areas have seen great success in the twentieth century. The health care crisis is not really about public health but rather about public policy regarding private health problems.

HEALTH INSURANCE

Health insurance coverage has advanced steadily along with advances in medical technology. Before the twentieth century the medical profession was able to offer relatively few medical services. Advances in drugs, medical technology, and diagnostic techniques during the twentieth century have continually increased average lifespans, not because the longest-lived are living longer but because more people are able to survive to reach old age. For serious injury or illness, the medical techniques that enhance the chances of survival are expensive, and because one cannot forecast who will be stricken or when, such risks are natural candidates for insurance.

Government involvement in health insurance began in the nineteenth century. In the United States, the government's first involvement began with Workers' Compensation for medical problems that occurred on the job. The common law tradition was to make workers liable for on-the-job injuries, presuming that employees were able to understand the risks when they took employment. Alabama made employers liable for on-the-job injuries in 1885, followed by Massachusetts in 1887. By 1915, 30 states had Workers' Compensation laws, and 42 states had them by 1920. At the same time there was increased demand for comprehensive government health insurance. Government health insurance was common in other industrialized nations, providing a model for U.S. policy. Organized labor in particular favored comprehensive health care underwritten by the government.[8]

While the U.S. government does not provide comprehensive health care to all of its citizens, the Medicare and Medicaid programs provide benefits to many, and organized labor was successful in getting employers to provide health insurance as a benefit to employees. Because they are privately-provided plans, the provisions vary, but in general, employer-provided health insurance is provided to all employees regardless of their health status (sometimes pre-existing conditions are not covered) and at a fixed cost. When an individual covered by insurance becomes ill or injured the insurance company pays the medical expenses, sometimes with a deductible or co-payment.

As medical insurance has covered more and more of the population, the incentives inherent in this type of coverage have lead to escalating medical costs. With full coverage any medical expenses incurred by an insured individual are not paid for by the individual receiving the treatment. As a result, there are no incentives to keep costs down. Nobody wants to become ill or injured, but this does not mean that people will demand less medical care if the price of the care falls. Individuals might choose more elective surgery if covered by insurance, and individuals will be less reluctant to visit the doctor for minor ailments that might keep them at home if they had to pay the full cost of an office visit. However, increased demand as a result of the low cost of visiting a doctor is not the major problem. The problem is more insidious because over a longer time period nobody has an incentive to see that medical costs are kept in check.

WHO IS ACCOUNTABLE FOR MEDICAL COSTS?

Consider the incentives facing employers, patients, and doctors in a situation where a patient's medical costs are fully insured through an employer's medical plan. Nobody wants high insurance costs, but employees do want comprehensive coverage in case they need medical care, and typically those health insurance costs will be untaxed benefits to the employee. While rising insurance costs are unpopular, they go hand in hand with rising medical costs. There is a continual spiral because the higher medical costs become, the more employees will want comprehensive coverage. Even the smallest injury or illness could inflict major financial harm.

Once an illness or injury occurs, insurance pays the benefits. Typically, the patient will know relatively little about available treatment options. When surveying the options, the physician has little incentive to consider the costs. If a test might turn something up then do it. If a treatment might help heal the patient then it will be used. Any medical expenses will be income for the physician or for others in the medical system but, because of insurance, will not cost the patient anything. The doctor may consult with the patient about available treatment options, but the individuals deciding on the actual treatment — the doctors and their insured patients — have little incentive to consider the costs of the options.

Since most patients now have medical insurance, the treatment given to them will determine the standards for medical treatment given to those without insurance. No medical professional would want to give substandard care to an individual simply because the individual has no insurance. In addition to purely professional reasons, there is the question of legal liability, and many patients without insurance end up not paying for treatment. This spreads their cost to paying customers, but more to the point, it leaves the doctor with the knowledge that the patient is unlikely to be directly responsible for the medical bill.

Therefore, nobody is accountable for medical costs. Those costs are paid for primarily through insurance premiums, but individuals who pay the premiums have nothing to say about the costs incurred. The doctors and their patients who incur the costs have no incentive to conserve because the costs of their decisions will be pushed onto others.

One of the fundamental problems with the incentive structure in the medical industry is that the insurance carrier pays for a patient's medical expenses while the patient is given complete freedom to select the provider of the services. This is changing to a degree with the introduction of Health Maintenance Organizations (HMOs) and preferred provider plans, but throughout most of the twentieth century, the standard method of providing medical care was to allow the patient to choose who provided treatment. This prevented insurance companies from bargaining with specific doctors or hospitals for favorable rates, and prevented insurance companies from providing their own doctors. Even with this limitation, throughout most of the twentieth century large insurers often acted counterproductively to create incentives for cost containment.

Prior to 1983, large insurers such as Medicare and Blue Cross reimbursed hospitals by paying that percentage of the hospital's costs accounted for by their patients' fraction of the hospital's total patient-days. For example, if Blue Cross patients were responsible for 30 percent of the hospital's patient-days, then Blue Cross would reimburse the hospital for 30 percent of its costs.[9] This method of reimbursement was the equivalent of writing a blank check to the hospital, because it tells the hospital that insurance will cover the costs, whatever they are. Hospitals have every incentive under those circumstances to find the most expensive treatment possible, and as a result a day's stay in the hospital cost five times as much in 1970 as it did in 1950.[10]

These incentive problems have existed since the advent of medical insurance, but the negative effects on overall health costs have only manifested themselves since World War II because health insurance was rare before that time. In 1940 less than 10 percent of the U.S. population had any health insurance, so while institutions responsible for reducing market forces in medicine were developed earlier in the century, they did not exert a major effect until insurance became more widespread.[11]

INCENTIVES PRODUCED BY THE LACK OF ACCOUNTABILITY

The lack of accountability for medical costs leads to increasing costs for several reasons. In the short run, there is no incentive to weigh the costs against the benefits for any medical treatment. If there may be some benefits, the treatment will take place because someone else will pay the costs. This increases the demand for medical services in the short run. People have more of an incentive to visit a doctor when it may not be necessary because cost is no factor. In addition, the doctor has every incentive to provide every available remedy because cost is no factor to the patient, and medical costs provide income to the doctor.

These short-run incentives are dwarfed by the long-run incentive problems, however. The short-run incentives mean that available treatments will be used without accountability for their costs. The long-run incentives mean that there is no competitive pressure to keep costs down, so existing medical services will increase in cost, and there are incentives to introduce new and expensive medical treatments for patients who can then use them because cost is no factor.

If the market for automobiles worked like the market for medical care, everyone would pay a regular automobile purchase premium, and then when a person needed a new car, he would be able to go to a dealer and pick one out at no additional cost because the premiums would cover the cost of the car. Under this situation everyone would drive Cadillacs. Chevrolets would not even be an option because when faced with the choice, and with cost as no factor, few would pick a Chevrolet over a Cadillac, eliminating the incentive to even manufacture a Chevrolet. The market for medical care is analogous. Through high premiums, everyone is charged Cadillac prices for the medical care that they might need in the future. When that time of need arrives, after patients have paid Cadillac prices they want Cadillac service. They get it, too, because the alternative is no medical care at all.

The lack of incentives to control costs means that physicians and their patients will treat medical care as if it were free because once the insurance premiums are paid any extra care is free to the people who choose to have it. Incentives for medical institutions, such as hospitals, are worse. As noted in the previous section, the methods by which insurance companies reimbursed hospitals meant they had no incentives to control their costs, and organizations generally can benefit from increasing their size under these conditions. Administrators tend to be paid in proportion to the size of hospital budgets, and larger budgets also mean more power and more prestige for hospital management. State-of-the-art technology is something an administrator can show off with pride, whereas one might be embarrassed (or sued) if the most advanced medical services were not available. Studies of incentives facing medical institutions demonstrate that hospitals exist in an environment where rewards are given for spending as much as can possibly be justified.[12]

UNIVERSAL COVERAGE

With medical costs at such high levels, people who can afford it have medical insurance. Medical benefits come with many jobs, and those persons who do not have medical benefits will usually have lower-paying or part-time work or may not have any steady job at all. What happens to medical bills for those individuals? Often, they are not paid. The largest hospital in Tallahassee advertised in 1992 that 43 percent of the hospital's bills are never collected.[13] In order for the hospital to continue operating, these costs must then be spread onto the users who do pay, which means the users who have insurance.

The problem of uncollectible bills is greater in urban hospitals for several reasons. First, there are more low-income individuals in urban areas who cannot afford medical treatment, and, second, accidents associated with urban violence can overwhelm some urban emergency rooms. If the problem of uncollectible bills were spread evenly among hospitals, then it might better be viewed as a cost of doing business, but when indigent care problems cluster at certain hospitals, the hardest-hit hospitals will find it difficult to finance their activities. One proposed solution is universal medical health insurance coverage, financed through taxes, to alleviate the problems associated with those who are uninsured and cannot afford the high cost of medical care.

Without increased insurance coverage, the problem of uncollectible accounts will reinforce itself. The costs incurred by those who do not pay must be incurred by those who do, which raises the bills of paying patients. This, in turn, makes care unaffordable to even more individuals, which raises costs again. While universal coverage could end this spiral, it would remove markets even further from the medical industry, which would provide even less incentive for cost containment.

A better solution would be to increase market forces in the medical industry to allow competition to hold prices down.

Note that there is an important difference between universal insurance coverage and universal availability of medical care. While there are a substantial number of individuals in the United States who lack health insurance, medical care is available to virtually everybody. People who show up at hospital emergency rooms are treated regardless of their ability to pay. (That is one reason why such a large percentage of a hospital's bills are uncollectible.) The issue of universal health insurance coverage primarily is a financial issue, then, rather than one dealing with availability of health care. Those who cannot afford to pay still get health care services. The distinction between the availability of health care and health insurance coverage is often blurred in discussions of the health care crisis.

An increased reliance on markets could make health care more affordable, thus reducing problems caused by the lack of universal coverage. Before turning to a discussion of how markets might be used consider the medical system in Canada, which is entirely government funded so every citizen has coverage. While the Canadian system is often viewed as a model for U.S. medical reform, it does not appear to be less costly for the services it provides, and it does not provide the same quality of service in many areas as the current U.S. system.

THE CANADIAN SYSTEM

In Canada the entire medical industry is government-financed and government-operated. Such a system obviously solves the problem of uninsured medical expenses and greatly simplifies the paperwork aspects of medical care delivery. Rather than filling out forms for various insurance companies, trying to collect bills, and so forth the government acts as a single payer that covers all medical expenses. Patients never have to worry about whether their medical expenses will be insured. Another alluring aspect of the Canadian system is that it appears to be considerably cheaper than the U.S. system. In 1987, the United States spent 11.1 percent of its GNP on health care while Canada devoted only 9.0 percent to health care.[14]

How can the Canadian system offer such cost advantages and, at the same time, offer the quality advantage of universal care? The apparent advantages of the Canadian system vanish under closer scrutiny. For one thing, care in some areas is rationed and is less available than it would be in the United States. For another thing, the lower level of expenditure on health care in Canada leaves out several factors that would bring the two figures more into balance.

In the United States, there is a large monetary advantage for physicians who specialize. Heart surgeons make more than general practitioners, for example. The socialized system in Canada does not offer the same financial advantages for specialists, with the result that general practitioners make up a much larger percentage of the medical profession in Canada. Whether this is beneficial depends upon the type of medical care that is called for. Most patrons of the Canadian medical care system say they have no trouble seeing a doctor whenever they want, and this is consistent with the larger relative population of general practitioners. If one has a minor ailment medical care will be readily available, and there will be no charge for a visit to the doctor. However, if one is in need of a specialist medical care is rationed, and Canadians must wait for care that would be available immediately in the United States.

Not infrequently, Canadians will cross the border to get specialized medical care that is not available at any price (or without a prolonged wait) in Canada. In some respects, Canadian medical care is similar to shopping in the former Soviet Union. Pricing is attractive, but consumers may not be able to get what they want at any price. While primary care in Canada is in abundant supply, specialized care is not.

In the United States, about 12 percent of individuals do not have medical insurance, but virtually every citizen has access to the health care system through a medical system that treats all patients and then absorbs the costs of those who cannot pay. Those without insurance are financed through charity, through direct government contributions, or by passing the costs on to those with insurance. In Canada, all citizens are insured through the government, but many are denied access to medical care because services must be rationed. Universal access to health care is much different from universal health care insurance. Canadians approach the goal of universal insurance, but the U.S. system, despite its problems, is better than the Canadian system at providing universal access to health care.

The cost advantages to the Canadian system are more apparent than real. One factor is that the United States is a world leader in medical research and development, and these costs are included in the U.S. figures. Another factor is that the demographic make-up of the United States differs from that of Canada, and the United States has a larger population of individuals who are more intensive users of the health care system. Violent injuries are more common, as are the medical side effects of drug use and other lifestyle choices. The Canadian system would be more expensive if it provided its current level of care to the health care problems associated with the demographic mix found in the United States.

Two important accounting differences also increase the apparent cost of the U.S. system when compared to the Canadian one. In the United States, a significant proportion of the hospitals and other medical capital equipment is financed, either through the private sector or through the issuance of government bonds dedicated to the purpose. The interest charges for financing the purchase of medical capital equipment are rightly included as a cost of the U.S. medical system. In Canada, the government pays the capital costs, and they are included without any associated financing costs. If capital expenditures were treated the same way in the two countries, the Canadian and U.S. costs would be closer together.

The second accounting difference is that the Canadian system is financed through tax collections, but the medical system's share of the cost of the tax system is not included in Canadian medical costs. In the United States, the cost of billing patients, of the insurance system, and so forth are included in the cost of the system. To put the Canadian system on an equivalent basis, the medical system's share of tax collection costs, including the excess burden of taxation (the disincentive effects of higher taxes, the use of tax shelters, and so forth) ought to be included in any comparison of costs.[15]

The Canadian system is often viewed as a better alternative to medical care than the current system in the United States. However, a closer comparison reveals that the apparent cost advantages of the Canadian system are not real, and in many areas the quality of medical care is inferior to that of the United States. Rather than move away from markets to a socialized system like Canada's, the United States would be better served to place more reliance on markets.[16]

MARKETS AND MEDICAL CARE

It is easy to imagine that if people paid directly for their own medical care they would be paying much less than under the current system of insurance-financed care. One could easily imagine walk-in clinics that advertise, "If you go to the emergency room with your child's high fever, it will cost you $300. At our clinic, the first visit is $50." This would allow the customer the choice of having the more complete support of a relatively large hospital or, at $250 saving, an initial look by a doctor who could refer a patient to the hospital only if the severity of the illness or injury seemed to warrant it. The current insurance system offers no such incentive. If the doctor says to come to the emergency room, the visit costs the insured patient nothing, but it does generate a $300 billing for the medical system. Everyone's premiums rise as a result.[17]

Critics of increased reliance on markets in medical care often cite the fact that most patients do not know very much about what type of medical care they need.[18] Instead, they rely on the advice of their doctor, and in this setting markets are inherently unsatisfactory. This criticism misses the mark because, in many markets, consumers do not have a good idea of what they need, but they do have some idea about whether they are satisfied with the service they received, and they can compare their experiences with the experiences of others.

If a person's car breaks down, or if a person's air conditioner stops working, most people would have little idea about what the underlying problem is or how to fix it. Nevertheless, they rely on an expert whom they hire in a free market setting. After the fact, they may have little idea about whether they were overcharged or even had the problem explained correctly to them. However, they can compare their experiences with others they know and can guess as to whether they were treated fairly. Such a system is not perfect. Some people may have had high repair bills because of a severe problem or may have had an unreliable repair done because of an underlying problem with the unit being repaired. However, repair personnel who generally do high quality work at fair prices will find their reputations enhanced, and regular customers will come to rely on them and refer them to others. This same type of system can work in medicine and can be combined with a market-oriented regulatory system like the one described in the previous chapter. The fact that the practitioner knows more about the problem than the person having the problem is no reason not to rely on markets to allocate the services of practitioners. In fact, one reason people choose specialists of any type, whether they are mechanics or physicians, is that the specialist knows more about the problem than the person who has the problem.

The role of brand names and market-based regulatory agencies, discussed in Chapter 7, also would be greater in a more market-oriented medical system, which would further increase the amount of information available to consumers. One can see how markets might work without insurance, but this does not solve the fundamental problem because people are not going to give up insurance. Thus, any meaningful change must restructure the way in which insurance is offered.

POSSIBLE INSURANCE REFORMS

Broadly stated, the solution to the health care crisis is to reintroduce markets into medical care in a way that makes the customer responsive to medical prices. But how? One of the key elements of the present insurance system is that often medical insurance is offered without taking into account the medical risks faced by the insured. Insurance plans are offered through employers, and all employees obtain coverage at the same basic rates. In many cases, there are only two rates: one for single people and one for families. A married couple pays the same rate as a family with several children. There is an obvious subsidy for those with children, paid for by those without, because everybody is insured under the same plan.

With auto insurance, people with different cars pay different rates, people with different driving records pay different rates, and people of different ages pay different rates. In short, rates are related to the perceived risk of a claim. Life insurance is the same way. In a more market-oriented approach to medical insurance, the same would be true. However, people would want insurance companies to ignore some risks when adjusting rates. For example, if a person developed cancer, few would think that the person's health insurance rates should go up as a result. Cancer is, after all, one of the risks people are insuring against, and most people would prefer to have an insurance company that did not raise rates for individuals who developed cancer while covered by the company. In competing for customers, insurance companies would structure policies so that customers would not lose coverage when illness or injury occurred.

Risks that can be foreseen might be treated differently. For example, an insurance company could offer lower rates to non-smokers or to people whose weight remained within 20 percent of an ideal weight according to some schedule of height, age, and gender. Special rates could give individuals an incentive to pursue healthier lifestyles or at least to bear more of the costs themselves for medical problems brought on by their own behavior. As it is, most employees have the option to take or refuse the employer's medical plan. There are no ways for someone taking the insurance to save costs.

While individuals have no way to save money in exchange for healthier lifestyles that lower medical costs, the same is not true for group policies. Employers who offer medical insurance are given an experience rating that reflects the claims experience of the group. A better experience rating can produce a lower rate. This helps to keep claims in line with insurance costs, but note that the experience rating lacks any individual incentives to reduce costs.[19] As long as the tax system provides big incentives for employer-provided insurance, and as long as individuals have no effective way of shopping for more economic coverage, the medical payment system will remain substantially insulated from market forces.

DEDUCTIBLES, COPAYMENTS, AND HEALTH MAINTENANCE ORGANIZATIONS

A common way of building incentives into health insurance is to provide a deductible for certain services. Thus, for example, the patient pays the first $20 for any office visit. This could work to discourage frivolous trips to the doctor, but it will do little to control higher-cost services where costs are escalating rapidly. After the deductible is paid, neither the patient nor the doctor have any incentive to cut costs, and the patient might even expect more in exchange for the out-of-pocket cost.

Copayments assign a certain percentage of the medical cost to the patient. For example, the patient will be responsible for 20 percent of the cost of medical care. This goes some distance toward giving both the patient and the doctor an incentive to look at the bottom line, but not much. A patient can incur $1.00 in costs for only $0.20. The incentives are still weak at the margin, and the copayment does away with some of what the insurance was wanted for in the first place. For large bills, the copayment could be substantial, leaving the patient only partially insured in an area where the patient might desire full insurance.

HMOs provide all the medical care an individual requires in exchange for a fixed fee that is paid like insurance. The difference is that an insurance company pools the premiums it receives and then pays them to medical care-givers when the services are rendered, whereas an HMO gets the money whether any services are provided or not. In an ordinary insurance situation, the medical professionals can make more profit by providing more medical care, which is then paid for by insurance. With an HMO, more profit is earned if less medical care is provided, because the HMO gets the money in any event and gets to keep the difference between its revenues and its costs.

HMOs have a financial incentive to give less medical care, whereas the traditional system provides an incentive to give more medical care. This might provide a problem to someone who needs medical care, but there are several reasons why HMOs have incentives not to give too little medical care. First is the issue of legal liability. The HMO has an incentive to avoid charges of medical malpractice, so it has every incentive to give standard medical care from this standpoint. Second is the issue of the brand-name reputation of the HMO. Typically, there will be alternatives to the HMO, either in the form of traditional insurance or other HMOs. To compete for business, the HMO has to develop a reputation as an organization that does not shortchange its patients when they need treatment.

Despite the improved incentives with HMOs, there is limited competition. Typically, employers can shop among available HMOs, but employees still must take the employer's plan. Thus, from the individual's viewpoint there is still no market and no ability to shop. In other cases, limited choices among HMOs are offered, but all with the same employer-paid premium. For markets to be effective, individuals must have the incentive to shop among alternatives.

HMOs are a step in the right direction to put market incentives in medical care. HMOs will not have much impact, however, until they gain more market share. Medical services of any type will tend to be produced to a current standard of care, and, because most health policies are standard insurance that pays a fee for service, HMOs competing in the same market will offer comparable services.[20] Should HMOs gain a more substantial share of the market, and should there be an opportunity for individual buyers of health insurance to choose among HMOs on the basis of price, then the competition among plans will have a greater impact.[21]

MEDICAL SAVINGS ACCOUNTS

One alternative to traditional health insurance that has been proposed is tax-free medical savings accounts that would work along the lines of individual retirement accounts that can now be used to save for retirement.[22] Under this alternative, individuals could buy tax-free catastrophic health insurance for coverage over some limit of expenditures. In addition to catastrophe insurance to cover large expenditures, individuals would be allowed to contribute up to a certain amount to a tax-exempt medical savings account. Money for medical expenditures under the catastrophic limit would then be paid out of the medical savings account. Expenditures more than the amount in the account would be paid directly by the patient, but money not spent would accumulate for future use. This plan would take the place of traditional insurance and would provide an incentive to conserve on medical expenditures while still providing protection against catastrophic illness or injury.

For sake of illustration, assume that a family's medical insurance coverage now costs $5,000 per year. For the same money, the family could buy a catastrophic coverage policy for $2,000 and put $3,000 into a medical savings account, all tax-free. If the family did not use the entire $3,000 in one year, the balance would be retained in the account, and the next year another contribution of $3,000 would be made into the account. This way, individuals are able to make tax-exempt medical expenditures, as they currently can with employer-provided insurance, but any money they save provides a direct benefit to them by being retained in their account. Individuals could shop for the best value in medical care, rather than being tied to a preferred provider or HMO, and have an incentive to save on medical expenses whenever possible.

This type of plan provides an example of how market incentives can replace the existing system, providing the right incentives to reduce health care expenditures where possible, but without reducing the coverage of individuals who are already covered. Governmentally financed medical savings plans could be provided to those who met some criteria of need, so the system could be extended to cover everybody. While market incentives would be possible and desirable — as the proposal outlined in this section shows — the current system has progressively limited market incentives in the health care industry and threatens to limit them even more as governmental health care reform pushes forward.

HOW DID WE GET INTO THIS MESS ANYWAY?

The health care crisis in the United States is a product of the institutional structure of the health care industry. To understand the problem fully, it is worthwhile to examine how the current institutions evolved. The medical industry was almost completely unregulated in the middle of the nineteenth century, but by the beginning of the twentieth century there was widespread regulation at the state level that controlled who could be licensed to practice medicine. The regulation was essentially controlled by the American Medical Association (AMA), so it was the doctors themselves, through the AMA, who were able to control admission to their profession. This led to a substantial reduction in the number of physicians and gave physicians a great deal of monopolistic power.

Monopolistic power conveys the ability to charge higher prices, but, in the case of medicine, it did much more for physicians. The structure of the medical industry was undergoing substantial changes, and the physicians were able to steer the entire industry to meet their goals and, as a by-product, to produce our contemporary system.[23]

Hospitals are an integral part of the contemporary crisis in health care, but in the nineteenth century hospitals were different kinds of institutions than they are today. Before the advent of antiseptic and aseptic techniques, anesthetics, and twentieth-century advances in surgery, hospitals were places for the sick to go if they had nobody else to take care of them. Doctors treated patients in their homes, even to the extent of performing surgery. Hospitals, because they were filled with sick people, were more likely to make those who entered sick rather than well. This situation changed in the twentieth century when the hospital evolved into what it is today.

As hospitals were transformed into institutions where doctors could practice medicine, doctors became more dependent on hospitals. At the same time, hospitals became dependent on doctors to bring in their patients. Under different circumstances, one could easily imagine hospitals as businesses, employing doctors the same way they employ other personnel to produce medical services. However, an overriding goal of the AMA has always been to maintain the professional independence of physicians and to oppose any institutional arrangement in which physicians are employed by non-physicians. As a matter of policy, doctors did not want to work for hospitals.

The threat that hospitals posed to the independence of physicians was recognized early in the century. In 1902, a physician writing in the *Journal of the American Medical Association* stated, "If we wish to escape the thralldom of commercialism, if we wish to avoid the fate of the tool-less wage worker, we must control the hospital."[24] Other workers who might have had the same goals could not control the nature of their employment, but physicians had enough monopolistic power that they could. Hospitals could not hire just anyone they wanted to practice medicine and could not train their own doctors. State certification required that doctors graduate from approved medical schools through a process controlled by the AMA. Because hospitals were dependent on physicians to bring in their patients, the hospitals were agreeable to accommodating doctors in this way and allowing them to work as independent contractors.

Other developments pointed in similar directions early in the twentieth century. The primary way in which businesses offered medical benefits to their employees at the turn of the century was through staff doctors. Railroads, mining companies, and other large concerns employed their own physicians, but such employment was opposed by the AMA. Similarly, throughout the twentieth century, physicians would offer prepaid medical care to groups, such as clubs or lodges. For a certain fee per person, physicians, acting either alone or with other physicians, would agree to provide complete medical care to everyone in the group, much like modern HMOs. All such arrangements were opposed by the AMA, which saw a fee-for-service system as the only acceptable way to finance medical care. Because of their monopolistic power, physicians were successful in maintaining their status as entrepreneurs, although these alternative institutional arrangements were never completely eliminated.

Physicians had help from unions in eliminating staff doctors from the companies that provided health care to their employees in that way. One of the important activities of staff physicians was treating on-the-job injuries, and, if lawsuits developed, the staff physician would testify on the side of the employer. While workers and their unions might dislike this, unions also wanted to gain control over the fringe benefit of health care that was not exclusively in the employer's domain. Thus, pressures were exerted from several sides to take the money companies put into their own medical staffs and to use them instead to buy private medical insurance, which would allow workers to see the doctor of their choice.

By the 1930s, the institutional structure of physician care was firmly established in favor of the independently-practicing physician. At the same time, rising medical costs and particularly the rising incidence of very expensive treatment caused people to demand more medical insurance. Before twentieth-century advances in medical technology, there were few costly procedures that could aid the injured, sick, or dying. As technology advanced, medical miracles meant an increased likelihood of financial disaster. With doctors firmly opposed to any type of prepayment in exchange for medical care and able to insist on the traditional fee-for-service arrangement, the structure of medical insurance was dictated by the structure of the industry.

Crisis did not follow immediately. Standards of medical practice change only over time, and health insurance did not become widespread until after World War II. As long as a relatively small percentage of the population was insured, incentives to keep costs down worked for most of the industry, and in 1940, only 10 percent of the population had medical insurance. However, with more of the population being insured and with insurance companies paying a fee for service whenever insured individuals demanded medical care, the institutional structure described earlier, in which nobody is accountable for costs, led to the escalation of medical costs and precipitated the crisis in health care. The crisis is a result of the institutional structure of the health-care industry, which, in turn, is a result of the demands of physicians who had enough market power to ensure that doctors remained firmly in control of their profession.

CONCLUSION

Ideally, this would be the point at which the chapter would draw all of its lessons together and present the comprehensive, easy-to-understand, readily implementable solution to the health care crisis. Alas, if such a solution existed, it would have already been suggested and implemented. There are no easy answers, but there are some principles that can point in the right direction.[25]

Moving in the right direction means relying more on market mechanisms to provide health care and making the recipients of health care more responsive to the health care costs they incur. The difficulties in establishing a more market-oriented health care system result from two main factors. First, the system cannot be designed from the ground up. There already is a health care system, and any modifications mean changes in the existing system. This, in turn, means dealing with the vested interests of doctors, patients, and health care administrators. Second, people want to be insured against the financial burdens that can arise from unexpected health problems, and insurance complicates the incentives to control costs.

The health care crisis is often couched in terms of individuals who do not have health insurance, but in the United States, the health care system is open to virtually everyone regardless of whether they are insured or can pay for the services they receive. Regardless of the merits of more comprehensive insurance coverage, the lack of insurance has not translated into a lack of access even when compared to countries that have universal health insurance. Compared to the Canadian system, for example, there is more access to specialized aspects of medical care for everyone in the United States. Health insurance is expensive, though, and one thing that hinders the extension of insurance to more people is its cost. If medical costs were brought down, insurance would be more affordable, and more people would have insurance. The problems in the medical industry tend to reinforce each other, but solutions would also tend to reinforce each other.

The key to instituting markets in health care is to make insured individuals responsible for choosing among insurance options. Presently, individuals take the insurance their employers offer because it is cheaper than independently buying a policy, largely because favorable tax treatment is given to employer-financed health insurance. This keeps the individual from shopping for insurance and explicitly being able to take advantage of a trade-off between quality and price. In addition to favorable tax treatment, employer-provided health insurance helps avoid a moral hazard that gives those most likely to have health problems an incentive to buy the most insurance coverage. There is no reason for employer-provided health insurance to be treated differently for tax purposes than privately purchased insurance. Moral hazard exists in all types of insurance, and insurance companies have been able to deal with it. Medical insurance should not be much different in this respect from auto or fire insurance.

If everyone shopped for their own insurance rather than taking what their employer had to offer, there would be much more competitiveness in the insurance industry. More to the point, there would be more competitiveness in the medical industry. People could accept lower premiums in exchange for higher deductibles or in exchange for agreeing to limit certain types of care, such as life-prolonging measures for the terminally ill. Individuals already sign living wills saying they do not want heroic medical intervention to keep them alive under certain circumstances, even though there will be no cost advantage to them. Auto insurance companies offer lower rates to non-drinkers, and health insurers could offer lower rates to people who agree not to be insured for certain treatments.

In communities with more than one hospital, insurance companies would have an incentive to bargain with hospitals to house their patients at discount costs. The savings would then be passed on in lower premiums. Insurance companies could strike similar bargains with ambulance companies and drug stores, passing the savings along in lower premiums. If an individual was willing to call the alternative ambulance company, insurance would pay, but the insured would have to pay for any ambulance called by dialing 911. Some people would opt for this in exchange for lower premiums, and the competitive forces would push all prices down as a result.

The factors producing the health care crisis built up over decades, but the problems have in the main already been recognized, and many changes in the health care industry beginning in the 1980s have reinstated market incentives. The problems took a long time to manifest themselves, and likewise, the beneficial effects of more market-oriented health programs will show up only over time. Medical care is still too insulated from market forces, and the solution is to subject the industry to more competitive pressure, not turn over the industry to the government either outright or through regulation.

As in other areas of public policy, many of the problems with the current health care system are a result of governmental interference in health care markets. The perception of the general public often is that health care is provided in the market and governmental regulation is what is required to improve the system. Thus, the government is asked to solve problems that largely resulted from past governmental intervention. Because much of the general public does not understand very clearly how markets work and, because they tend to place too much confidence in government's ability to control the allocation of resources, problems caused by governmental intervention lead to the demand for more governmental intervention, which then leads to more problems. Greater reliance on markets would improve the quality of life in this very important area, but public policy seems to be moving toward more governmental control.

Another way to help contain costs is to redefine public health so it means the same thing in the twenty-first century as it did in the nineteenth century. Communicable diseases are legitimate public health concerns. Diseases brought on by lifestyle choices such as smoking, drinking, and obesity are not. Under the current health care system, the costs of these lifestyle choices are borne by everyone, rather than only by those who make those choices. In a free society, people should have the right to choose their lifestyle, but they should also bear the full cost of their lifestyle choices. If people bore the full cost they would have the incentive to choose healthier lifestyles. In all likelihood, this would mean higher insurance premiums for smokers and for people who are overweight. The higher premiums are warranted. Why should non-smokers bear the health care costs of those who choose to smoke?[26]

Perhaps as significant, when people's lifestyles impose costs on others, those choices become a part of the public policy debate. People want to regulate behavior that imposes costs on them, so individual freedom is diminished in the process. The next chapter deals directly with one of those lifestyle choices that imposes costs on others — the use of recreational drugs.

NOTES

1.   Perhaps the health care system has always been viewed as being in crisis. Regulation of the industry, dating from the nineteenth century, has been portrayed as response to crises, and Rosemary Stevens, *American Medicine and the Public Interest* (New Haven, Conn.: Yale University Press, 1971) described the sense of crisis in medicine more than two decades ago.

2.   Burton A. Weisbrod, "The Health Care Quadrilemma: An Essay on Technological Change, Insurance, Quality of Care, and Cost Containment," *Journal of Economic Literature* 29 (June 1991): 523–52 analyzes the problem a little differently but sees many of the same problems discussed in this chapter.

3.   Health care expenditures might be measured in different ways, which could make this number larger or smaller. For example, this figure on expenditures from personal income excludes some public health programs, as well as medical research costs not passed through to consumers. These numbers are conservative; for example, Karen Davis, Gerard F. Anderson, Diane Rowland, and Earl P. Steinberg, *Health Care Cost Containment* (Baltimore: Johns Hopkins University Press, 1990) cite 1950

health care expenditures as 4.4 percent of GNP and 1987 expenditures as 11.2 percent. Regardless of the way they are measured, however, the trends would be the same. The numbers in the text were calculated by the author from raw data in *The Statistical Abstract of the United States*, various issues.

4.   Rexford E. Santerre, Stephen G. Grubaugh, and Andrew J. Stollar, "Government Intervention in Health Care Markets and Health Care Outcomes: Some International Evidence," *Cato Journal* 11 (Spring–Summer 1991): 1–12 give figures for the United States and other countries and argue that increased governmental involvement in health care produces poorer care.

5.   A history of public health in the United States appears in Odin W. Anderson, *Health Services in the United States: A Growth Enterprise Since 1875* (Ann Arbor, Mich.: Health Administration Press, 1985), Chap. 4.

6.   See Paul Starr, *The Social Transformation of American Medicine* (New York: Basic Books, 1982), Chap. 5 for a history of the concept of public health.

7.   Robert D. Tollison and Richard E. Wagner, "Self-Interest, Public Interest, and Public Health," *Public Choice* 69 (March 1991): 323–43 discuss the differences between public health and private health issues.

8.   Anderson, *Health Care Services in the United States* describes the evolution of U.S. health policy from its origins to the latter part of the twentieth century.

9.   See National Center for Policy Analysis, "An Agenda for Solving America's Health Care Crisis," Task Force Report, rev. June 1991, for a discussion of this system.

10.   See Martin Feldstein, "Hospital Cost Inflation: A Study of Nonprofit Price Dynamics," *American Economic Review* 61 (December 1971): 853–72.

11.   The statistics on the extent of health insurance in the United States are reviewed by Weisbrod, "The Health Care Quadrilemma." Weisbrod also notes that tax incentives have contributed to the reduction of market forces in the medical industry.

12.   See Michael D. Rosko and Robert W. Broyles, *The Economics of Health Care* (Westport, Conn.: Greenwood Press, 1988), Chap. 4 for a discussion of studies in this area. Davis, Anderson, Rowland, Steinberg, *Health Care Cost Containment* argue that the most significant problem leading to uncontrolled health care costs is the payment system used to reimburse hospitals.

13.   This information is from a two-page advertisement placed by the Tallahassee Memorial Regional Medical Center in the *Tallahassee Democrat*, March 13, 1992. Part of this 43 percent of bills that were not paid includes payments from groups that were able to negotiate a more favorable payment schedule from the hospital.

14.   This section is based primarily on Jaques Krasny, "Searching for Solutions to the Health Care Crisis," *Backgrounder* (James Madison Institute) 4 (1991).

15.   These factors are documented in Krasny, "Searching for Solutions to the Health Care Crisis."

16.   Arthur Seldon, "The Lessons of Centralized Medicine," in *New Directions in Public Health Care: An Evaluation of Proposals for National Health Insurance*, ed. Cotton M. Lindsay (San Francisco: Institute for Contemporary Studies, 1976), Chap. 3 comes to similar conclusions in analyzing the British health care system.

17.   This $300 figure was not chosen arbitrarily. In 1991, when the first draft of this chapter was being written, my three-year-old son had a high fever on a Sunday. We called his doctor, who said to meet him at the emergency room of the local hospital. The doctor examined him and found no serious problem, prescribed an over-the-counter medication, and said to call him if the fever persisted. My son recovered uneventfully, and the bill for the emergency room visit was $300, covered by our insurance.

18.   This point is made by Kenneth J. Arrow, "Uncertainty and the Welfare Economics of Medical Care," *American Economic Review* 53 (December 1963): 941–73.

19.   Starr, *The Social Transformation of American Medicine*, pp. 329–31 discusses some issues related to experience ratings.

20.   Paul J. Feldstein, *Health Care Economics*, 3rd ed. (New York: John Wiley & Sons, 1988), Chap. 12 offers some evidence that HMOs are more cost-effective and shows that despite their small presence in the market they are growing rapidly.

21.   According to Starr, *The Social Transformation of American Medicine*, pp. 422–27 HMOs constitute a small but growing part of the market but less than 10 percent in the 1980s. Davis, Anderson, Rowland, and Steinberg, *Health Care Cost Containment* state that HMOs cover 8 percent of the population and give some evidence that they cost less than traditional insurance, although HMO costs tend to rise at about the same rate.

22.   See John C. Goodman and Gerald L. Musgrave, *Patient Power: Solving America's Health Care Crisis* (Washington, D.C.: Cato Institute, 1992) for a discussion of this idea.

23.   Starr, *The Social Transformation of American Medicine* discusses the evolution of modern medical institutions in detail. Much of this section is based on his history.

24.   This quotation appears in Starr, *The Social Transformation of American Medicine*, p. 165.

25.   The crisis view of the health care industry will undoubtedly increase the demand for solutions. The essays in George Teeling Smith, *Health Economics: Prospects for the Future* (London: Croom Helm, 1987) suggest that health economics is a booming field as a result of perceived problems with health care.

26.   Charles J. Dougherty, *American Health Care: Realities, Rights, and Reforms* (New York: Oxford University Press, 1988) argues that individuals have a moral right to health care. In this case, the general public must bear the cost of personal choices in order to grant the right to health care. One might question, however, how some can claim the right to have others take care of them.

10

The Drug Problem

The use of illegal drugs has a significant effect on the quality of life for many Americans. Drug use has a major effect on the users themselves, but from a public policy standpoint it is probably more significant that the negative effects of drug use that spill over to non-users. Family members will often be affected, and neighborhoods in which sales of illegal drugs take place become infested with violent crimes. Often, criminal activity increases far from the areas in which drug use is most concentrated as users engage in burglary and robbery to help finance their drug use.

The public policy response to the drug problem has been to make recreational drug use illegal and then to enforce drug laws by arresting both users and sellers, even going overseas to nations supplying the underground drug markets to try to stop the supply at the source. This legal strategy has been accompanied by a public rela-tions campaign opposing drug use. Former First Lady Nancy Reagan's crusade, when she was in the White House, to get people to "Just Say No" to drugs was a good example. The war on drugs is now decades old, and, as the problems cited above illustrate, there is no evidence that the war is being won, or can be won.

As the very limited success of the war on drugs shows, drug use will continue to be extensive although drugs are illegal. Along with the law enforcement campaign against underground drug markets has come a public relations campaign to dissuade people from drug use. The public relations campaign appears more successful than the law enforcement campaign, and public relations campaigns can help to curtail the use of both illegal drugs and legal drugs such as alcohol and tobacco. This shows that there are alternative strategies to legal prohibition for those who want to use the government to reduce drug use. The costs of continuing to make recreational drug use illegal are many. The war on drugs is taking its toll on the individual rights our Constitution was designed to protect. Many of the negative consequences of illegal drug use stem from the fact that illegal drugs are illegal rather than that they are drugs. Because of the history of the legal prohibition on recreational drug use, it is reasonable to consider alternatives to help solve many of the problems that are a part of the drug problem.[1]

Exploring the idea of legalizing the use of recreational drugs is not meant to imply that recreational drug use is harmless. The use of legalized drugs such as alcohol and tobacco is harmful, and the same would be true of recreational drugs if they were legalized. My own personal recommendation is to combine the wisdom of two great American women, Nancy Reagan and Miss Manners, and advise those tempted to use drugs to "Just Say No, Thank You." Society is worse off as a result of individuals' use of recreational drugs, and, in my view, the drug users themselves are worse off. However, in a free society, people should have the right to make their own choices so long as those choices do not harm others. Even while recognizing the potential harm that can come from recreational drug use, the arguments that follow in this chapter suggest that the harm would be smaller if recreational drugs are legalized than if they remain illegal. This conclusion is controversial, to be sure, but the arguments are worth considering, not only narrowly within the drug issue but also more broadly in considering the rights and responsibilities that go along with living in a free society.

CAN THE WAR ON DRUGS BE WON?

Before considering some of the pros and cons of legalization, consider the question of whether it would ever be possible to win the war on drugs. One of the problems often cited in fighting the war on drugs is that users tend to be relatively insensitive to the price of drugs. If drugs become more costly, users will engage in various types of theft to acquire them. In the terminology of economists, the demand for recreational drugs is relatively inelastic, so that even a relatively large increase in the price will result in only a small decrease in the quantity of drugs demanded by users. The evidence on the elasticity of demand for recreational drugs does not point clearly in one direction. For one thing, since markets are illegal, data are hard to get and surely will never be comprehensive. In addition, the elasticity of demand for drugs probably varies from one drug to another. Nevertheless, this section explores the consequences of fighting a war on drugs assuming that drug users will not change their demands very much in response to price changes.[2]

If users in the recreational drug market do not want to alter their consumption habits very much in response to price changes, consider the results of winning some battles in the war on drugs. Surely, sellers in the black market for drugs will charge whatever the market will bear, and if government efforts succeed in removing a small percentage of the supply of drugs from the market, competition among buyers for drugs will push prices up by a greater percentage than the decline in quantity, with the result that the drug market will take in more total money by selling fewer drugs. A numerical example can illustrate this principle.

Assume that cocaine sells for $1 per gram and that the total market at this price is 100 grams of cocaine, meaning that total revenue from the sale of cocaine is $100. (I am keeping the numbers small in this example to make the principle easier to understand. Readers who want more realism can substitute bigger numbers.) Now assume that the government is successful in eliminating 10 percent of the market, reducing the total supply to 90 grams. Because buyers will compete for the remaining supply, and because buyers are relatively insensitive to price changes, the price might now increase to $1.50 per gram. Selling 90 grams at $1.50 brings in $135, compared to $100 for selling 100 grams at $1. Although fewer grams are being sold at the higher prices, the total revenue from the sales rises because the price increase more than compensates for the reduced volume of sales.

If buyers do not change the amount they want to buy very much in response to price changes, then a reduced supply of drugs will actually bring in more revenue to the drug industry. In other words, the more successful the war on drugs is in keeping supplies of drugs down, the more money drug dealers will make. The higher prices they charge will more than compensate for the reduced quantity they have to sell.

Returning to the economist's jargon, if the demand for recreational drugs is inelastic, then the war on drugs may be inherently unwinnable. Every little victory in intercepting drug supplies drives prices higher and actually puts more profits into the pockets of drug dealers. Because there is no clear agreement among experts on the characteristics of the demand for drugs, the above scenario may not describe the actual underground drug market. However, that scenario is consistent with the apparently increasing profits of drug dealers as the war on drugs has intensified. At a minimum, it is a scenario worth considering, especially because many who favor legal measures to reduce supplies fail to consider the effects of those efforts on the profits of suppliers.

DRUG PROFITS: WHAT ARE THE SOCIAL CONSEQUENCES?

The consequences of the illegal profits in drug markets are overwhelmingly negative. The location of drug markets tends to be in poorer neighborhoods and in inner cities. The resulting crime harms those who do not participate in the markets but have a limited ability to move from the area. However, in poor neighborhoods, there is also the negative side effect of the incentives established by drug markets. In areas where unemployment may be high and employed people work for relatively low wages, much more money can be made by dealing in drugs than working in legal markets. The people with the new cars and the people with the gold chains will likely be those involved in the drug market. This entices others to enter the market and makes those who deal in drugs neighborhood role models. Why work for low wages, if one can find a job at all, when by working for drug dealers one can make more money?

The social consequences in these neighborhoods must be substantial. What are the lessons that young people in this environment learn? If one wants to drive a new car and make lots of money getting into illegal drug sales is the way to go. Staying in school to get a job that requires an education must look foolish compared to the alternatives in the drug market. The incentives of illegal profits, inflated because of the government's war on drugs, pushes people into criminal activity. Drug profits pave the road to material well-being, as one can see just by looking around. Of course, with law enforcement efforts, those profits do not come without risk, but look at the alternatives. When the odds eventually catch up with the individual lured into dealing drugs, a prison term is likely, after which the individual will be uneducated and have a criminal record. Because of the alternatives for an individual with a criminal record, a return to the drug market may be the most attractive possibility.

If recreational drugs were legal, there would be no high profits to lure individuals into the market. There would still be drug users, to be sure, but those individuals would tend to be the losers — the equivalent of the skid row alcoholic — rather than the people to envy. Without the illegal profits, those involved in drugs would no longer look like role models to individuals in drug-infested neighborhoods. This is one argument for legalization.[3] If all drugs were legalized, the drug culture would not look nearly as attractive because it would be stripped of its excess profits caused by government efforts to reduce supply.

DRUG PROFITS AND LAW ENFORCEMENT

Another negative aspect of the profits generated by drug prohibition is they create an opportunity for corrupting law enforcement officers. Law enforcement is not a notably high-paid profession, and drug profits can be spent to pay law enforcement officers for protection or to look the other way while drug dealers transact their business.

Corruption of law enforcement officers is most serious with victimless crimes, such as drug sales, prostitution, gambling, and the like. Crimes with victims, like assault and burglary, have individuals who want to cooperate with law enforcement officers and who have an incentive to monitor the law enforcement system to see that justice is done. With victimless crimes nobody directly involved in the activity wants law enforcement. If an individual who commits an assault is able to buy his way out of an arrest, the assault victim will want to call that corruption to the attention of someone higher up in the political chain of command. The potential problems would be severe enough that there would be a high likelihood that the corrupt law enforcement officer would not benefit from the corrupt activity. With victimless crimes, nobody directly involved in the crime has an incentive to complain about corrupt activity. Therefore, corruption is more likely.

One of the costs of the war on drugs is to make the law enforcement system more susceptible to corruption. To the credit of law enforcement officers, corruption is relatively rare although not completely absent. One reason why corruption may be rare is that drug use violates the law at many levels of government, so local, state, and federal law enforcement officers pursue drug crimes. If law enforcement officers at one level of government were bought off, this might be detected by those at another level.[4] Still, the incentives for corruption remain. Corrupt law enforcement has costs that spill over into non-drug areas, so another reason to legalize drug use — and legalize victimless crimes in general — is to reduce the incentives for corruption in law enforcement.[5]

Corruption may not be the major problem related to the legal enforcement of drug crimes. Incentives in the legal system may lead law enforcement officers to pursue drug crimes at the expense of other types of crime, with the result that other crimes increase.[6] The most obvious incentive is that often property confiscated by law enforcement officers through drug arrests remains with the law enforcement agency. Law enforcement officers will have more incentive to pursue these types of crimes if the budgets of their agencies can be directly enhanced as a result. There are other more subtle incentives at work as well.

The demand for law enforcement activity comes as a result of the criminal activity it is trying to prevent. Some crimes, such as burglaries, will create a demand regardless of police activity. Burglaries are reported by victims, giving police crimes to solve and future crimes to prevent. While some burglaries will go unreported, statistics are relatively easy to compile. Drug crimes are different. There will be relatively little reporting of the crime because both buyer and seller are consenting parties to a drug transaction. In order to demonstrate a drug problem police need to pursue it and make arrests. More drug arrests will demonstrate a growing drug problem, which then demonstrates the need for more money spent on law enforcement.[7]

The incentives are structured so law enforcement officers can benefit from putting more law enforcement effort into drug crimes and less effort into property crimes. As a result of reduced effort fighting property crimes robbery and burglary will become less risky, and crime rates in those areas will increase. Many people believe that illegal drug use leads to property crimes. This line of reasoning shows why that may be the case although not through the logic usually employed. More drug use leads law enforcement officers to pursue property crimes less vigorously, which causes an increase in property crimes.[8]

A FRAMEWORK FOR ANALYZING THE DRUG PROBLEM

As the above discussion makes clear, there are a number of costs associated with the enforcement of laws against the use of recreational drugs. This section will offer a framework for analysis of the problem to better identify who is harmed by the use of illegal drugs and why they are harmed. The framework divides the negative consequences of illegal drug use in the following ways: some of the harm comes directly from the use of the drugs, some of the harm comes from the consequences of dealing in illegal markets, some of the harm is felt by the drug user directly and some of the harm from drug use is felt by others who do not use drugs. That framework is depicted in Figure 10.1.

FIGURE 10.1
The Negative Consequences of Illegal Drug Use

Negative Consequences of

	Drug Use	Trade in Illegal Markets
Costs Borne By Users	A	C
Others	B	D

The top of Figure 10.1 divides the negative consequences of illegal drug use into the negative consequences of using drugs versus the negative consequences of trade in illegal markets. The left side of the figure divides the costs into those borne by users and those borne by others. This creates a matrix with four cells, labeled A, B, C, and D, for each of the different types of costs imposed by the use of illegal drugs. Costs falling into cell A are those costs of drug use that are borne by drug users themselves. Costs falling into cell B are the costs borne by non-users because of drug use. The costs represented by cell C are those costs users bear solely because they are trading in an illegal market and are not related to the actual effects of drug use. Those costs in cell D are the costs borne by non-users because drugs are traded in illegal markets. The next four sections analyze each of these four different types of costs with the hope of understanding why recreational drug use has a negative impact on the quality of life and whether legalization could potentially lower the costs of the drug problem.

THE EFFECTS OF DRUGS ON USERS

This section considers whether drug users benefit from laws against the use of the drugs they take. This is the analysis of the contents of cell A in Figure 10.1. When considering only the costs in cell A, the strongest argument against legalization is that it will prevent more people from becoming users. Presently, some people are users; some are not. If drugs were legalized, this would eliminate one of the costs of becoming a user and would increase the number of users. How would these costs be affected if drugs were legalized?

Earlier, it was argued that the demand for recreational drugs is relatively inelastic meaning that a reduction in the price would not cause large increases in consumption. This suggests that legalization would have relatively little effect on drug use taking only the money price into account. For some people, however, the violation of drug laws might appear as a powerful and prohibitive deterrent because legalization would entice people who never had a desire to do so to try recreational drugs.

Simply trying recreational drugs is likely to cost relatively little compared to becoming a regular user, so an important question is, how likely is it that someone who tries a drug will develop into a regular user? There are two considerations here. One is the issue of physical addiction. Different drugs might be considered differently here, but there is some evidence that about half of all heroin users are only occasional users as opposed to regular users, and heroin is one of the most physically addicting drugs.[9] Psychedelic drugs are not physically addictive, but users might develop a psychological dependence that would encourage regular use.[10] Alcohol is physically addictive, and some people become addicts to the extent their quality of life is lowered. Other people can use the drug occasionally without becoming addicted. There is little evidence that the legal prohibition of alcohol consumption during the 1920s lowered addiction rates, which is at least suggestive of how effective current drug laws might be at lowering the incidence of drug addiction.[11]

An important argument in favor of legalization, regardless of how many new users would be created, is that in a free society people should have the right to behave as they choose as long as their behavior does not harm others. People engage in many activities that are hazardous to their health, but society does not ban skydiving or motor-cycle riding. One of the casualties of the war on drugs has been individual rights. While the topic of rights will be discussed more fully later, note that if a society is based on the principle of individual liberty the government has no right to decide what an individual can or cannot do. This is perhaps the strongest argument against the notion that legalization is undesirable because it would increase the number of drug users. How many more users are created is irrelevant if we believe that individuals have the right to make choices without the government deciding what is best for them.

While there may be some costs within cell A of Figure 10.1, there would be overwhelming benefits to drug users if drugs were legalized. Keeping in mind that cell A isolates the costs of taking drugs from the costs of trading in illegal markets, the benefits of legalization would be that the drugs offered in a legal market would be less harmful to the user. There are several reasons why this is the case.

If drugs were legalized, their quality would be controlled better because they would be sold in commercial markets. Firms would have an incentive to develop reputations for quality, and drugs would be packaged in standardized doses, which would reduce the incidence of accidental overdoses. Because drugs would be sold under brand names, sellers would have an incentive to distinguish their products and to be concerned about the health of their customers.

If drugs were legalized, there would not be the same incentives to produce drugs in concentrated doses. Transportation is more costly for illegal drugs because they must be concealed from law enforcement officers. Drugs that can contain more doses in a given volume will be more valuable, and one of the motivations of designer drugs is to allow easier transportation through more concentrated doses. Using alcohol as an example, high-proof liquor was more often produced than beer with low alcohol content during prohibition. Legalization would result in drugs that are not as strong.

If drugs were legalized, there would be an incentive for research and development in the recreational drug industry to produce designer drugs that cause better feelings but with fewer harmful side effects. The designer drug industry today shows the possibilities for research and development in recreational drugs, but, as just noted, the incen-tives today are to produce more concentrated drugs rather than less harmful drugs. This push toward less harmful designer drugs would be amplified if drug manufacturers were allowed to advertise their products.

When recreational drugs are illegal, it is impossible to undertake third party testing of drugs. Drug categories are tested now so that, for example, we have some understanding about the differences between the harmful effects of marijuana and heroin. However, from dealer to dealer and from day to day the quality of marijuana and heroin can vary, and there is no way to evaluate the products of particular producers. If drugs were legalized, periodicals such as *Consumer Reports* would report on the qualities of various drugs and give an overall evaluation for potential users.[12] Third party evaluation would go a long way toward increasing information and safety for drug users.

Finally, if drugs were legalized, manufacturers would have an incentive to innovate because they could take advantage of patent protection and other legal protections that would go to producers in any legal industry. As it is, the incentives do not exist because drugs are illegal.

To sum up the conclusions from analysis of cell A in Figure 10.1, under legalization drug users would find drug use safer and less addictive. Looking only at the effects from drug use on the drug users themselves the arguments lean toward legalization.

THE EFFECTS OF DRUGS ON NON-USERS

This section examines cell B — the effects of drug use on non-users. The issues relevant to the incidence of drug use, discussed in the previous section, are perhaps most relevant here. The only real ways that legalization of drugs can harm non-users is if the population of users increases or if their drug use imposes more costs on non-users. It is important to recognize the distinction between the costs represented in cell B and those represented in cell D. Because the gang violence and the effects of illegal profits belong in cell D this section is confined only to considering the effects of drug use on non-users.

Legalization would bring the same benefits to users and non-users. Violence and unpredictable behavior from drug use should be reduced because of better information about drugs, quality control, increased variety, and the tendency for drugs to be packaged in less potent forms. Accidental deaths should fall, which would reduce costs to those with drug users in the family. Thus, the effects of drug use should be less burdensome to non-users if drugs were legalized.

Non-users would also have to consider the likelihood that if drugs were legalized non-users would become users.[13] For people who know little about drugs, this can be a frightening prospect, but consider this problem in the context of drugs that are currently legal, like alcohol and tobacco. Surely there are some users of these drugs who would be non-users if they were illegal, but the prohibition of the 1920s can again be instructive in considering the effects of legalization when compared to the current regime. Again, consider the issue of individual rights. In a free society, individuals should have the right to make choices, even if those choices might harm them. With freedom comes responsibility, and if we turn our responsibility over to the government, we turn our freedom over at the same time.

Considering this section and the previous one, there are good arguments that the negative effects of drug use would be lessened if recreational drugs were legalized.

USERS AND ILLEGAL MARKETS

This section moves over to cell C of Figure 10.1 to consider the negative effects on drug users of trade in illegal markets. In this cell, there are overwhelming arguments supporting legal over illegal markets. Consider, first, the simple economic effects.

The creation of illegal markets for recreational drugs has the obvious effect of making prices higher than they would be with legal markets. Because buyers would benefit from lower prices, this is an obvious cost to users. Higher prices also contribute to property crime because high prices can push users into criminal activity to finance their drug purchases. The news often portrays drug users as criminals who steal to support their habit but rarely shows stories of alcoholics who steal to support their addictions. One reason is that alcohol prices are not forced upward artificially by legal prohibition.

Trade in illegal markets creates huge profits that entice people into the market. It is worth noting that if drugs were legalized and treated the same way as alcohol there would be less incentive to involve children in the drug industry. As it is, drugs are illegal, so the legal consequences of involving minors in the distribution network are not much different from employing adults. If anything, minors may be more attractive as drug couriers and sellers because if minors get caught they are more likely to be treated leniently. Legalization would take the glamour out of drug dealing, it would eliminate the problems produced by the profitability of dealing, and it would be more likely to keep children out of the drug market.

Another disadvantage to users of trading in illegal markets is that there is no legal protection for the transaction. This means, at a minimum, that there is no recourse in case of a faulty product but also means that a buyer risks being the victim of other crimes in an attempt to purchase drugs. Users might be reluctant to tell the police that they were robbed by someone from whom they were trying to buy drugs.

One major disadvantage to drug users of trading in illegal markets is that their activities make them criminals. There are several negative side effects. First, there is a stigma attached to drug use simply because it is illegal. One need only remember the 1980s to recall that Judge Douglas Ginsberg's nomination to the Supreme Court was torpedoed because he had used marijuana. There was no evidence that it had affected his legal activities or his judgment in any other way. Simply the stigma attached to marijuana use was enough to keep him off the Supreme Court. If, instead, he had admitted to trying bourbon there would have been no issue raised.

This stigma can extend to a wide variety of business and social situations. Because recreational drug use is illegal users have an incentive to keep their use hidden from their employers and business associates. Drug use might be a source of blackmail or other pressure. People are reluctant to mention it to acquaintances. This will tend to push drug users into their own social circles where drugs become the major common interest of the group, which is likely to reinforce their behavior. The stigma attached to drug use is likely to make the problem worse for the user.

This stigma will also make users more reluctant to seek treatment. People must admit not only that they cannot seem to get off drugs but also that they have been violating the law. Legalization would make it easier for people to seek treatment for drug problems if they desired it.

Yet another drawback to the user of trading in illegal markets is that it lowers the barriers toward entering into other forms of crime. Because criminal elements deal in drugs, by definition, the drug market will attract individuals who have criminal experience. Experience in evading the law might give them a comparative advantage in this type of work, but a criminal background also makes it more difficult to find a legitimate job. Users must associate with these individuals in order to obtain their drugs, giving them ready access to information about how to commit criminal activities. Furthermore, from a moral standpoint there may be less aversion to breaking the law by stealing property if the person is already breaking the law by taking drugs.

This discussion on the costs to drug users of trading in illegal markets would not be complete unless it mentioned the obvious costs involved if one is arrested or sent to prison. There are no advantages to trading in illegal markets. Thus, cell C of Figure 10.1 points unambiguously in favor of legalization.

NON-USERS AND ILLEGAL MARKETS

This section considers cell D of Figure 10.1 and analyzes the effects of illegal markets for recreational drugs on non-users. This aspect of the drug problem is probably the least well understood by those who favor drug prohibition. Non-users suffer considerably because drugs are bought and sold on black markets, which offers no legal protection to those who deal in them. There is big money to be made dealing in drugs, and, without legal protection, those dealing in the markets must find ways to protect themselves. This is what leads to the gang warfare, the drive-by shootings, and the unsafe neighborhoods filled with criminal activity.

Dealing in illegal drugs is a very profitable business for the dealers, but it is a business that has no access to legal protection. Whereas the legal system is, for the most part, designed to protect property and to defend the rights of individuals to engage in voluntary exchange and retain ownership over what they receive through market transactions, in the drug market, the legal system is worse than neutral toward protecting participants. Rather than just not offering those transactions any protection, the legal system actively seeks to confiscate any money and goods exchanged in the market. Because the government's legal system is openly hostile to drug markets those who participate in those markets must take steps to actively protect themselves.

Businesses in legal markets have property rights to their place of business and often to the types of products they sell. They can use the legal system to protect themselves from trespassers, and, through trade marks and brand names, they can establish product identities associated with what they sell. If they have disputes with other businesses over anything from trademark infringement to trespassing to unfair pricing policies they can go to court to settle their disputes through the legal system. No such protection exists in underground drug markets. To protect one's place of business, which may only be a certain street corner (and which cannot be too prominently marked in any event), dealers must use force. To protect themselves from what they view as unfair competition they must use force. To protect their money and goods they must employ their own protection because the police protection that works for legal businesses works against drug dealers. Under these circumstances, one should not be surprised that illegal markets are characterized by violence.

Imagine that jewelry sales were made illegal, just as recreational drug sales are today. One would expect to find the same types of markets and the same types of violence. People could not sell jewelry from fixed locations because the police would find out. They would hang out on street corners pedaling their wares but would be potential victims themselves to robbers who know that sellers would have no legal recourse if their black market goods were stolen. The jewelry salespeople would have to hire their own protection, would have to enforce their own rights to markets, and so forth just like drug dealers today.

Imagining jewelry sold in underground markets with no legal protection, but, rather, with legal opposition shows that much of the harm from current drug markets comes not from the fact that drugs are sold but from the fact that the trades are taking place without the same legal protection as for other goods. The bulk of the adverse effects of illegal drugs on non-users comes from the side effects of trade that is occurring in illegal markets, not the drugs that are being traded.

The framework in Figure 10.1 shows that legalization would, overall, benefit both drug users and non-users. Most non-user harm results from laws rather than from drugs, and if drugs were legal they would be safer for users and would probably have fewer side effects that would be harmful to non-users. Users choose to use drugs, so it is relatively easy to say that they should be responsible for bearing the consequences for those choices, whether or not drug use is legal. Non-users must bear some of the costs of drug use, and the costs borne by non-users will be lower if drugs are legalized. Many innocent bystanders in the war on drugs want protection from the harm caused by the drug trade, and legalization is the best way to protect those innocent bystanders. However, in a free society, the most important arguments are not those that can be cast strictly in terms of quantifiable costs and benefits. Free societies give people the right not to make the best choices or the choices everyone else thinks should be made. One of the big costs of drug laws is the resulting reduction in individual freedom.

ILLEGAL MARKETS AND INDIVIDUAL RIGHTS

Victimless crimes, whether they involve drugs, prostitution, gambling, or anything else, distinguish themselves because the participants have no incentive to reveal the crimes. Rather, the participants take measures to conceal the activities from law enforcement officers. If a burglary occurs, the victim will summon law enforcement officers, but without a victim none of the participants to a drug deal will notify the police. Therefore, law enforcement officers must actively seek out the activities that participants are trying to conceal. The privacy of individuals must be invaded for law enforcement officers to investigate drug crimes, so the rights of individuals are bound to suffer.[14]

As a result of the war on drugs, the Supreme Court has constantly and consistently widened the ability of law enforcement officers to legally conduct searches for drugs without search warrants. The court has approved of a warrantless search of an open field, of aerial surveillance of private property, of a barn, of a motor home that was somebody's residence, and search of a public school student's purse.[15] The details in each specific case are less relevant than the principle that covers them all. Because of the war on drugs, the rights of individuals are being systematically narrowed, and the power of government law enforcement agencies is being consistently broadened. The constitutional rights of the citizens of the United States, which have been jealously guarded for two centuries, are now being sacrificed to fight a war on drugs.[16]

Law enforcement officers are seizing vehicles — cars, boats, airplanes — if they have found drugs on them, regardless of whether the owner is found responsible. A shrimp boat based in Key West was seized when three grams of marijuana were found on board, although no evidence was found that the boat owner was responsible for the drugs. A Michigan woman, returning from Canada with her husband, lost her car when customs agents discovered that her husband was carrying two marijuana cigarettes.[17] The Supreme Court has affirmed the right of law enforcement officers to establish roadblocks to check everyone for drugs without any probable cause for search. Law enforcement agencies have developed profiles of likely drug carriers and have singled out those individuals for surveillance and searches for no other reason than that their outward appearances match characteristics associated with drugs.

The encroachment of the war on drugs has already had a substantial impact on individual rights in the United States. If some individuals can be singled out now for searches and for surveillance, and if the war on drugs is not won, then rather than just single out certain individuals the activities of everyone could be kept under constant surveillance. The principles to do so are already affirmed by the Supreme Court. The quality of life that U.S. citizens have enjoyed throughout the first two centuries of this country has been largely a result of a limited government dedicated to protecting the rights of individuals. The war on drugs, by reducing the rights of individuals, will have a negative impact on the quality of life.

The enforcement of laws against victimless crimes in general has a detrimental effect on individual rights because law enforcement must intrude into individuals' private lives to discover violations. This is a strong argument in favor of legalizing all drug use.

OPTIONS FOR LEGALIZATION

An argument for legalization is that most of the harm caused by recreational drug use comes from the fact that drugs are illegal, not that they are drugs. This implies that to minimize this harm completely free and open markets for drugs should be established. As with alcohol, there are arguments in favor of restricting the market to adults, but the market for alcohol itself provides an example of goods being produced by private producers and sold to those who wish to purchase.

Other less drastic alternatives have been suggested and tried. The use of certain drugs might be decriminalized, for example, while making production and sale illegal. This would remove sanctions against users while retaining the current legal system that pursues sellers. Another alternative would have the state control the production and sale of drugs. Yet another would require people to register if they wanted to use legally restricted drugs. Sometimes people not completely convinced by arguments for legalization want to phase it in.

The problem with all of these proposals is they leave the problems of illegal drug use intact. The problems are caused by the existence of underground markets. The only way to truly eliminate those problems is to legalize the sale of drugs. If half-way measures do not succeed, there will be a renewed push for stronger drug laws using the argument that decriminalization was tried and did not work. Half-way measures are not likely to work, because they retain the incentives to trade in illegal markets.

CONCLUSION

The ideas presented in this chapter can be developed into conclusions at three different levels. At the first level, the chapter concludes that the costs of fighting the war on drugs exceed the benefits, and the quality of life of everyone would be enhanced if recreational drugs were legalized. Users would benefit from better products with more quality control and from not having to participate in illegal activities to get drugs. The biggest benefits, however, would come to non-users, because most of the harm to non-users from drugs comes from underground markets rather than drugs per se. At the second level, this analysis can be extended to legal prohibitions on market exchanges of all types. Prohibitions impose costs on non-users, undermine the legal system, and lower the quality of life.

The third level at which conclusions can be drawn is with regard to the larger issues of individual rights and individual responsibilities. The prosperity and quality of life that Americans have enjoyed since the founding of the United States has been a result of a government instituted primarily to protect the rights of individuals and to allow them to pursue their own self-interests, as they understand them, without interference from government or from other individuals. A society cannot be free unless it allows individuals enough latitude to make wrong as well as right choices, and a society cannot be free if it allows the majority to make choices for everybody else.

This discussion of drug policy considers a controversial issue but one that is worthwhile considering within the context of an examination of public policy and the quality of life. For one thing, a general framework should be able to deal with controversial issues, but a larger reason is that the issue of drug policy directly confronts the issue of the degree to which individual freedom contributes to the quality of life. Freedom is important enough to the quality of life to want to defend it as a goal of its own, but the protection of individual freedoms also indirectly enhances the quality of life. Freedom allows people to pursue their own interests as they understand them, and it allows them to profit from activities that benefit others. The protection of individual rights is necessary for a market system to operate, and the market system has proven itself to be an indispensable component in enhancing the welfare of a nation's citizens. Freedom is an end in itself. It is also a means for improving the standard of living and enhancing the quality of life.

NOTES

1.   Some of the costs of the drug war are reviewed by Chester Nelson Mitchell, *The Drug Solution* (Ottawa: Carleton University Press, 1990); Arnold S. Trebach, *The Great Drug War* (New York: Macmillan, 1987). Both volumes stop short of recommending outright legalization but go into detail about the harm caused by the twentieth-century drug policy in the United States. Richard Lawrence Miller, *The Case for Legalizing Drugs* (New York: Praeger, 1991) presents the case of legalization but does not dwell as hard on the harm caused by current laws.

2.   Robert J. Michaels, "The Market for Heroin Before and After Legalization," in *Dealing With Drugs: Consequences of Government Control*, ed. Ronald Hamowy (Lexington, Mass.: Lexington Books, 1987), Chap. 8 suggests that the demand for heroin is very inelastic even while noting that hard numbers are difficult to obtain. Michael D. White and William A. Luksetich, "Heroin: Price Elasticity and Enforcement Strategies," *Economic Inquiry* 21 (October 1983): 557–64 also examine the question but do not arrive at a conclusion about the elasticity of demand. They do discuss law enforcement strategies under different assumptions about elasticity.

3.   Charles Murray, "How to Win the War on Drugs," in *The Crisis in Drug Prohibition*, ed. David Boaz (Washington, D.C.: Cato Institute, 1990) argues against this point of view. Murray asserts that, as long as the welfare system continues to insulate individuals from the consequences of their actions, there will be little incentive for those suffering from drug use to straighten out their lives and become productive citizens. Thus, he reluctantly favors legal prohibitions on recreational drug use.

4.   This idea is explored in more detail by Peter Reuter, "Police Regulation of Illegal Gambling: Frustrations of Symbolic Enforcement," *The Annals of the American Academy of Political and Social Science* 474 (July 1984): 36–47.

5.   While corruption is relatively rare, Steven Wisotsky, *Beyond the War on Drugs* (Buffalo, N.Y.: Prometheus Books, 1990), pp. 145–50 recounts enough instances to illustrate that it does occur on a regular basis.

6.   Isaac Ehrlich, "Participation in Illegitimate Activities: A Theoretical and Empirical Investigation," *Journal of Political Economy* 81 (May–June 1973): 521–65 gives evidence of the deterrent effect of law enforcement, suggesting that a substitution of resources into drug crimes would increase the incidence of other crimes.

7.   This line of reasoning is explored in Bruce L. Benson and David W. Rasmussen, "Relationship Between Illicit Drug Enforcement Policy and Property Crimes," *Contemporary Policy Issues* 9 (October 1991): 106–15. The notion that bureaucracies of any kind have an incentive to act in ways that increase their budgets was a theme of William A. Niskanen, *Bureaucracy and Representative Government* (Chicago: Aldine-Atherton, 1971).

8.   Benson and Rasmussen, "Relationship Between Illicit Drug Enforcement Policy and Property Crimes" present some evidence that this is the case.

9.   See Michaels, "The Market for Heroin Before and After Legalization"; James B. Bakalar and Lester Grinspoon, *Drug Control in a Free Society* (Cambridge: Cambridge University Press, 1984) who also note that most users of hard drugs are not addicts.

10.   See Robert Byck, "Cocaine, Marijuana, and the Meanings of Addiction," in *Dealing With Drugs: Consequences of Government Control*, ed. Ronald Hamowy (Lexington, Mass.: Lexington Books, 1987).

11.   Once, while speaking on this subject, I discussed the effects of the drug laws on preventing people from becoming drug addicts as in the previous paragraphs, and then asked my audience how many of them believed that if drugs were legalized they would become drug users. Nobody volunteered that drug laws kept them from being

addicts. Essentially, these laws kept other people from being addicts. These people might not have known themselves well, and some of them might have become drug abusers, but the point is that most people who favored legal control of drugs in the audience I was addressing wanted these laws to control the behavior of other people, not themselves.

12. This has been done already. See Edward M. Brecher and *Consumer Reports* Editors, *Licit and Illicit Drugs: The Consumers Union Report on Narcotics, Stimulants, Depressants, Inhalants, Hallucinogens & Marijuana — Including Caffeine, Nicotine, and Alcohol* (Boston: Little, Brown, 1972).

13. Rodney T. Smith, "The Legal and Illegal Markets for Taxed Goods: Pure Theory and an Application to State Government Taxation of Distilled Spirits," *Journal of Law & Economics* 19 (August 1976): 393–429 develops a framework for analyzing the effects of legalization on use but does not provide evidence on the likelihood of becoming a user. Richard H. Thaler and H. M. Shefrin, "An Economic Theory of Self-Control," *Journal of Political Economy* 89 (April 1981): 392–406 suggest circumstances under which people may wish to have some restrictions placed on their behavior to prevent them from undertaking some activities they might later regret. A model along these same lines is presented in Mark Crain, Thomas Deaton, Randall Holcombe, and Robert Tollison, "Rational Choice and the Taxation of Sin," *Journal of Public Economics* 8 (1977): 239–45. Thomas C. Schelling, "Self-Command in Practice, in Policy, and in a Theory of Rational Choice," *American Economic Review* 74 (May 1984): 1–11 considers these same issues.

14. This point is made by Randy E. Barnett, "Curing the Drug-Law Addiction: The Harmful Side Effects of Legal Prohibition," in *Dealing With Drugs: Consequences of Government Control*, ed. Ronald Hamowy (Lexington, Mass.: Lexington Books, 1987).

15. These Supreme Court cases are documented in Steven Wisotsky, "Zero Tolerance, Zero Freedom." Paper presented at the Critical Issues Symposium, Florida State University, March 1991.

16. Edward J. Epstein, *Agency of Fear: Opiates and Political Power in America* (New York: G. P. Putnam's Sons, 1977) discusses the way in which the government, in the name of protecting society from the evils of drugs, is able to increase its power at the cost of sacrificing the rights of its citizens. Epstein's book deals with specific drug policies during the Nixon administration, but has general applicability.

17. These events are cited in Wisotsky, "Zero Tolerance, Zero Freedom," p. 22.

11

Responsibility:
Public and Private

Much of what has appeared in the previous ten chapters is controversial. Why? The theme of this volume is the use of public policy to improve the quality of life. The goals set out in each chapter are relatively noncontroversial. Most people want to protect the environment. Most people want to improve the quality of life in developed areas and to provide affordable housing to all. Most people want high quality medical care but want to keep health care costs under control. Most people want to be protected from problems caused by illegal drugs, and they especially want to protect non-users from any harm inflicted by users. The goals expressed in this volume are widely shared. The controversial aspects of this analysis are the means suggested to achieve widely agreed-upon ends rather than the ends themselves.

Improvements in the quality of life are not automatic. They have to be produced by somebod;, therefore, somebody has to take the responsibility. The current direction of public policy in all of these areas is to increase government involvement. If current policy direction is an indication, improving the quality of life has become the government's responsibility. The alternative is to make improvements in the quality of life a matter of private responsibility rather than public responsibility.

Giving the government the responsibility to enhance the quality of life might, in a sense, be comforting, because individuals have government to look out for their well-being rather than having to bear the responsibility themselves. The comfort of having the government take care of them can quickly fade when one reflects on the government's record of achievement. The collapse of the savings and loan industry, with its huge associated costs, was overseen by the government that regulates and insures the nation's banking system. The federal government that cannot balance its budget is the same government that, in 1985, passed the Gramm-Rudman-Hollings Act legally mandating a balanced budget by 1991. The military procurement system provides our armed services with toilet seats that cost hundreds of dollars and fax machines that cost more than a new car. Considering the government's record, do we really want to entrust the government with enhancing our quality of life if it is not absolutely necessary? Why should we think that legislation to improve the quality of life would be any more effective than the Gramm-Rudman-Hollings legislation was at balancing the budget?

Consider how ironic it is that people want the government, that appears so inept at so many of the things it does, to enhance their quality of life. Too often, when people want the government to enhance the quality of life, they envision a government that would perfectly implement policies that best advance their vision of the public interest. In reality, democratic government always produces policies that are compromises, and political power has as much to do with what policies are implemented as does the public interest. Politicians typically consider the effects of supporting legislation on their prospects for reelection in addition to considering legislation on its own merits, and bureaucrats consider the effects of policies on their agencies and their careers in addition to considering the public interest. One must be cautious in arguing that the government should pursue some policy initiative when, essentially, that means that policies will be determined by those who have the most political influence.

The government is not perfect, to be sure, but perhaps government policy must be relied on when there is no alternative. An important message in this volume is that there are alternatives and that the market can be used effectively to further the quality of life. Market decisions are not always perfect, either, but it would be unfair to compare the imperfect market with some idealized perfect government. Rather, market institutions must be compared to the actual performance of government. In this comparison, the market looks very good as a vehicle for improving the quality of life. Those who live in predominantly market economies have consistently had a quality of life superior to those who have relied on government for their quality of life.

It is remarkable that, at the end of the twentieth century when markets have been shown superior to government planning in so many instances throughout the world, people who have benefited so much from the market allocation of resources in the market economies argue that their quality of life would be enhanced by giving the government increased control over resources. Amazingly, many people in the United States argue that their quality of life can be enhanced by relying more on the system that caused the collapse of the Soviet Union.

It does not follow logically, of course, that, just because less government would have been desirable in the pre-1989 Eastern European socialist countries, more government would be undesirable in more market-oriented economies. There may be an optimal middle ground between the extremes of complete laissez faire and complete socialism. At the same time, one must always reject the argument that the optimal government policy has to be a compromise between the extremes. While politics tend to work through compromise, the optimal policy might be at the extremes or might be somewhere in between. The issue cannot be resolved by accepting some middle ground, then, but rather by analyzing the issues to identify how public policy can best further the quality of life.

QUALITY-OF-LIFE ISSUES

The discussion of the previous chapters has established that there is an alternative to government planning to enhance the quality of life. Too often, when environmental, housing, or health problems appear the reaction is that government has to step in and allocate resources to solve the problem. Whether one agrees with the preceding analysis, one must at least recognize that there are other possible solutions and that quality-of-life issues are not necessarily best handled through government. The preceding chapters have examined a number of specific issues in which there are clear market alternatives to government control.

Perhaps the clearest examples of the way in which markets can work to enhance the quality of life were in the applications to environmental protection and land use planning. The two areas might be viewed as similar, because, in the one case, the issue is protecting the natural environment, while, in the other, it is creating a desirable man-made environment. The general principles are the same in both cases. The goal is to utilize resources in such a way as to maximize their value to all individuals, and that can be done when property rights are clearly defined, giving the owners an incentive to maintain the value of their property. With government control of resources, a constant political battle for resources will ensue — a battle that nobody ultimately can win.

With private property rights, owners have ownership rights until they voluntarily decide to give up ownership to someone who values the property more. This provides the incentive to maintain the property's value. With government control, today's victor never has secure rights, because people with opposing views can mount a political challenge tomorrow, or next year, or any time in the future. This gives people the incentive to quickly exploit their political victories while they have the opportunity rather than to consider the future impacts of their actions. People who win logging rights on federal land have the incentive to take the lumber quickly, and have little incentive to consider the value of someone else's land after they leave it. With privately owned land, the owner always has the incentive to consider the future value of resources.

PUBLIC POLICY AND THE QUALITY OF LIFE

Markets provide incentives for orderly and efficient development of both urban and suburban areas. Business and commercial users of land naturally want to locate at main intersections and on heavily travelled roads. Residential users naturally want to locate in less busy locations but still nearby the business and commercial establishments they expect to visit often. Thus, without government planning, efficient land use patterns will develop because of market incentives. Often, well-intentioned government land use planning is counterproductive and creates the land use problems people complain about.

People argue that the government should do something to solve a problem, when the government is actually the cause of the problem. Unless the underlying causes are clearly recognized, the problems caused by government intervention tend to lead to the demand for more government intervention, which then causes more problems.

The same principles were applied to the regulation of quality standards, both in general and specifically in the health care industry. Government regulation is often counterproductive and serves the interests of those who are being regulated, rather than those who consume the production of the regulated industry. In the absence of government regulation, private sector regulatory agencies will monitor product quality. Organizations such as Best Western and Underwriters Laboratories are examples. However, where government regulation is already in place — the health care industry is an excellent example — there is little incentive for private sector regulators to operate. Chapters 8 and 9 illustrated that government involvement in the health care industry has made health care more expensive and, in many ways, less effective.

Chapters 4 through 10 examined a number of specific quality-of-life issues to demonstrate how market mechanisms can work to enhance the quality of life. Clearly, there is an alternative to government planning and control in these areas, and the analysis in those chapters used specific examples to show how increased reliance on market mechanisms can improve the quality of life.

OTHER QUALITY-OF-LIFE ISSUES

There are many other aspects to the quality of life besides those discussed in Chapters 4 through 10. Those chapters provided some examples, applying the theoretical foundation laid in Chapters 1 through 3. That theoretical foundation could have been extended to cover any number of additional issues.

A pressing issue at the end of the twentieth century is the quality of public education. One can hardly argue that education is being under-funded. As increasingly more money is being spent, the problems with the educational system seem to get progressively worse. Following the same principles applied to other areas discussed here, the solution is to allow markets into education and allow students and their parents to choose where to spend their education dollars. The voucher system has been proposed by many people for many decades, but teachers (and teachers' unions) resist it.[1] Why should they do otherwise? Even though the educational system seems to be failing, it is not going out of business like a failing institution would in the private market. To the contrary, the worse schools do, the more money we want to give them. What possible incentive do they have to produce high-quality education?

It is interesting to contrast U.S. elementary and secondary education with the U.S. college and university system. While the high schools seem to be failing, U.S. universities are considered the best in the world. Students from throughout the world come to the United States to get a university education, but nobody would consider coming to the United States to get a good high school education. Why is it that our elementary and secondary schools perform so poorly while our universities do so well?

Our high schools and colleges have many similarities. Both rely primarily on the same teaching method — a teacher instructing a classroom of students. Both draw from about the same pool of students. College students are for the most part, the same people who were high school students a few years previously. In both cases, there is a mix of private and public institutions. The big difference is that markets operate much more extensively at the college level than at the high school level.

First, students have a choice of which college to attend, whereas in the typical public school system, they go to the school in the district in which they live. If students have no choice in which school to attend, they have no incentive to shop around to find the school that best fits their needs and desires. Every student in a college is there because, for some reason, the student chose that college over all others.

Students might choose a college simply because it is conveniently located, but they might also choose a college offering courses that they want to take, or that has a level of rigor compatible with their abilities and desires. Whatever the reason, colleges have the incentive to give students what they want so that they will choose to go to that school rather than another, and because students can transfer from one school to another colleges have an incentive to maintain their quality.

Simply being able to choose one's college gives students an identification and a degree of pride in that school that is hard to come by in a public high school. One's college is one's college by choice. One's high school is the school in one's district. A person who does not like her college can leave. A person who does not like her public high school cannot leave. Of course, one can always choose a private high school at extra cost, but there are always other colleges available at about the same cost. Because students can choose their colleges, colleges must make their schools appealing to students.

A second place where markets are more active at the college level is with regard to faculty. Typically, high school teachers get paid on a scale. They get paid more the more years they have been teaching, and they get paid more if they have more advanced degrees, but, in most cases, there is no extra pay for people who excel at teaching. Typically, an English teacher gets paid the same as a science teacher who gets paid the same as a physical education teacher. At the college level, there is an active market for faculty, and faculty are paid based on their merits as perceived by the college's administrators. More productive faculty get paid more. Also, faculty in some disciplines get paid more than others. Engineering professors, in general, get paid more than English professors. This is not because colleges like engineering professors more but because engineering professors have better job opportunities outside the college environment, so it costs more to hire an engineering professor than to hire an English professor of the same quality.

Thus, markets operate in two crucial areas at the college level — areas that are absent at the high school level. Students choose their schools, and there is an active market for faculty, with salary levels determined competitively. Admittedly, there are many other differences between high schools and colleges, and the doubter can always cite these as the reason for the difference in quality between high schools and colleges. However, there are also many similarities, and, in keeping with the principles discussed throughout this volume, it is worth considering that there are major differences in the degree of market incentives. Perhaps more reliance on markets in elementary and secondary education would improve matters. We have already tried spending more money on schools and have seen that more money did not lead to improvement.

What about quality-of-life issues of a more cultural nature, such as art galleries, symphony orchestras, libraries, and museums? As noted in Chapter 1, these tend to be subsidies to the rich because they are financed by taxpayer revenue but utilized mostly by upper-income people. There seems to be little reason to finance symphony orchestras but not country-western music with taxpayer dollars. Even from a cultural standpoint, symphonies are an import from Europe whereas country-western music originated in the United States.

When facilities, such as art galleries and civic centers, are produced in the public sector, there will always be political debate about their use. Should controversial artists have their work displayed in public galleries? Should controversial music groups be allowed to perform in publicly owned civic centers? On the one hand, being publicly owned, the public should have a say in how the facilities are used, but this often means something like majority rule or the establishment of community standards. On the other hand, because all taxpayers are asked to finance the facilities, these facilities should be open to shows that appeal to all segments of society, regardless of whether the shows would be controversial. Nobody is forced to view controversial art or listen to controversial music. Because the facilities are financed by all there seems to be an argument for allowing all types of entertainment in them. The controversy would never arise if these facilities were privately owned, however.

Chapter 6 considered homelessness, and, with more space, this topic might have been expanded to consider the problem of poverty. The issues are difficult, but with hindsight, it is apparent that the welfare state erected in the United States bears at least some responsibility for establishing incentives that keep people dependent on welfare.[2] The market mechanisms that have been applied to other quality-of-life issues could also be used to design transfer programs that give people an incentive to become independent, rather than foster welfare dependency.

While several quality-of-life issues were discussed in chapters 4 through 10, the same principles applied there could be extended to other issues affecting the quality of life from education to cultural activities to poverty. The specific issues covered in the earlier chapters were used to illustrate the application of the general principles laid out in chapters 1 through 3, and the overall lesson does not apply so much to any one quality-of-life issue but rather to the broader idea that increased reliance on the market mechanism, which has worked so successfully to increase our standard of living, can also increase the quality of life in areas that go beyond just producing more goods and services.

THE GOVERNMENT'S ROLE: DEFINE
AND PROTECT PROPERTY RIGHTS

One of the key points illustrated throughout this book is that government ownership of resources and government planning in the allocation of resources are often counterproductive. This should not be taken to mean that there is no role for government. The operation of markets depends upon having clearly defined property rights and a legal system that protects people from being harmed by others. The role of government in the process is, first, to establish clearly defined property rights, and, second, to protect them.[3]

Many of the quality-of-life problems considered throughout this book are a result of poorly defined property rights. The protection of endangered species is difficult because there are no clearly defined property rights to those species. The chapter on environmental protection showed how such property rights could be established, and in the case of the African elephant showed how clearly defined and enforced property rights have produced impressive results in increasing herd sizes where rights to elephants are clearly defined. Where they are not elephant populations are declining. Similarly, environmentally sensitive lands are best protected when they are privately owned, as, for example, the land owned by the Audubon Society or the Nature Conservancy. Government-owned land is always subject to political pressure, and there can be no real guarantee that it will be preserved.

Similarly, highway congestion in developed areas results from poorly defined property rights to roads. Roads might be viewed as a publicly owned common resource in urban areas in a manner similar to viewing rivers as publicly owned resources in undeveloped areas. In each case, the same principles apply to effective use of the resources. Likewise, housing problems arise when property owners are not given clear ownership rights to their property. For example, rent controls in New York City have created the paradoxical situation of thousands of abandoned apartment buildings in a city that has thousands of homeless people. The government has an important role to play in protecting and enhancing the quality of life, but that role is not to take over resources or engage in central planning to enhance the quality of life. Rather, it is to define and enforce property rights.

One of the key aspects in the legal system that can protect the quality of life is the law of nuisance. Individuals cannot engage in activities on their own property that create a nuisance for their neighbors. In a market setting, what would keep someone from building a garbage dump next to your house? In the past, this has been a clear cut application of the law of nuisance. If the garbage dump attracts pests or creates an odor or does anything else that makes it a nuisance to you then you would have legal recourse. Recognizing this, people have traditionally avoided locating incompatible uses of property near each other.

Ironically, government regulation has served to weaken the law of nuisance because, through zoning and other regulations, people can obtain government permits to use property in certain ways that might create a nuisance to neighbors. The creator of the nuisance can then use the government permits as a defense for the use, saying that the government granted permission ahead of time and that all applicable laws have been complied with.

One might, at first, view government regulation as better protection than the law of nuisance, but upon closer inspection this is not the case. While one would hope that the government would prevent the nuisance from being created in the first place, rather than having to sue to stop it after it has already been created, government decisions are subject to political pressures. People with political power can get government approval to create nuisances, leaving those who are bothered with little recourse. With a well-established law of nuisance, few nuisances would actually be created, because those creating them would know that the legal system would rule against them. Resources are most efficiently allocated when property rights are clearly defined and legally protected, and the law of nuisance could play a bigger role if government mandates did not provide protection for those creating nuisances.

If the solution to quality-of-life issues were simply to eliminate government involvement, then the issue would be simpler from a policy-making perspective. However, the overall solution does involve government protection of property rights to facilitate the operation of markets. The government has an important role, and the quality of life depends not only on keeping the government from doing the wrong thing but also on getting the government to do the right thing.

CAVEAT EMPTOR

One of the principles of the marketplace is caveat emptor: Buyer Beware! This is a good rule because it makes the consumer responsible for quality-of-life decisions. Whether individuals are buying lunch or a new house, it is up to the buyers to make sure that what they are purchasing meets their expectations. This rule gives buyers an incentive to take care of themselves and take the responsibility for the decisions they make. Every transaction is policed by the people who are directly involved.

Just as the law of nuisance protects people from being harmed by others, the law of fraud protects both buyers and sellers in transactions. It is, and should be, illegal to fraudulently represent goods and services offered for sale. Thus, under the law of fraud, it would be illegal to misrepresent pork as beef or to misrepresent a car as in good condition when it had a defect that was known (or should have been known) by the seller. However, as long as both parties to a transaction accurately represent what they have to exchange, it should be up to the parties themselves to ascertain that what they are getting is what they want to get.

It is interesting to observe that many retailers have a policy of offering more reassurance than is legally necessary by offering an unconditional money-back guarantee on merchandise. If a customer is not completely satisfied, he or she can bring the merchandise back for a refund. This policy apparently is effective — retailers adopting the policy seem to thrive — and is a market-generated reassurance. All other things equal, an uncertain consumer would rather buy from a retailer offering a money-back guarantee than not.

Government regulation often attempts to create the same type of assurance. Restaurants are inspected by government health inspectors, banks are regulated by government regulators, doctors are certified competent by state boards of health, and food processors are approved by the U.S. Food and Drug Administration. With such regulation, consumers are given government assurance of the quality of their

purchases, so they do not need to check on them so carefully themselves. This may provide a false sense of security, though, for several
reasons. First, government regulators do not have as much of an
incentive to look out for your well-being as you do, so the government
guarantee that the consumer receives may be less than it appears at
first. Second, without reading all of the fine print, people might assume
that the government is taking care of them in ways that it is not.

When the savings and loan (S&L) industry collapsed in the 1980s, a
number of depositors were caught off guard because they did not
recognize the limited extent of government protection they were being
afforded. In one instance, a retired couple who lost their life savings in
a failed S&L was interviewed on television. "We thought our deposits in
this savings and loan were government-insured," they claimed. However, the S&L had offered a higher interest rate on securities that were
not government-insured, and this couple took the higher interest rate,
apparently unaware that they were foregoing federal deposit insurance
in the process. When the S&L collapsed, they lost everything.

It is easy to argue that this couple should have read the fine print or
should have known that a higher interest rate could be obtained only
by giving up something else, which, in this case, was federal deposit
insurance. However, it is also easy to see that in an S&L prominently
displaying evidence that its deposits are federally insured, the couple
would have been led into a false sense of security, thinking that this
industry is government-regulated and that the government would take
care of them. If caveat emptor were more generally the rule, then the
couple would have had a greater incentive to make sure that their
savings really were safe, because they would have known the government was not taking care of them. In this case, the existence of widespread government protection created the opportunity for individuals
to be taken advantage of because they did not know where the line of
government protection ended.

If buyers have to look out for their own well-being, and cannot
presume that the government is doing it for them, ultimately, the
marketplace will be much better policed because people have more of
an incentive to look out for their own well-being than government
employees do. In cases where it is difficult for buyers to see that their
interests are being served, private sector regulatory agencies will arise
to police the market. Best Western and Underwriters Laboratories are
two examples of private sector regulatory agencies discussed in
Chapter 7, and there would be many more organizations of this type
were government regulation not so prominent. As explained in Chapter
7, private sector regulatory agencies have much more incentive to look
out for the interests of consumers than do government regulators.

Ultimately, the policy of caveat emptor places the responsibility for
an individual's well-being with the individual. The individual has more
incentive to look out for his well-being than does a government

regulator, and the policy of caveat emptor also creates incentives for market institutions that look out for the individual's well-being to emerge. The big advantage of private sector regulatory agencies over government regulation is that private sector institutions depend upon satisfying their customers for their incomes whereas government institutions get their income from forced taxation. Worse yet, government institutions failing at their mission often prompts a call for them to spend more money. Unsafe products are still coming to market? The Consumer Product Safety Commission needs more money to do its mission. In a perverse way, government agencies are often rewarded for failure by receiving larger budgets, which takes away some of the incentive to succeed.

Individuals have the incentive to look out for their own well-being, and when it is costly to do so in certain instances, there is an incentive for private firms like Best Western and Underwriters Laboratories to help them. Caveat emptor is a policy that fosters individual responsibility and enhances the market's ability to improve the quality of life.

THERE ARE NO GUARANTEES

A century ago, life was much more uncertain, and individuals knew they faced risks that they would have to deal with. In addition to the risk in the marketplace of making purchases they would later regret, they faced risks of illness, injury, and the likelihood of early death much more so than today. People faced economic risks of unemployment, either because they were laid off or because their businesses went bankrupt. Farmers faced economic risks associated with the weather and the demand for their products. Advances in public health and sanitation and in drugs and medical care have produced a society where, for the first time in history, people can expect to live their natural life span. Unemployment compensation, farm price supports, and government crop insurance have helped to insulate people against economic misfortune, and welfare programs — Social Security, Medicare, and Medicaid — have helped take care of people who were unable to take care of themselves. Early in the twentieth century, people could hope to live out their natural life spans and to have the means to take care of themselves until the end. Now, people can expect these things.

As prosperity and good health have become increasingly accessible to all individuals, peoples' attitudes about them have changed. At the beginning of the twentieth century, people had to be responsible for their own futures, and if luck was with them, they could succeed. However, around the turn of the century, the progressive movement brought with it the idea that the government should play a major role in furthering peoples' economic well-being. The nineteenth century idea was that government enforced the rights of individuals and gave them the opportunity to enhance their quality of life. The twentieth century idea became that government was responsible for enhancing peoples' quality of life. In the nineteenth century people were responsible for their own successes and failures. In the twentieth century the government is viewed as responsible for mitigating the effects of peoples' failures and, increasingly, for the production of peoples' successes as well.

The government's responsibility begins before birth and continues through death. Did a pregnant mother abuse alcohol and drugs during her pregnancy? If so, the government will take care of her premature infant. Does a child live in an environment where his parents do little to stimulate his emotional and intellectual development? If so, the government will enroll the preschooler in a Head Start program to compensate for the lack of parental attention. Has a person lost his job? If so, the government will compensate the person for being unemployed. Is a single mother with small children unable to earn enough to live independently? If so, the government will support her. Is a farmer unable to sell his crops in the market at prices that will sustain him in agriculture? If so, the government will buy those crops. Is a person who has smoked cigarettes all his life now dying of lung cancer? If so, the government will pay his medical bills.

The wide range of government programs to provide food, health care, and economic well-being to people in the United States has created the attitude that, when people have problems, the government is obliged to take care of them. No matter how hard the government tries, however, there are no guarantees. People get sick. People run into economic problems. The more the government accepts the responsibility for these problems, the harder they will be to solve. When the government takes care of the health problems of smokers and drug abusers, it reduces the individual incentives to engage in responsible behavior. When the government agrees to take care of those who run into economic misfortune, it takes away some of the incentive for people to work to enhance their lives on their own.

When the government tries to provide guarantees, the quality of life is lower because individuals have less incentive to take care of themselves. Misfortune is an unavoidable fact of life, but the successes of the twentieth century have made misfortunes that were common a century ago much more rare. There is every reason to expect that continued progress will make them even more rare but only if individuals take the responsibility for their own lives. Giving the government responsibility not only creates a convenient scapegoat — one's failures are no longer one's individual responsibility — but also creates a lower quality of life for everyone.

PERSONAL FREEDOM AND PERSONAL RESPONSIBILITY

One of the triumphs of American government is the degree of freedom that is enjoyed by its citizens. Along with freedom comes responsibility, however. If one has the freedom to make choices, one must at the same time accept the responsibility for the consequences of those choices. The alternative is to push the costs of one individual's freedom onto other people.

In a free country, people should have the right to choose to smoke or to overeat, but they also should bear the health care costs that result from their choices. If the public is expected to bear the cost of smoking, for example, then because everyone bears the cost it is a small step to take to say that the government should regulate (or outlaw) that costly behavior.

Similarly, in a free country people have the right to own and use property. Along with the right to use that property as they want comes the responsibility not to use it in a way that creates a nuisance for their neighbors. Increasingly, the government is involving itself in land use decisions, taking away some of the freedom of property owners but, at the same time, taking away some of the responsibility for the consequences of those decisions. Individual freedom and individual responsibility allow the individual to benefit from good decisions, but individual responsibility also implies that the individual bears the cost of bad decisions. When the government accepts responsibility, the cost of bad decisions is borne by all.

The S&L scandal of the 1980s provides a good example of government mistakes resulting in costs borne by everybody. Why would one expect the government to be able to manage the environment any better than it can manage the S&L industry? Private property coupled with a legal system that makes individuals liable for the costs they impose on others means that individuals must consider the costs of their actions and be concerned about the consequences if their actions cause harm. With public ownership, if a bureaucrat makes a decision that imposes costs on others, the public bears those costs. The incentives created by private ownership and clearly defined property rights help preserve the environment. When the government makes mistakes in the environmental arena the costs are borne by everybody.

The government plays an important role in enhancing the quality of life, by defining and enforcing property rights, and by making individuals bear the responsibility for the costs that their choices place on others. Along with freedom comes responsibility.

DOING THE RIGHT THING

Every day, every individual relies on others to do the right thing. Drivers count on other drivers to stay on their side of the road and to obey traffic signals. Patrons at movie theaters count on other patrons queuing in an orderly fashion while waiting for tickets, and customers in grocery stores rely on other customers not to get in the express lane for ten items or less if they have more than ten items. These rules of conduct are violated on occasion, to be sure, but they are observed by most people when there might be some advantage gained from not observing them.

Years ago, I worked in the Roslyn section of Virginia, just across Key Bridge from Washington, D.C., and lived in Maryland. Every evening after work, I would take the George Washington Parkway home. The traffic on the parkway was always bumper to bumper, and there was always a long line of cars waiting on the ramp to get on the parkway. How could they merge into bumper to bumper traffic? The cars on the parkway would let them in. In general, each car on the parkway would let one car in from the ramp. A car from the parkway would go, followed by a car from the ramp, followed by a car from the parkway, and so forth. Cars on the parkway did not have to let cars on from the ramp, and, indeed, sometimes a car on the parkway would not. However, most cars did, and the traffic flowed smoothly, although not rapidly.

Why would a car on the parkway let one on from the ramp? Certainly not because the driver was expecting the favor to be returned. Every day the same people were on the parkway and the same people were on the ramp, so it was always one set of people doing favors for another set, and those on the ramp would not ever even have the opportunity to return the favor. Of course, in a more general sense, people might hope that charitable behavior might spread and eventually come back to benefit them, but the answer certainly cannot be expected reciprocity. Basically, the drivers on the parkway were just doing the right thing to keep traffic moving in an orderly fashion.

People choose to do the right thing in other contexts when the costs are higher. Americans contribute generously to private charitable organizations, and their generosity is more noteworthy considering that they are forced to contribute a large amount of tax dollars to help the needy. In the case of charitable organizations, individuals have the opportunity to make a choice to help out those in need. They have the opportunity to engage in moral and virtuous behavior, and they have the right to feel good about themselves for the role they have chosen to play in helping others. When they pay their tax dollars to help others, they have no such opportunity to feel virtuous about doing the right thing because they have no choice. There is nothing moral or virtuous about paying the taxes that the government says you have to pay or go to jail. There is something virtuous about choosing to help others.

The government's heavy involvement in ensuring that people have an adequate quality of life takes away a substantial amount of opportunity for virtuous and moral behavior. When paying their taxes, individuals do not have to think about whether it would be the right thing to contribute toward the medical care of the needy, or whether it would be the right thing to use some of their income to build low income housing, or whether it would be the right thing to spend some of their money to purchase and protect environmentally sensitive land. The government has made this choice for them. Even if the result were the same (which, as the previous chapters have illustrated, it is not), the mechanism that is used robs people of the opportunity to behave in a virtuous manner.

A good society cannot operate solely by forcing people to obey laws. Societies work because their members want to cooperate to produce a better society for everybody, and the greater the opportunity for people to contribute, the higher the quality of life will be. Despite heavy government involvement in activities that compete with all types of charities, there is still a substantial amount of charitable activity in the United States, and one must be careful about squeezing out that charitable impulse by having the government manage quality-of-life issues that could and should be a matter of individual responsibility. People give to charities because they want to. People pay taxes because they have to.

By placing quality-of-life issues in the government's hands we are creating a system where enhancing the quality of life is something people try to avoid rather than something they try to contribute to. Instead of feeling good about their generosity, taxpayers are likely to feel resentment that their incomes are forcibly being taken from them and given to someone else. There is no virtue in being forced to do a good deed. If quality-of-life issues were a matter of private responsibility rather than public responsibility, an environment in which people have the opportunity to do the right thing would be created, and people can accept the satisfaction of virtuous behavior rather than being pushed into something whether they like it or not.

THE GENERAL WELFARE

The push to get government involved in areas to enhance the quality of life might be categorized under the more general heading of employing the government to promote the general welfare, as called for in the Constitution of the United States. However, the idea that the government has a broad mandate to promote the general welfare was not accepted until the twentieth century. In the nineteenth century, the government promoted the general welfare through the measures recommended in this volume — defining and enforcing the rights of individuals — rather than through actively planning to allocate resources.[4]

Following a literal interpretation of the Constitution, one must question whether the government has a mandate to promote the general welfare. Questions arise on at least three grounds. The Constitution gives Congress the power "To lay and collect Taxes, Duties, Imposts, and Excises, to pay the Debts and provide for the common Defence and general Welfare of the United States." The wording seems to suggest that taxes are to be collected to promote the general welfare, as opposed to using revenues to target benefits to particular interest groups. Taken in context, this general welfare clause does not seem to imply that the federal government can do whatever it deems prudent to promote the general welfare.[5] A second ground for questioning the claim that the government has a general mandate to promote the general welfare is that the Constitution goes on to enumerate the activities the federal government can engage in. There would be no need to enumerate these activities if, in addition, the government was given permission to do anything it felt would promote the general welfare. A third reason is that the Tenth Amendment to the Constitution specifically limits the government to those activities enumerated in the Constitution, reserving all other activities to the states or individuals. Such a limit would be meaningless in the context of an unconstrained mandate to promote the general welfare.

From a constitutional standpoint, there are convincing reasons to believe that the founding fathers did not intend to give the federal government a general mandate to promote the general welfare.[6] Nevertheless, popular opinion at the end of the twentieth century seems to be that our democratic government is within its bounds to do whatever it believes will promote the general welfare. Even more extreme than this, popular opinion often seems to suggest that the government has an obligation to promote whatever popular opinion deems will further the general welfare. The call for increased government involvement in the health care industry provides a good example. One must look very hard in the Constitution to find where it is stated that the government should be involved in providing health care.

The founding fathers intended to create a limited government and were wise enough to see that, unless government power was constrained by constitutional rules and by other checks and balances, government would tend to extend its sphere of influence. The founders recognized the important role that the government could play in creating an environment where individuals would be free to pursue life, liberty, and happiness, but even as they recognized that individuals should have the right to enhance their quality of life, they also recognized that government could not provide enhancements to the quality of life. The government's role, according to the founders, was to prevent some people from harming the quality of life of others, not to be involved directly in enhancing the quality of life.

POLITICS AND RESOURCE ALLOCATION

While the argument might be made that the government should be responsible for enhancing the quality of life, there is no single entity that can be identified as the government. The government is actually lots of governments, and the actions of those governments are determined by a political decision-making process that involves a large number of people inside and outside the government. To give the responsibility to government is to turn the decision over to the political decision-making process and to allow those with the most political power the right to determine public policy.

When some people are given the right to decide how the resources of others are to be used, it is almost certain that those resources will be used ineffectively. Private owners of resources have an incentive to maximize the value of the resources they own, both now and in the future, because any enhancement in the value of the resources will go to the owner. Owners of valuable environmental assets have an incentive to preserve them because they can be sold. Private owners of wilderness can profit from selling camping and hunting rights but only if the resource is preserved. Income is earned by charging for hunting privileges, for example, but that income will be lost unless the wildlife on the property is preserved. Private owners have an incentive to prevent over-hunting and overutilization in general.

Public wilderness areas charge low admissions — generally too low even to recover the direct expenses of running the areas — with the result that more people are attracted to them because of the low price, which further harms the natural environment. Private owners of wilderness areas have an incentive to preserve the resources unless the value of the resources exceeds its opportunity cost. Chapter 4 explained how the Audubon Society leases mineral rights on its lands and uses the income to buy more environmentally sensitive land. With public land, loggers, oil companies, hunters, and environmentalists all vie for uses of scarce resources. The winner is not determined by whose use would be more valuable but rather by who has more political power.

In addition to the obvious inefficiency of this system, where the wrong decision can often be made, no decision is permanent. The loser in the political arena today can always return to do battle tomorrow. With private ownership, property owners have a secure right to use the property however they want and have the incentive to use it in a value-maximizing way.

The same principle that applies to the natural environment also applies to the man-made environment. Private owners have an incentive to develop their property in a way that maximizes its value to the people who use it, both now and in the future. Public planning for the use of private property allows people to use the political process to further their own ends and gain some value from the use of the property of others, without having to consider the costs. In an idealistic setting, the government might always make the best possible land use decisions. In reality, people in government have little incentive to consider the costs of the decisions they make, and decisions tend to be made to further the interests of those who have political power.

In every issue we have examined, the quality of life would be enhanced by allowing a greater role for market mechanisms. The optimal policy for government is to define and enforce the rights of individuals and let market mechanisms operate in order to enhance the quality of life. Yet, in all these issues, there is an increasing call for direct government involvement to further the quality of life. The collapse of the centrally planned economies in Europe in 1989 and the demise of the Soviet Union in 1991 brought clear evidence that government planning is counterproductive and that it lowers the standard of living and harms the quality of life. The lessons learned so painfully in Europe apply just as forcefully to the United States. The way to improve the quality of life is to rely less on government, not more.

NOTES

1.   Milton Friedman, *Capitalism and Freedom* (Chicago: University of Chicago Press, 1962) was an early proponent of a voucher system for education.

2.   The topic is discussed in more detail by Charles Murray, *Losing Ground* (New York: Basic Books, 1984).

3.   Even here, private contractual activity might be used in place of governmentally determined laws. See Bruce L. Benson, *The Enterprise of Law: Justice Without the State* (San Francisco: Pacific Research Institute, 1990) for a development of this idea.

4.   Terry L. Anderson and Peter J. Hill, *The Birth of a Transfer Society* (Stanford: Hoover Institution Press, 1980) suggest that changes were brought about by Supreme Court decisions that have continued to broaden the mandate of the federal government. Robert Higgs, *Crisis and Leviathan: Critical Episodes in the Growth of American Government* (New York: Oxford University Press, 1987) traces the change to the progressive era at the turn of the twentieth century. Richard E. Wagner, *To Promote the General Welfare: Market Processes vs. Political Transfers* (San Francisco: Pacific Research Institute, 1989) also notes the change in the government's mandate from one of protecting market exchange to one of engaging in transfers of income.

5.   Further comments and evidence on this point can be found in Randall G. Holcombe, "The Distributive Model of Government: Evidence from the Confederate Constitution," *Southern Economic Journal* 58 (January 1992): 762–69.

6.   The approval of the Constitution did considerably extend the discretion of those in the federal government, however. For a discussion, see Randall G. Holcombe, "Constitutions as Constraints: A Case Study of Three American Constitutions," *Constitutional Political Economy* 2 (Fall 1991): 303–28.

Bibliography

Ahlbrandt, Roger. "Efficiency in the Provision of Fire Services." *Public Choice* 16 (Fall 1973):1–15.

Anderson, Martin. "The Federal Bulldozer." In *Urban Renewal: The Record and the Controversy*, edited by James Q. Wilson, Chap. 19. Cambridge, Mass.: MIT Press, 1966.

Anderson, Odin W. *Health Services in the United States: A Growth Enterprise Since 1875*. Ann Arbor, Mich.: Health Administration Press, 1985.

Anderson, Terry L. "The Market Process and Environmental Amenities." In *Economics and the Environment: A Reconciliation*, edited by Walter E. Block, Chap. 4. Vancouver, B.C.: The Fraser Institute, 1989.

Anderson, Terry L., and Peter J. Hill. *The Birth of a Transfer Society*. Stanford: Hoover Institution Press, 1980.

Anderson, Terry L, and Donald R. Leal. *Free Market Environmentalism*. San Francisco: Pacific Research Institute for Public Policy, 1991.

Arrow, Kenneth J. "Uncertainty and the Welfare Economics of Medical Care." *American Economic Review* 53 (December 1963): 941–73.

Babcock, Richard F. *The Zoning Game: Municipal Practices and Policies*. Madison: University of Wisconsin Press, 1966.

Baden, John, and Richard L. Stroup, Eds. *Bureaucracy vs. Environment: The Environmental Costs of Bureaucratic Governance*. Ann Arbor: University of Michigan Press, 1981.

Bakalar, James B., and Lester Grinspoon. *Drug Control in a Free Society*. Cambridge: Cambridge University Press, 1984.

Bassuk, Ellen L., Ed. *The Mental Health Needs of the Homeless*. San Francisco: Jossey-Bass, 1986.

Bellush, Jewel, and Murray Hausknecht, Eds. *Urban Renewal: People, Politics, and Planning*. Garden City, N.Y.: Anchor Books, 1967.

Bennett, James T., and Manuel H. Johnson. "Tax Reduction Without Sacrifice: Private Sector Production of Public Services." *Public Finance Quarterly* 8 (October 1980): 363–96.

Benson, Bruce L. *The Enterprise of Law: Justice Without the State*. San Francisco: Pacific Research Institute, 1990.

Benson, Bruce L., and David W. Rasmussen. "Relationship Between Illicit Drug Enforcement Policy and Property Crimes." *Contemporary Policy Issues* 9 (October 1991): 106–15.

Blair, Roger D., Paul B. Ginsberg, and Ronald J. Vogel. "Blue Cross-Blue Shield Administration Costs: A Study of Non-Profit Health Insurers." *Economic Inquiry* 13 (June 1975): 237–51.

Block, Walter E., Ed. *Economics and the Environment: A Reconciliation.* Vancouver, B.C.: Fraser Institute, 1990.

Boaz, David, Ed. *The Crisis in Drug Prohibition.* Washington, D.C.: Cato Institute, 1990.

Borcherding, Thomas E. "Natural Resources and Transgenerational Equity." In *Economics and the Environment: A Reconciliation,* edited by Walter E. Block, Chap. 2. Vancouver, B.C.: Fraser Institute, 1990.

Brecher, Edward M., and *Consumer Reports* Editors. *Licit and Illicit Drugs: The Consumers Union Report on Narcotics, Stimulants, Depressants, Inhalants, Hallucinogens & Marijuana — Including Caffeine, Nicotine, and Alchohol.* Boston, Mass.: Little, Brown, 1972.

Brickner, Philip W., Linda Keen Sharer, Barbara A. Conanan, Marianne Savarese, and Brian C. Scanlan. *Under the Safety Net: The Health and Social Welfare of the Homeless in the United States.* New York: W.W. Norton, 1990.

Buchanan, James M. "Politics, Policy, and the Pigouvian Margins." *Economica* n.s. 29 (February 1962): 17–28.

_____. "Public Finance and Public Choice." *National Tax Journal* 28 (December 1975): 383–94.

Buchanan, James M., and Gordon Tullock. "Polluters' Profits and Political Response: Direct Controls Versus Taxes." *American Economic Review* 65 (March 1975): 139–47.

Buchanan, James M., Robert D. Tollison, and Gordon Tullock. *Toward a Theory of the Rent-Seeking Society.* College Station: Texas A&M University Press, 1980.

Campbell, Rita Ricardo. *Drug Lag: Federal Government Decision Making.* Stanford, Calif.: Hoover Institution Press, 1976.

Campion, Frank D. *The AMA and U.S. Health Policy Since 1940.* Chicago: Chicago Review Press, 1984.

Clarkson, Kenneth W. "Some Implications of Property Rights in Hospital Management." *Journal of Law & Economics* 15 (October 1972): 363–84.

Coase, Ronald H. "The Problem of Social Cost." *Journal of Law & Economics* 3 (October 1960): 1–44.

Cooper, John W., Ed. *Private Property, Land-Use Policy, and Growth Management.* Tallahassee, Fla.: Montpelier Books, 1990.

Crain, Mark, Thomas Deaton, Randall Holcombe, and Robert Tollison. "Rational Choice and the Taxation of Sin." *Journal of Public Economics* 8 (1977): 239–45.

Crain, W. Mark, and Asghar Zardkoohi. "A Test of the Property Rights Theory of the Firm: Water Utilities in the United States." *Journal of Law & Economics* 21 (October 1978): 395–408.

Davies, David G. "The Efficiency of Public versus Private Firms, The Case of Australia's Two Airlines." *Journal of Law & Economics* 14 (April 1971): 149–65.

_____. "Property Rights and Economic Efficiency — The Australian Airlines Revisited." *Journal of Law & Economics* 20 (April 1977): 223–26.

Davis, Karen, Gerard F. Anderson, Diane Rowland, and Earl P. Steinberg. *Health Care Cost Containment.* Baltimore: Johns Hopkins University Press, 1990.

Downs, Anthony. *An Economic Theory of Democracy.* New York: Harper & Row, 1957.

_____. *Inside Bureaucracy.* Boston: Little, Brown, 1967.

Dougherty, Charles J. *American Health Care: Realities, Rights, and Reforms.* New York: Oxford University Press, 1988.

Ehrlich, Isaac. "Participation in Illigitimate Activities: A Theoretical and Empirical Investigation." *Journal of Political Economy* 81 (May/June 1973): 521–65.

Epstein, Edward Jay. *Agency of Fear: Opiates and Political Power in America.* New York: G. P. Putnam's Sons, 1977.

Feldstein, Martin S. "Hospital Cost Inflation: A Study in Nonprofit Price Dynamics." *American Economic Review* 61 (December 1971) 853–72.

Feldstein, Paul J. *Health Care Economics,* 3rd. ed. New York: John Wiley & Sons, 1988.

Florida Department of Community Affairs. *Technical Memo* 4 (undated, but released in 1989).

Frech, H. E., III. "The Property Rights Theory of the Firm: Empirical Results from a Natural Experiment." *Journal of Political Economy* 84 (February 1976): 143–52.

Friedman, Milton. *Capitalism and Freedom.* Chicago: University of Chicago Press, 1962.

Friedman, Milton, and Rose Friedman. *Free to Choose.* New York: Harcourt Brace Jovanovich, 1980.

Goodman, John C., and Gerald L. Musgrave. *Patient Power: Solving America's Health Care Crisis.* Washington, D.C.: Cato Institute, 1992.

Gordon, Peter, and Harry Richardson. "You Can't Get There From Here." *Reason* (August/September 1989): 34–37.

Grabowski, Henry G. *Drug Regulation and Innovation: Empirical Evidence and Policy Options.* Washington, D.C.: American Enterprise Institute, 1976.

Grabowski, Henry G., and John M. Vernon. "Consumer Protection Regulation in Ethical Drugs." *American Economic Review* 67 (February 1977): 359–64.

Greer, Scott. *Urban Renewal and American Cities.* Indianapolis: Bobbs-Merrill, 1965.

Hamowy, Ronald, Ed. *Dealing With Drugs: Consequences of Government Control.* Lexington, Mass.: Lexington Books, 1987.

Hartman, Chester W. "The Housing of Relocated Families." In *Urban Renewal: People, Politics, and Planning,* edited by Jewel Bellush and Murray Hausknecht, pp. 315–53. Garden City, N.Y.: Anchor Books, 1967.

Hayek, Friedrich A.. *The Road to Serfdom.* Chicago: University of Chicago Press, 1944.

____. "The Use of Knowledge in Society." *American Economic Review* 35 (September 1945): 519–30.

Higgs, Robert. *Crisis and Leviathan: Critical Episodes in the Growth of American Government.* New York: Oxford University Press, 1987.

Hinich, Melvin J., and Richard Staelin. *Consumer Protection Legislation and the U.S. Food Industry.* New York: Pergamon Press, 1980.

Holcombe, Randall G. "Constitutions as Constraints: A Case Study of Three American Constitutions." *Constitutional Political Economy* 2 (Fall 1991): 303–28.

____. "The Distributive Model of Government: Evidence from the Confederate Constitution." *Southern Economic Journal* 58 (January 1992): 762–69.

____. *An Economic Analysis of Democracy.* Carbondale: Southern Illinois University Press, 1985.

____. *Economic Models and Methodology.* New York: Greenwood, 1989.

____. "Growth Management in Florida: Lessons for the National Economy." *Cato Journal* 10 (Spring/Summer 1990): 109–25.

____. *Public Finance and the Political Process.* Carbondale: Southern Illinois University Press, 1983.

Holcombe, Randall G., and Lora P. Holcombe. "The Market for Regulation." *Journal of Institutional and Theoretical Economics* 142 (December 1986): 684–96.

Joeres, Erhard R., and Martin H. David. *Buying a Better Environment: Cost-Effective Regulation through Permit Trading*. Madison: University of Wisconsin Press, 1983.

Kneese, Allen V. *Economics and the Environment*. New York: Penguin Books, 1977.

Krasny, Jaques. "Searching for Solutions to the Health Care Crisis." *Backgrounder* (James Madison Institute) 4 (1991).

Lange, Oskar, and Fred M. Taylor. *On the Economic Theory of Socialism*. Minneapolis: University of Minnesota Press, 1938.

Lindsay, Cotton M., Ed. *New Dimensions in Public Health Care: An Evaluation of Proposals for National Health Insurance*. San Francisco: Institute for Contemporary Studies, 1976.

____. "A Theory of Government Enterprise." *Journal of Political Economy* 84 (October 1976): 1061–77.

Malthus, Thomas Robert. *An Essay on Population*. New York: E. P. Dutton, 1914 (originally published in 1798).

Marx, Karl. *Capital*. New York: Modern Library, 1906 (originally published in 1867).

Meiners, Roger E., and Bruce Yandle. "Common Law Solution for Water Pollution: The Path Not Taken." Working Paper 92-6. Bozeman, Montana: Political Economy Research Center.

____. "Constitutional Choice for the Control of Water Pollution." *Constitutional Political Economy* 3 (Fall 1992): 359–80.

Miller, Richard Lawrence. *The Case for Legalizing Drugs*. New York: Praeger, 1991.

Mitchell, Chester Nelson. *The Drug Solution*. Ottawa: Carleton University Press, 1990.

Mumy, Gene E. "Long-Run Efficiency and Property Rights Sharing for Pollution Control." *Public Choice* 35 (1980): 59–74.

Murray, Charles. *Losing Ground*. New York: Basic Books, 1984.

Niskanen, William A. *Bureaucracy and Representative Government*. Chicago: Aldine-Atherton, 1971.

____. "Bureaucrats and Politicians." *Journal of Law & Economics* 18 (December 1975): 617–43.

____. "The Peculiar Economics of Bureaucracy." *American Economic Review* 58 (May 1968): 293–305.

Opaluch, James J., and Richard M. Kashmanian. "Assessing the Viability of Marketable Permit Systems: An Application to Hazardous Waste Managment." *Land Economics* 61 (August 1985): 263–71.

Osborne, David, and Ted Gaebler. *Reinventing Government: How the Entrepreneural Spirit is Transforming the Public Sector*. Reading, Mass.: Addison-Wesley, 1992.

Ostrom, Elinor. *Crafting Institutions for Self-Governing Irrigation Systems*. San Francisco: Institute for Contemporary Studies, 1992.

Peltzman, Sam. "An Evaluation of Consumer Protection Legislation: The 1962 Drug Amendments." *Journal of Political Economy* 81 (September 1973): 1049–91.

____. *Regulation of Pharmaceutical Innovation*. Washington, D. C.: American Enterprise Institute, 1974.

____. "Toward a More General Theory of Regulation." *Journal of Law & Economics* 19 (August 1976): 211–40.

Posner, Richard A. *Economic Analysis of Law*. Boston: Little Brown, 1972.

____. "Theories of Economic Regulation." *Bell Journal of Economics and Management Science* 5 (Autumn 1974): 335–58.

Priest, George L. "The Common Law Process and the Selection of Efficient Rules." *Journal of Legal Studies* 6 (January 1977): 65–82.

Reuter, Peter. "Police Regulation of Illegal Gambling: Frustrations of Symbolic Enforcement." *The Annals of the American Academy of Political and Social Science* 474 (July 1984): 36–47.

Rosko, Michael D., and Robert W. Broyles. *The Economics of Health Care*. Westport, Conn.: Greenwood Press, 1988.

Rothenberg, Jerome. *Economic Evaluation of Urban Renewal*. Washington, D. C.: Brookings Institution, 1967.

Rubin, Paul H. "Why is the Common Law Efficient?" *Journal of Legal Studies* 6 (January 1977): 51–63.

Santerre, Rexford E., Stephen G. Grubaugh, and Andrew J. Stollar. "Government Intervention in Health Care Markets and Health Care Outcomes: Some International Evidence." *Cato Journal* 11 (Spring/Summer 1991): 1–12.

Schelling, Thomas C. "Self-Command in Practice, in Policy, and in a Theory of Rational Choice." *American Economic Review* 74 (May 1984): 1–11.

Seldon, Arthur. "The Lessons of Centralized Medicine." In *New Directions in Public Health Care: An Evaluation of Proposals for National Health Insurance*, edited by Cotton M. Lindsay, Chap. 3. San Francisco: Institute for Contemporary Studies, 1976.

Siegan, Bernard H. *Land Use Without Zoning*. Lexington, Mass.: D. C. Heath, 1972.

____. "Nonzoning in Houston." *Journal of Law & Economics* 13 (April 1970): 71–147.

Smith, George Teeling, Ed. *Health Economics: Prospects for the Future*. London: Croom Helm, 1987.

Smith, Rodney T. "The Legal and Illegal Markets for Taxed Goods: Pure Theory and an Application to State Government Taxation of Distilled Spirits." *Journal of Law & Economics* 19 (August 1976): 393–429.

Starr, Paul. *The Social Transformation of American Medicine*. New York: Basic Books, 1982.

Stevens, Rosemary. *American Medicine and the Public Interest*. New Haven: Yale University Press, 1971.

Stigler, George J. "The Theory of Economic Regulation." *Bell Journal of Economics and Managment Science* 2 (Spring 1971): 3–21.

Stroup, Richard L., and John A. Baden. *Natural Resources: Bureaucratic Myths and Environmental Management*. San Francisco: Pacific Institute for Public Policy Research, 1983.

Svorny, Shirley. "Should We Reconsider Licensing Physicians?" *Contemporary Policy Issues* 10 (January 1992): 31–38.

Tang, Shui Yan. *Institutions and Collective Action: Self-Governance in Irrrigation*. San Francisco: Institute for Contemporary Studies, 1992.

Temin, Peter. "The Origins of Compulsory Drug Prescriptions." *Journal of Law & Economics* 22 (April 1979): 91–105.

____. "Regulation and the Choice of Prescription Drugs." *American Economic Review* 70 (May 1980): 301–5.

Thaler, Richard H., and H. M. Shefrin. "An Economic Theory of Self-Control." *Journal of Political Economy* 89 (April 1981): 392–406.

Thomas, Lisa, Mike Kelly, and Michel Cousineau. "Alchoholism and Substance Abuse." In *Under the Safety Net: The Health and Social Welfare of the Homeless in the United States*, edited by Philip W. Brickner, Linda Keen Scharer, Barbara A. Conanan, Marianne Savarese, and Brian C. Scanlan, Chap. 13. New York: W. W. Norton, 1990.

Thorne, Rolando, Catherine Zandler, John B. Walker, Jr., Linda Keen Scharer, and Marisa Canto. "Entitlements," In *Under the Safety Net: The Health and Social Welfare of the Homeless in the United States*, edited by Philip W. Brickner,

Linda Keen Scharer, Barbara A. Conanan, Marianne Savarese, and Brian C. Scanlan, Chap. 20. New York: W. W. Norton, 1990.

Tollison, Robert D., and Richard E. Wagner. "Self Interest, Public Interest, and Public Health." *Public Choice* 69 (March 1991): 323–43.

Trebach, Arnold S. *The Great Drug War*. New York: Macmillan, 1987.

Tucker, William. *The Excluded Americans: Homelessness and Housing Policies*. Washington, D. C.: Regnery Gateway, 1990.

Tullock, Gordon. *The Politics of Bureaucracy*. Washington, D. C.: Public Affairs Press, 1965.

von Mises, Ludwig. *Bureaucracy*. New Haven: Yale University Press, 1944.

_____. *Human Action*, 3rd rev. ed. Chicago: Henry Regnery Company, 1966.

_____. *Planned Chaos*. Irving-on-Hudson, New York: Foundation for Economic Education, 1947.

_____. *Socialism*. New Haven: Yale University Press, 1951.

Wagner, Richard E. *To Promote the General Welfare: Market Processes vs. Political Transfers*. San Francisco: Pacific Research Institute, 1989.

Weingast, Barry R., Kenneth A. Shepsle, and Christopher Johnsen. "The Political Economy of Benefits and Costs: A Neoclassical Approach to Distributive Politics." *Journal of Political Economy* 89 (August 1981): 642–64.

Weisbrod, Burton A. "The Health Care Quadrilemma: An Essay on Technological Change, Insurance, Quality of Care, and Cost Containment." *Journal of Economic Literature* 29 (June 1991): 523–52.

White, Michael D., and William A. Luksetich. "Heroin: Price Elasticity and Enforcement Strategies." *Economic Inquiry* 21 (October 1983): 557–64.

Wilson, James Q., Ed. *Urban Renewal: The Record and the Controversy*. Cambridge, Mass.: MIT Press, 1966.

Wisotsky, Steven. *Beyond the War on Drugs*. Buffalo, N.Y.: Prometheus Press, 1990.

_____. "Zero Tolerance, Zero Freedom." Paper presented at Critical Issues Symposium, Florida State University, March 1991.

Worthy, William. *The Rape of Our Neighborhoods: And How Communities are Resisting Take-Overs by Colleges, Hospitals, Churches, Businesses, and Public Agencies*. New York: William Morrow and Company, 1976.

Yandle, Bruce. *The Political Limits of Environmental Regulation*. New York: Quorum Books, 1989.

Index

ABOUT THE AUTHOR

Randall G. Holcombe is Professor of Economics at Florida State University. He is also chairman of the Research Advisory Council of the James Madison Institute for Public Policy Studies, a think tank that specializes in issues facing state governments. He is the author of six books, including most recently, *Economic Models and Methodology* (Greenwood, 1989) and *The Economic Foundations of Government* (1994).

ISBN 0-313-29358-9

90000>

EAN

9 780313 293580

HARDCOVER BAR CODE